D1253011

THE
BRAZEN FACE
OF HISTORY

Also by Lewis P. Simpson

The Dispossessed Garden:
Pastoral and History in Southern Literature

The Man of Letters in New England and the South:
Essays on the Literary Vocation in America

Edited by Lewis P. Simpson

The Possibilities of Order:
The Work of Cleanth Brooks

Profile of Robert Frost

The Poetry of Community:
*Essays on the Southern Sensibility of
Literature and History*

The Federalist Literary Mind:
Selections from the Monthly Anthology
and Boston Review

Lewis P. Simpson

THE
BRAZEN FACE
OF HISTORY

Studies in the Literary Consciousness

in America

LOUISIANA STATE UNIVERSITY PRESS / BATON ROUGE AND LONDON

PS
88
.S45

Copyright © 1980 by Louisiana State University Press
All rights reserved
Manufactured in the United States of America

Designer: Albert Crochet
Typeface: VIP Trump
Typesetter: LSU Press
Printer and Binder: Thomson-Shore, Inc.

LIBRARY OF CONGRESS CATALOGING IN PUBLICATION DATA
Simpson, Lewis P
    The brazen face of history.

    Includes bibliographical references
    1. American literature—History and criticism.
2. United States—Intellectual life.   I.   Title.
PS88.S45   810'.9   80–12940
ISBN 0–8071–0752–2

In Memory of Arlin Turner
Student of American Letters

01734

One rubbed one's eyes, but there, at its highest polish, shining in the beautiful day, was the brazen face of history, and there, all about one, immaculate, the printless pavements of the State.

—Henry James at the national Capitol
(*The American Scene*, 1907)

Contents

Preface

In his Introduction to *Democracy in America* (1835), Alexis de Tocqueville sums up the development of the modern mind as follows: "Gradually enlightenment spread, a reawakening of taste for literature and the arts became evident; intellect and will contributed to success; knowledge became an attribute of government, intelligence a social force; the educated man took part in affairs of state." A century and a half after the initial publication of Tocqueville's famous work, the metaphor of a dawning secular intelligence slowly spreading its light into every corner of a society and its governance hardly seems adequate to describe the modern increase of mind's dominion. The portrayal of this phenomenon requires an image more suggestive of the dynamic intensification of the link between intellect and will than the conventional one of dawning day. It is interesting that in a subsequent part of his book Tocqueville does come up with such an image. Although he seems to do so almost incidentally, and in fact the image is to be found in a footnote, its context in Tocqueville's discussion affords it arresting significance.

The context is a chapter in which the author tells about his penetration of the marginal area of the rapidly developing American continental settlement. Here he found physical existence to be crude; yet, in striking contrast to many other travelers in America, Tocqueville discovered no lubberlanders or semibarbarians in the log huts along the frontier. The typical hinterlander is, he says, a full-fledged descendant of the Old World culture, the self-conscious "result of the labor and experience of eighteen centuries." Wearing the dress and speaking the "language of cities," he is "acquainted with the past, curious about the future, and ready for argument about the present." In short, he is a "highly civilized being" who has voluntarily transferred himself into the New World wilderness. With no intention of cutting himself off from the settled world out of which he has come, he has brought with him not only his ax and his Bible, but his newspapers as well. "It is difficult to imagine," Tocqueville exclaims in amazement, "the incredible rapidity with which thought circulates in these deserts. I do not think so much intellectual activity exists in the most enlightened and populous districts of France." He documents this observation in the footnote I have alluded to:

> I traveled along a portion of the frontier of the United States in a sort of cart, which was termed mail. Day and night we passed with great rapidity along the roads, which were scarcely marked out through immense forests. When the gloom of the woods became impenetrable, the driver lighted branches of pine, and we journeyed along by the light they cast. From time to time we came to a hut in the midst of the forest; this was the post-office. The mail dropped an enormous bundle of letters [to be taken in the general sense of the term] at the door of this isolated dwelling, and we pursued our way at full gallop, leaving the inhabitants of the neighboring log houses to send for their share of the treasure.

Does not this little story about the swift transmission of thought in America—with its Poesque, even its Kafkaesque flavor—indicate a profound intuition of the meaning of the Enlightenment in America? In its deepest sense it is a metaphor of what, from a philosophical and psychological, and not less poetic, perspective, the American phase of modern history fundamentally represents: the climactic stage of mind's willful transference of nature, man, and society—and eventually of God, and finally of mind itself—into itself.

First clearly symbolized in the career of Sir Francis Bacon, this massive subjectification constitutes the inner—the determinative—motive of modern history. Becoming so incorporated with willing that it cannot be distinguished from this faculty, secular intelligence has assumed that it is indeed what it has willed itself to be: the immanent model of a society essentially different from any society that has before existed—a society, that is to say, of history and science. The literary—in the broad sense of the term, the poetic—response to the modern motive has been to identify mind with self. Although the most distinguishable response in nineteenth-century America to the experience of subjectification, Emersonian transcendentalism, was masked as a struggle between materialism and idealism, fact and mind, Thoreau and others of the Concord school knew that their experience of (to use Emerson's words in "The Transcendentalist") "this transfer of the world into the consciousness, this beholding of all things in the mind" was not definable in terms of what had been known as idealism. They knew that they belonged to a movement out of the dominion of idealism into a new realm where reality would be defined (as Emerson says in "Historic Notes of Life and Letters in New England") in the image of "the mind that had become aware of itself." This dominion of the "new consciousness" demanded a radical ethic centered in the self. In "The Transcendentalist" Emerson declares: "Everything real is self-existent. . . . I— this thought which is called I—is the mould into which the world is poured like melted wax. The mould is invisible, but the world betrays the shape of the mould. You call it the power of circumstance, but it is the power of me."

Dealing with certain aspects of the experience of the Great Transference as it is embodied in the American manifestations of the modern literary consciousness, the following studies are particularly concerned with the agency of transference, the Third Realm, or the Republic of Letters; and with the major consequence of the transference: loss of transcendent reference for being and a tendency (defined cogently by Eric Voegelin) toward the closure of history in the self of the writer. The focus is on various eighteenth- and nineteenth-century American men and women of letters (Washington, Hamilton, John Adams, Jefferson, Paine, Breckenridge, Brown, Hawthorne, George Fitzhugh, George Washington Harris, Mark Twain, Henry James, and Kate Chopin) and on several twentieth-century writers (Edmund Wilson, Malcolm Cowley, Faulkner, Davidson, Tate, Warren, and Walter Sullivan). Although originally shaped to some extent by the requirements of differing occasions, the essays have in common my long interest in the symbolism of literary order and the nature and meaning of the literary vocation in America. Some of the pieces have been considerably revised; in two instances they represent combinations of articles that appeared independently. As structured here they make, I trust, an implicitly coherent series of chapters in a book that comprehends, however sketchily, some important facets of the inner history of American letters. This book, I hope, both complements and expands three earlier works: *The Federalist Literary Mind, The Man of Letters in New England and the South,* and *The Dispossessed Garden: Pastoral and History in Southern Literature.*

In the brief space I have at my disposal here I cannot begin to mention the names of all the persons who have been of assistance to me in my recent work. I shall set down only a few of them. I am in special debt to certain officials of Louisiana State University: Darwin H. Shrell, chairman of the Department of English (1973–80); Irwin H. Berg, dean emeritus of the College of Arts and Sciences; James M. Traynam, vice-chancellor and dean of the Graduate School; Otis B. Wheeler, vice-chancellor for Academic Affairs; and Chancellor Paul W. Murrill. Their approval of a sabbatical leave for 1977–78 greatly facilitated my efforts in research and writing.

The dedicatory page to this volume expresses thanks, personal and professional, to a wise and exceedingly kind and gracious individual who was at the center of American literary studies for many years. It is impossible to imagine how academic scholarship in our letters could have been carried on without him. Let me acknowledge, too, my extraordinary debt to three other friends now deceased: Theodore Hornberger, Allen Tate, and Gordon Mills. In their own ways both Ted Hornberger and Allen Tate exemplified the man of letters as a member of a community and in so doing shared their devotion to literature with many of us. My obligation to my contemporary, Gordon Mills, is profound. For over thirty years I was privileged to enjoy not only an intellectual companionship but a close friendship with this eminently intelligent and marvelously patient scholar, critic, and teacher.

Finally I must express my thanks to the National Foundation for the Humanities for supporting my studies with a Fellowship for Independent Study and Research.

Acknowledgments

The first appearance of the chapters in this volume is cited below. Permission to reprint is gratefully acknowledged.

"The Printer as Man of Letters" (under the title "The Printer as Man of Letters: Franklin and the Symbolism of the Third Realm"), in *The Oldest Revolutionary: Essays on Benjamin Franklin*, ed. J. Leo Lemay (Philadelphia: University of Pennsylvania Press, 1975).

"The Symbolism of Literary Alienation in the Revolutionary Age," in *200 Years of the Republic in Retrospect*, ed. William C. Havard and Joseph L. Bernd (Charlottesville: University Press of Virginia, 1976).

"The Fiction of the Real American Revolution," *Studies in the Literary Imagination*, IX (Fall 1976).

"Slavery and Modernism" (under the title "The Southern Reaction to Modernism"), in *Southern Literary Study: Problems and Possibilities*, ed. Louis D. Rubin, Jr., and C. Hugh Holman (Chapel Hill: University of North Carolina Press, 1975).

"The Act of Thought in Virginia," *Early American Literature*, XIV (Winter 1979–80).

"The Civil War and the Failure of Literary Mind in America," *Southern Literary Journal*, VII (Fall 1974).

"The Southern Exodus from Arcadia" (under the title "The Southern Literary Imagination and the Pastoral Mode"), *Southern Humanities Review* (Fall 1976). Unnumbered Bicentennial extra issue.

"The Will to Art in Postbellum America," as the Introduction to *Kate Chopin* by Robert Arner, issued as Vol. XIV, *Louisiana Studies* (Spring 1975). This journal is currently issued as *Southern Studies: An Interdisciplinary Journal of the South*.

"The Spectatorial Attitude" (under the title "Malcolm Cowley and the American Writer"), *Sewanee Review*, LXXXIV (Spring 1976).

"The Decorum of the Writer," *Sewanee Review*, LXXXVI (Fall 1978).

"The Bard and the Clerk," as the Foreword to *The Literary Correspondence of Donald Davidson and Allen Tate*, ed. John Tyree Fain and Thomas Daniel Young (Athens: University of Georgia Press, 1974).

"The Legend of the Artist" (under the title "Faulkner and the Legend of the Artist"), in *Faulkner: Fifty Years After the Marble Faun*, ed. George H. Wolfe (Tuscaloosa: University of Alabama Press, 1976).

"A Fable of Civilization," adapted from "Southern Fiction" in *Harvard Guide to Contemporary American Writing*, ed. Daniel Hoffman (Cambridge, Mass.: Harvard University Press, 1979); "Faulkner's Fable of Civilization," in *The Maker and the Myth: Faulkner and Yoknapatawpha*, ed. Evans Harrington and Ann J. Abadie (Jackson: University Press of Mississippi, 1978); and "The Loneliness of William Faulkner," *Southern Literary Journal*, VII (Fall 1975).

"What Survivors Do" (under the title "The Southern Aesthetic of Memory"), in *Essays in American Literature in Memory of Richard P. Adams*, issued as Vol. XXIII of *Tulane Studies in English* (1978).

"The Closure of History in a Postsouthern America," adapted from "Walter Sullivan and the Southern Possibility" and "A Necrology of the Southern Renascence," *Southern Literary Journal*, V (Spring 1973); IX (Spring 1977).

Part I

But in the night of thick darkness enveloping the earliest antiquity, so remote from ourselves, there shines the eternal and never-failing light of a truth beyond all question: that the world of civil society has certainly been made by men, and that its principles are therefore to be found within the modifications of our own human mind. Whoever reflects on this cannot but marvel that the philosophers should have bent all their energies to the study of the world of nature, which, since God has made it, He alone knows; and that they should have neglected the study of the world of nations or civil world, which, since men had made it, men could hope to know. This aberration was a consequence of that infirmity of the human mind . . . by which, immersed and buried in the body, it naturally inclines to take notice of bodily things, and finds the effort to attend to itself too laborious; just as the bodily eye sees all objects outside itself but needs a mirror to see itself.

—Giambattista Vico, *The New Science* (1744), translated by
Thomas Goddard Bergin and Max Harold Fisch

"The revolution," said Mr. Adams
"Took place in the minds of the people."
—Ezra Pound, *Cantos*, No. XXXII

1 / The Printer as American Man of Letters

I Benjamin Franklin, of Philadelphia, printer, late Minister Pleni-
potentiary for the United States of America to the Court of
France, and President of the State of Pennsylvania . . ."[1]
Although he had not followed the printing trade since 1748, when
he had withdrawn from active participation in a printing and bookselling house to enter upon his various and widely influential public
life as man of letters and statesman, Franklin recognized in his last
will and testament in 1788 that the second part of his career was at
one with the first. He confirmed the prophecy of his career made at
the age of twenty-two, when, as a youthful Philadelphia printer suffering from pleurisy, he had somewhat prematurely composed his
own epitaph:

The Body of
B Franklin Printer
(Like the Cover of an old Book
Its Contents torn out
And stript of its Lettering & Gilding)
Lies here, Food for Worms.
But the Work shall not be lost;
For it will, (as he believ'd) appear once more,
In a new and more elegant Edition
Revised and corrected
By the Author.

In this "most famous of American epitaphs,"[2] as Carl Van Doren
calls it, Franklin exemplifies his ability to make homely apostrophe

1 Quoted in Carl Van Doren, *Benjamin Franklin* (New York: Garden City Publishing
Company, 1941), 123.
2 *Ibid.*, 123. Epitaph quoted on p. 124.

the ironic mask of sophisticated cultural observation. When the individual existence inevitably falls into disrepair, according to Franklin's vision of things, it will be brought out in a new and more beautiful edition by a God who, like Franklin, is not only an author but also a printer. He will both correct the errata of the first edition and make the new edition typographically elegant. In Franklin's epitaph, salvation by faith in the regenerating grace of God becomes faith in the grammatical and verbal skills and in the printing shop know-how of a Deity who is both Man of Letters and Master Printer.

This symbolic representation of the God of Reason is as appropriate to the Age of the Enlightenment as the more familiar symbolism depicting Him as the Great Clock Maker. In proclaiming his adherence to deism, Franklin implies his rejection of the order of existence under which he had been reared, that of the New England theocracy. He suggests an awareness of his affiliation with an order of mind and spirit that as yet existed only in tentative ways in colonial America: an order additional to the realms of Church and State—the autonomous order of mind, the Republic of Letters, a Third Realm, being made manifest as never before in Western civilization by the advancing technology of printing. Franklin's epitaph signifies the historical engagement of his whole career with the articulation, expansion, and consolidation of the Third Realm in America.

Although the differentiation of the Third Realm in the Western symbolization of the orders of existence is difficult to document with any degree of exactitude, three phases in the history of this process may be briefly noted. In the first we discover the remoter origins of the Third Realm in a "Second Realm" of Grecian and Roman times. This was first instituted in the Athens of Socrates, Plato, and Aristotle, where a society of philosophers formed a realm apart from the religious and political power constituting the government of the city-state. Later, in the Rome of Cicero and Virgil, the Second Realm was ideally constituted in two visions of intellectual and literary community: the Stoic vision of a cosmopolis of mind and the pastoral vision of Arcadia. These were the invisible homelands of spiritual elites removed from the conjoined politics and religion of the imperial state.

The more immediate origins of the Third Realm are to be located in the intellectual and literary existence of the later Middle Ages. Then, as a result of the differentiation of a power struggle between Church and State—a struggle, not previously known in history, between a transcendent order of Being and the temporal order of existence—a Republic of Letters emerged from the Republic of Christ. In the grand design of the medieval papacy, this Third Realm would find its function in the assimilation of Church and State—in effecting, as Christopher Dawson remarks, "the intellectual organization of Christian civilization." The rise of the universities and the complementary efforts centering in the quest for a unified Christian Republic, however, tended in the twelfth and thirteenth centuries to place an emphasis on intellect and verbal skills that disrupted the very quest. When the papacy began to seek to elevate the orders of friars within the university corporations, the secular clergy of the corporations resisted. The result was a quarrel that, Dawson observes, "foreshadows the future secularization of Western culture." As the design of unity came more and more into crisis, both as a result of pressures from within the realm of the Church and of events from without, the secularization of mind was specifically, if ironically, foreshadowed in the vision of Joachim of Flora. Joachim saw "the coming of a new age, the Age of the Spirit and the Eternal Gospel in which the Church will be renewed in the liberty of the spirit under the leadership of the new order of Spiritual Contemplatives." [3]

This vision of Christendom dominated by a community of spiritually perfected monks—which harks back to the Stoic vision of a

---

3 Christopher Dawson, *Religion and the Rise of Western Culture* (New York: Image Books, 1958), 197, 204. The theory of history advanced by Eric Voegelin is basic to an understanding of the Third Realm. See especially his *The New Science of Politics: An Introduction* (Chicago: University of Chicago Press, 1952), 107–32. Bizarre though they may be at times, the theories of Marshall McLuhan must be recognized as highly significant. See in particular *The Gutenberg Galaxy: The Making of Typographic Man* (Toronto: University of Toronto Press, 1962). Also see Lewis P. Simpson, "Literary Ecumenicalism of the American Enlightenment," in *The Ibero-American Enlightenment*, ed. A. Owen Aldridge (Urbana: University of Illinois Press, 1971), 317–32; Simpson, "Federalism and the Crisis of Literary Order," *American Literature*, 32 (November, 1960), 253–66; and Simpson, "The Satiric Mode: The Early National Wits," in *The Comic Imagination in American Literature*, ed. Louis D. Rubin, Jr. (New Brunswick: Rutgers University Press, 1973), 49–61.

community or Second Realm of sages—could be adapted to variant concepts of secular intellectual order. It offered an image of an ecumenicalism of mind apposite to the image of the university; and, as the latter image declined in importance, it supported the rise of a dominion of humanists as the Third Realm. This is the character of the Republic of Letters as it is represented, say, by a great Renaissance scholar such as Julius Caesar Scaliger, or in a less determinate but possibly more significant way by Erasmus. But the representation of the Third Realm became more various as the secularization of thought progressed and, with the loss of Latinity and the acceptance of the vernacular modes, its languages became manifold. It came to embrace the new science as well as classical humanism—although it is of fundamental importance to observe, all activity of mind, down through the eighteenth century, continued to be viewed under the aspect of the use of letters. And through the eighteenth century this aspect continued to be seen as comprehensive.

Meanwhile, the third, and most decisive, phase in the development of the Republic of Letters was inaugurated by the invention of printing in the fifteenth century. This eventually caused the fragmentation and diffusion of the Third Realm but the initial result was its expansion and growth in power. In the seventeenth and eighteenth centuries the Third Realm embraced a "classless" and crucial group of world-historical men of letters: among them, Francis Bacon, Newton, Milton, Locke, Pope, Voltaire, Diderot, Hume, Franklin, John Adams, Jefferson. These intellectuals, together with numerous equal or lesser counterparts, over a period of a century and a half elaborated a comprehensive and searching inquiry into the meaning of the orders of existence. They shaped a Great Critique of Church and State.

The uniformity and repeatability of the printed word opened up the Great Critique, and the Third Realm as a whole, to the general society, creating a relationship between literacy and society never before known. Making for a more absolute distinction between literacy and illiteracy—between the man of letters and the man of no letters—the expansion of the Third Realm at the same time introduced a distinction between degrees of literacy. This obtained between the man *of* letters and the man *with* letters; between the man who practices the art of letters (the man who has a vocation to letters) and persons whose use of letters ranges from that of the "general reader" to that of the person who cannot do more than inscribe his name. Under such cultural conditions the man *of* letters could seek to extend and enhance the quality of the literacy of the man *with* letters; he could seek, up to a point at least, to democratize the dominion of letters as an exclusive, elitist polity of mind. In either case the nature of literacy as a dominion became a historical issue in which the liberation of the general mind through the extension of the Republic of Letters found itself in opposition to an effort to confine letters and learning to the approximate scope they had achieved before the age of printing. These polar impulses were present in seventeenth- and eighteenth-century America, but Franklin's expression of them has to be understood in connection with a special differentiation of the Third Realm under the conditions of New England Puritanism.

The founding of Harvard College in 1636 embodied the Third Realm in New England. Established to perpetuate a learned ministry in the Puritan theocracy, Harvard descended from the conception of the realm of letters and learning as the servant of the autonomous Church. But Puritanism—and indeed the whole dissenting and reformist movement lumped under the head of Protestantism—developed after humanism had become identified with the rise of the Third Realm. The New England assimilation of Church and Letters showed increasing evidences of humanistic leavening in the later seventeenth century. Moreover, the New England clergy, in common with the Puritan clergy as a whole, had originated as a learned class—an intelligentsia—alienated from an official Church and State. The Puritan clerics in England assumed the role, Michael Walzer says, "of a clerical third estate," and in this capacity "tended to anticipate the intellectual and social changes characteristic of a secular third estate."

Their "plain-speaking" and matter-of-fact style; their insistence upon education and independent judgment; their voluntary association outside the corporate church; their emphasis upon methodical, purposive endeavor, their narrow unemotional sense of order and discipline—all this clearly suggested a life-style very different from that of a feudal lord, a Renaissance courtier or even an Anglican archbishop. This new style was first tested on the margins and in the interstices of English society by men cut off from the traditional world, angry and isolated clerics, anxiously seeking a new order. It was by no means the entirely spontaneous creation of those sturdy London merchants and country gentlemen who later became its devoted advocates; it was something they learned, or rather, it was something some of them learned. The automatic burgher values—sobriety, caution, thrift—did not constitute the significant core of Puritan morality in the seventeenth century; the clerical intellectuals had added moral activism, the ascetic style, and the quality of high-mindedness and taught these to their followers.[4]

Among those followers was John Milton, the greatest exemplar of the lay intelligentsia among the Puritans. In *Areopagitica*, a classic document of the effort to establish the autonomy of the Third Realm, Milton defended the "truth" of the "commonwealth of learning" and attacked the fallacy of censorship imposed in the name of religious authority. In New England the life-style of the third estate of Puritanism was more circumscribed than it was in England, but a basic disposition to respect the Republic of Letters is evidenced not only in the history of Harvard but also in the development of the Boston-Cambridge community as the seat of the Enlightenment in New England. By the end of the first quarter of the eighteenth century, the rise of an independent order of secular men of letters was a possibility in the Boston world. One of its first manifestations was the appearance in 1721 of the *New England Courant*, edited by Benjamin Franklin's older brother James, who had returned to Boston after completing an apprenticeship to a London printer. During his connection with this little paper, Benjamin Franklin began his personal representation of the Third Realm in New England and in America.

Franklin's fundamental response to the Age of Printing was his discovery that it opened to the person of talent and ambition a self-education in letters and learning. His initiation into the actual techniques of the printing trade was no more than secondary to his unfolding vision of the intellectual resources of the printer's product and commodity.

The description of how he made himself into a scholar and writer

4 Michael Waltzer, *The Revolution of the Saints: A Study in the Origins of Radical Politics* (New York: Atheneum, 1968), 124.

is a noted passage in the *Autobiography*. Before he was twelve he began to read as chance and fortune brought books into his hands, investing whatever small sums of money he acquired in books, selling a set of Bunyan to purchase "R. Burton's historical collections," making his way through volumes of polemic divinity in his father's library when nothing else was available, reading "abundantly" in Plutarch, and eventually falling upon Defoe's *Essay on Projects* and Cotton Mather's *Essays to Do Good* (which he apparently assumed emphasized good works instead of saving grace). After he was apprenticed he secured books clandestinely from acquaintances among apprentices to Boston booksellers—"Often I sat in my room reading the greatest part of the night, when the book was borrowed in the evening and to be returned early in the morning, lest it should be found missing or wanted." At length a merchant, Mr. Matthew Adams, "an ingenious, sensible man" who frequently visited the printing house and who had "a pretty collection of books," invited the youth to make use of them. Assiduously pursuing the role of scholar, Franklin conceived the greater possibility of becoming a self-made writer. After he had enjoyed some success with two Grubstreet ballads hawked about Boston (only to be admonished by his father that "verse-makers were generally beggars"), Benjamin turned to "prose writing" as the discipline offering the "principal means of Advancement." When he found his style "far short in elegance of expression, in method and in Perspicuity," as compared to that of his friend John Collins (with whom he had contested in a written debate), young Franklin—in an age when the fortuity of print made history subject to the chance encounter between a mind and a book—"met with an odd volume of the *Spectator*."

> It was the third. I had never before seen any of them. I bought it, read it over and over, and was much delighted with it. I thought the writing excellent and wished if possible to imitate it. With that view, I took some of the papers, and making short hints of the sentiment in each sentence, laid them by a few days, and then without looking at the book, tried to complete the papers again by expressing each hinted sentiment at length and as fully as it had been expressed before, in any suitable words that should occur to me.[5]

5 Franklin, *Autobiography and Other Writings*, ed. Russel B. Nye (Boston: Houghton Mifflin, 1958), 10–13. A detailed and interesting study of Franklin's journalistic career—from a point of view different from that stressed in the present study

Franklin's imitation of the *Spectator* became more elaborate and arduous. To force himself to seek a greater variety in his vocabulary, he transformed some of Mr. Spectator's stories into verse and, subsequently, when he had "pretty well forgotten the prose, turned them back again." He scrambled the organization of thoughts and topics in the original papers and then sought to restore them to wholeness. Thus he taught himself "method in the arrangement of the thoughts." Franklin was, he says, "extremely anxious" to become "a tolerable English writer."[6] But in shaping himself into an author, Franklin learned something more important to success than felicity of style. He learned that in the Age of Print a successful style involves a strategy of intimacy. This strategy is important in the *Spectator*, but it may be that the precocious Franklin discerned its significance earlier through his reading of a pure exemplification of the self-taught writer in the Age of Print, John Bunyan. That this could be the case is indicated in Franklin's recollection of an incident aboard a boat when he was on his way to Philadelphia to seek his fortune:

> In crossing the bay we met with a squall that tore our rotten sails to pieces, prevented our getting into the kill, and drove us upon Long Island. On our way a drunken Dutchman who was a passenger, too, fell overboard; when he was sinking, I reached through the water to his shock pate and drew him up so that we got him in again. His ducking sobered him a little, and he went to sleep, taking first out of his pocket a book which he desired I would dry for him. It proved to be my old favourite author Bunyan's *Pilgrim's Progress* in Dutch, finely printed on good paper with copper cuts, a dress better than I had ever seen it wear in its own language. I have since found that it has been translated into most of the languages of Europe, and suppose it has been more generally read than any other book except, perhaps, the Bible. Honest John was the first that I know of who mixes narration and dialogue, a method of writing very engaging to the reader, who in the most interesting parts finds himself, as it were, admitted into the company and present at the conversation. Defoe has imitated him successfully in *Robinson Crusoe*, in his *Moll Flanders*, and other pieces; and Richardson has done the same in his *Pamela*, etc.[7]

In discovering the reader "admitted into the company, and present

---

—is to be found in James A. Sappenfield, *A Sweet Instruction: Franklin's Journalism as a Literary Apprenticeship* (Carbondale: Southern Illinois University Press, 1973).
6 Franklin, *Autobiography*, 15.
7 *Ibid.*, 19.

at the conversation," Franklin grasped one of the key motives of modern literacy: the identity of author and reader. Under an imperative of intimacy, the postbardic author imitates the life of the "general reader." The author wears the guise of the reader or, in a more intricate sense, disguises himself as the reader.

How well Franklin early comprehended the novel role of the writer in the extension of literacy through printing is illustrated in the *Dogood Papers*, which he contributed anonymously to the *New England Courant* in 1722, when he was sixteen years old. Silence Dogood—a feminine Mr. Spectator carefully localized in manner and conversation—is a sophisticated persona; she is the youthful genius Franklin, the apprentice "leather-apron man" (printer), masquerading as the moral identity of the "common reader" in the age when secular moralism began to dominate post-theocratic New England. Silence begins her career as a writer by acknowledging the changing role of the author: "And since it is observed, that the Generality of People, now a days, are unwilling either to commend or dispraise what they read, until they are in some measure informed who or what the Author of it is, whether he be *poor or rich, old or young, a Schollar or a Leather Apron Man, &c.* and give their Opinion of the Performance, according to the Knowledge which they have of the Author's Circumstances, it may not be amiss to begin with a short Account of my past Life and present Condition, that the Reader may not be at a Loss to judge whether or no my Lucubrations are worth his reading."[8]

Born on shipboard while her parents were emigrating from England to New England and almost at once orphaned when her father was swept overboard by a wave while he stood on the ship's deck rejoicing at her birth, Silence is the widow of a country minister to whom she was once apprenticed. The minister had acquired a library, "which tho' it was but small, yet it was well chose, to inform the Understanding rightly and enable the Mind to frame great and noble Ideas"; and in this little dominion of the mind Silence has become a student of letters. She is, one supposes, insufficiently liberated by present-day standards to be referred to as a "person of letters" instead of a "woman of letters," but such a term, used without pejo-

8 *The Papers of Benjamin Franklin*, ed. Leonard W. Labaree, *et. al.* (20 vols. to date; New Haven: Yale University Press, 1959–), I, 9. Referred to hereafter as *Papers*.

rative implication, is a reasonably exact description of her status in society. Although Franklin conceives her as having womanly traits, she is relatively desexed and unclassed, a participant in her society and yet the observer of it. She is significantly aware, furthermore, of her role as self-made author whose authority to write—the right to be an author—derives from her self-admission into the Third Realm. The most substantial essay Silence writes in her brief career is, as a matter of fact, a satirical commentary on the changing nature of this authority and takes the form of a well-known satire on Harvard College in the fourth number of the *Dogood Papers*.

Silence, who has been urged by Clericus, a clergyman boarder in her home, to give her son an education at Harvard, soon afterward seeks her "usual Place of Retirement under the *Great Apple-Tree*," where she falls asleep and has a dream about the Temple of Learning. The "stately edifice" turns out to be in fact a seat of dullness, inhabited by a tribe of students who, finding that learning is difficult and demanding, make the ascent to the throne of Learning only through following well-established modes of cheating. The chief import of the dream vision is "the extream Folly of those Parents, who, blind to their Childrens Dulness, and insensible to the Solidity of their Skulls, because they think their Purses can afford it, will needs send them to the Temple of Learning, where for want of a suitable Genius, they learn little more than how to carry themselves handsomely, and enter a Room genteely, (which might as well be aquir'd at a Dancing-School) and from whence they return, after Abundance of Trouble and Charge, as great Blockheads as ever, only more proud and self-conceited." Silence, it is to be noted, does not discover in her vision that college is a worthless institution, merely that its true value is limited to the few who have the capacity for it. But the poor among these few cannot gain admittance. The entrance to the Temple of Learning must be made past two guards: Riches, who admits applicants who can pay, and Poverty, who denies those who cannot. The result is the bourgeois employment of the college as a finishing school. And yet hidden in the satire on the corruption of the true meaning of learning by money values is a revelation of a profound change in the relation of letters and learning to society. This occurs when Silence makes the curious discovery that Learning "in awful

State" on her "magnificent Throne" is "very busily employ'd in writing something on a half a Sheet of Paper." Upon inquiry Silence is
told that Learning is "preparing a Paper, call'd *The New-England
Courant*." Meanwhile,

> on her Right Hand sat *English*, with a pleasant smiling Countenance, and
> handsomely attir'd; and on her left were seated several *Antique Figures*
> with their Faces vail'd. I was considerably puzzl'd to guess who they were,
> until one informed me, (who stood beside me,) that those Figures on her
> left Hand were *Latin, Greek, Hebrew, &c.* and that they were very much
> reserv'd, and seldom or never unvail'd their Faces here, and then to few or
> none, tho' most of those who have in this Place acquir'd so much Learning
> as to distinguish them from *English* pretended to an intimate Acquain-
> tance with them. I then enquir'd of him, what could be the Reason why
> they continu'd vail'd, in this Place especially: He pointed to the Foot of the
> Throne, where I saw *Idleness*, attended with *Ignorance*, and these (he in-
> formed me) were they, who first vail'd them, and still kept them so.[9]

This is a symbolization (it may well be the first in American literature) of the expansion of the Third Realm—of the triumph of the
vernacular languages and of the periodical press. We note that the satire does not present Learning as prostituted to the press. On the contrary, Learning has accepted her new role as printer-editor-publisher
of a newspaper. If Idleness and Ignorance have veiled the learned languages, they have not veiled the goddess herself. She still reigns. The
implication is that the center of the Republic of Letters has shifted
from the university to the printing shop and the self-made author
like Silence Dogood. Franklin does not imagine his little satire as a
miniature *Dunciad* about the progress of dullness and the triumphant inversion of the progress of literature.[10] Instead, he offers a
kind of celebration of the freeing of letters and learning from the authority of the university, realizing at the same time that this has occurred at the expense of a certain degradation of the initial embodiment of the polity of letters.

The implied elevation of the role of the self-made author in Silence
Dogood is still more forcibly, if more subtly, suggested in the character and work of the philomath Richard Saunders, the editor of *Poor*

9 *Papers*, I, 15–16.
10 See Aubrey L. Williams, *Pope's Dunciad: A Study of Its Meaning* (Baton Rouge:
Louisiana State University Press, 1955), esp. pp. 42–59.

Richard's Almanack, which Franklin commenced in Philadelphia ten years after the brief run of the *Dogood Papers.* A poverty-stricken countryman who is a lover of learning, Poor Richard enters into the business of writing after, as he says, his wife has threatened "to burn all my Books and Rattling-Traps (as she calls my Instruments) if I do not make some profitable Use of them for the Good of my Family." With the assurance of a printer that he will derive "some considerable share of the Profits," Poor Richard begins the publication of an almanac.[11] The result is a decided easing of his economic condition. His improved circumstances are more confirmed than denied when, after a few years of publication, Poor Richard is found complaining that the printer is running away with most of the profits of the almanac enterprise. The real meaning of Poor Richard's grievance, however, lies in his qualification of it: the printer, he adds, "is a Man I have a great Regard for, and I wish his Profit ten times greater than it is."[12] This suggestion of the identity of Poor Richard and Franklin is more than waggish humor. In the fiction of Poor Richard, Franklin the printer and Franklin the man of letters are imaginatively united—more so than in Silence Dogood—as a representation of the expanding literacy of print. As a purveyor of information, wit, and philosophical and scientific argument, Poor Richard represents the domestication of the Third Realm in a world moving toward the democratic literacy inherent in the technology of print. (The full democratization of literacy would take place in the nineteenth century with the industrialization of the printing business.) Poor Richard, to be sure, recognizes the totality of the dominion of print and its replacement of the world of the manuscript and the oral mode; in four lines of doggerel verse that he offers as one of his quotations he bids farewell to the world of anonymous minstrels and bards and summarizes a world dominated by publication:

> If you wou'd not be forgotten
> As soon as you are dead and rotten,
> Either write things worth reading
> Or do things worth the writing.[13]

11 *Papers,* I, 311.
12 *Ibid.,* II, 218.
13 *Ibid.,* II, 194.

The opening up of the Third Realm is symbolized more dramatically in *Poor Richard's Almanack* of 1746 by the identification of Poor Richard with the tradition of the literary rural retreat.

> Who is *Poor Richard*? People oft inquire,
> Where lives? What is he? never yet the nigher.
> Somewhat to ease your Curiositee,
> Take these slight Sketches of my Dame and me.
>   Thanks to kind Readers and a careful Wife,
> With plenty bless'd, I lead an easy Life;
> My Business Writing; hers to drain the Mead,
> Or crown the barren Hill with useful Shade;
> In the smooth Glebe to see the Plowshare worn,
> And fill the Granary with needful Corn.
> Press nectareous Cyder from my loaded Trees,
> Print the sweet Butter, turn the Drying Cheese.
> Some Books we read, tho' few there are that hit
> The happy Point where Wisdom joins with Wit;
> That set fair Virtue naked to our View,
> And teach us what is *decent*, what is *true*.
> That Friend sincere, and honest Man, with Joy
> Treating or treated oft our Time employ.
> Our Table next, Meals temperate; and our Door
> Op'ning spontaneous to the bashful Poor.
> Free from the bitter Rage of Party Zeal,
> All those we love who seek the publick Weal.[14]

In a sense the image of Poor Richard on his farm, pleasantly engaged in the "Business" of writing while his wife tends to the agricultural tasks, presents a striking variation of the ideal of literary retirement. Poor Richard's mercenary literary activity may be regarded as a violation of the integrity of the idealized pastoral dominion of mind as this descends into eighteenth-century literature from Virgil and Horace. The location of the almanac-maker's business in a pastoral setting may even be construed as a somewhat cynical pastoral strategy—that is, as affording a pastoral ratification of Grubstreet, or bourgeois, enterprise. No doubt this motive exists in the depiction of Poor Richard's Pennsylvania Twickenham, but the complex-

14 *Ibid.*, III, 60. Important aspects of the retirement theme in the eighteenth century are discussed in Maynard Mack, *The Garden and the City: Retirement and Politics in the Later Poetry of Pope, 1731–1743* (Toronto: University of Toronto Press, 1969).

ity of that image must be taken into account. Poor Richard is not only a hack, but a man of letters and a moral preceptor as well. A counselor in the use of money and time, he harmoniously joins the idea of financial independence gained through intellectual work and the concept of pastoral leisure defined in literary tradition. Poor Richard has *earned* his Arcadia, but it is not the less Arcadia for having been thus acquired. His affluence merely enhances his moral independence.

Two years before he forsook an active part in the business of printing and bookselling, Franklin established Poor Richard securely in a symbolic home of the moral philosopher and man of letters. This was, one surmises, a deliberate act on Franklin's part. Removed from the city and worldly affairs, Poor Richard becomes distinctly a voice carrying the authority of pastoral detachment. Although he identifies the literary vocation with that of the farmer and thus appears as a common man articulating the values of the common reader, Poor Richard is not fused with the common mind. For all his expression of bourgeois-democratic attitudes, he speaks from the Third Realm. In his representation of the literary vocation, knowledge, wisdom, and wit do not spring from common literacy. He does not equate the man *of* letters and the man *with* letters.

There is more than a little justification for the view that, with whatever wry, ironic humor, Poor Richard symbolizes in provincial microcosm the cosmopolitan figure of letters and learning that Franklin was becoming during the years between the almanac-maker's inception and the middle of the eighteenth century. This was the figure that David Hume acclaimed in 1762 when he learned of the American's imminent departure from the post he had held in England as colonial agent of Pennsylvania. At this time Hume wrote to Franklin: "I am very sorry, that you intend soon to leave our Hemisphere. America has sent us many good things, Gold, Silver, Sugar, Tobacco, Indigo, &c.: But you are the first Philosopher, and indeed the first Great Man of Letters for whom we are beholden to her: it is our own Fault that we have not kept him: Whence it appears that we do not agree with Solomon that Wisdom is above Gold: For we take care never to send back an ounce of the latter, which we once lay our Fingers upon." [15]

Hume's graceful but sincere compliment not only recognized Franklin as a peer of the Third Realm but also acknowledged the rise of the Republic of Letters in the colonial mind. But David Hume, it must be said, had little if any notion of the Franklin who wore the mask of Poor Richard. Hume, who was fearful lest his theoretical destruction of the soul be bruited among the common people, considered speculation and knowledge to be the proper province of the community of the lettered—"a closed and interlocked system of mutual admiration and criticism," as Basil Willey described it. He knew only the Franklin who invited colonial Americans "in circumstances that set them at Ease, and afford Leisure" to "cultivate the finer Arts, and improve the common Stock of Knowledge" by forming a society of "Virtuosi or ingenious men." This would be called the American Philosophical Society, and it would be dedicated to maintaining "a constant Correspondence" on a great variety of subjects. [16] Hume scarcely understood that in the eighteenth century the self-articulation of the Third Realm through the correspondence of the learned could not be separated from the widening literacy of print.

Still less did Hume grasp that in this expansion of literacy the Great Critique of Church and State was being translated into an active politics of literacy. This was a politics based not on the idea of a conquest of illiteracy—of the achievement of universal literacy by means of gross diffusion of elementary reading and writing skills— but on the concept of achieving universal freedom of the educated secular mind by means of an extension of the Republic of Letters and an enhancement of its historical reality. This would be accomplished through the larger association of men of letters in a worldwide community created by a diffusion of pamphlets, magazines, and books and through an increase of the influence of men of letters.

15 *Papers*, X, 81–82.
16 Basil Willey, *The Eighteenth Century Background: Studies in the Idea of Nature in the Thought of the Period* (Boston: Beacon Press, 1961), 123. Also, see page 122. *Papers*, II, 380–81.

Which is to say, through an increase in the persons they can influence—in the number of men *with* letters who can be directed in the formation of an informed public opinion. The goal of the politics of literacy as it took shape in the Age of the Enlightenment was the domination of Church and State by the Third Realm, or—if it cannot be put quite so explicitly—the domination of history based on a cosmopolitan acquirement of rational power over nature and man. The quest for such a dominion—for a moral government of the world by men of letters—was rooted in the faith that nature and man exist in a rational and (because it is rational) a moral universe; either nature or man is subject to explication in a rational employment of language.

As it became increasingly localized in a multiplicity of institutions such as the French Academy, the Royal Society, and the American Philosophical Society, the Republic of Letters became a realm operating within the conjoined realms of Church and State—in a loose but vital way a symbolic *imperium in imperio* in Western civilization. But the Third Realm became world-historical in a definite sense only when it became operative and active in the determination of events in specific historical situations—for example, the relationship of the American colonies to the British Empire.

Representing the American expression of the Third Realm as an *imperium in imperio* of the British Empire, Franklin assumed his full role as a world-historical man of letters. Or, it is possibly more accurate to say, as a world-historical printer. For in Franklin's view the vocation of the man of letters subsumed the vocation of the printer; that is, in the case of the printer as Franklin knew him—the printer in the eighteenth-century printing house, a combined technician, editor, publisher, and bookseller. From the beginning of his career Franklin conceived the representation of the Third Realm in the Age of Print to be the leather-apron man at the printing press screw, just as in the age of the manuscript the Third Realm had been represented by the figure of the copyist in the *scriptorum*. Franklin's sense of the communication of the word is that it depends on the skill and integrity with which it is reproduced and disseminated. The politics of literacy—the examination of the truth of Church and State in a free debate of ideas—is singularly subject to the printer's perception of his moral responsibility for his task. Franklin made a declaration of his own moral commitment to printing in 1731, when, under pressure of an attack on his press, he wrote "An Apology for Printers." Among the particulars of Franklin's defense of printers the following are exceptionally noteworthy:

> Printers are educated in the Belief, that when Men differ in Opinion, both sides ought equally to have the Advantage of being heard by the Publick; and that when Truth and Error have fair Play, the former is always an overmatch for the latter: Hence they chearfully serve all contending Writers that pay them well, without regard on which side they are of the Question in Dispute.
>
> Being thus continually employ'd in serving both Parties, Printers naturally acquire a vast Unconcernedness as to right or wrong Opinions contain'd in what they print; regarding it only as the Matter of their daily labour: They print things full of Spleen and Animosity, with the utmost Calmness and Indifference, and without the least Ill-will to the Persons reflected on; who nevertheless unjustly think the Printer as much their Enemy as the Author, and join them both together in their Resentment.
>
> That it is unreasonable to imagine Printers approve of every thing they print, and to censure them on any particular thing accordingly; since in the way of their Business they print such great variety of things opposite and contradictory. It is likewise as unreasonable what some assert, *That Printers ought not to print any Thing but what they approve*, since if all of that Business should make such a Resolution, and abide by it, an End would thereby be put to Free Writing, and the World would afterwards have nothing to read but what happen'd to be the Opinion of Printers.[17]

Yet another major particular in Franklin's list of ten in "An Apology for Printers" concerns the limits of a printer's moral tolerance:

> That notwithstanding what might be urg'd in behalf of a Man's being allow'd to do in the Way of his Business whatever he is paid for, yet Printers do continually discourage the Printing of great Numbers of bad things, and stifle them in the Birth. I my self have constantly refused to print anything that might countenance Vice, or promote Immorality; tho' by complying in such Cases with the corrupt Taste of the Majority I might have got much Money. I have also always refus'd to print such things as might do real Injury to any Person, how much soever I have been solicited, and tempted with Offers of Great Pay; and how much soever I have

---

17 *Papers*, I, 195.

by refusing got the Ill-will of those who would have employ'd me. I have
hitherto fallen under the Resentment of large Bodies of Men, for refusing
absolutely to print any of their Party or Personal Reflections. In this Manner I have made my self many Enemies, and the constant Fatigue of deny-
ing is almost insupportable. But the Publick being unacquainted with all
this, whenever the poor Printer happens either through Ignorance or much
Persuasion, to do any thing that is generally thought worthy of Blame,
he meets with no more Friendship or Favour on the above Account, than
if there were no Merit in't at all.[18]

A declaration of practice founded on his own experience, "An
Apology for Printers" is as well a statement reflecting the experience of the Third Realm in its struggle for self-articulation in history.
It is both a practical and a symbolic statement: an announcement of
a clear differentiation of the Third Realm in colonial American history. From this point on, a colonial press—although it was always
affected by governmental censorship—would provide for the local-
ization of the politics of literacy in America. This is the development
brilliantly described in Bernard Bailyn's *The Ideological Origins of
the American Revolution*. Bailyn discovers a primary rationale of
the American Revolution in a colonial pamphlet literature that afforded "the clarification and consolidation under the pressure of
events of a view of the world and of America's place in it." This literature (Bailyn does not discuss it in quite the same terms used here)
was an offshoot of the expansion of the Third Realm in the England
of the Commonwealth and of the Glorious Revolution. These were
the times of Milton, James Harrington, Henry Neville, and Algernon
Sidney. The diffusion of the politics of literacy by these men of letters and "heroes of liberty" was carried further by their inheritors in
the early eighteenth century. Among these were John Trenchard,
Thomas Gordon, Bishop Hoadly, and other pamphleteers who followed a "country" as opposed to a London vision of government and
social order and thereby further widened the influence of the Third
Realm. Republished by American printers, the English pamphleteers
became the core of an American pamphlet literature that advanced

18 *Ibid.*, I, 196.

the tendency to democratize the mind and prepared the way for the Revolution—not to speak of sustaining it once it began.[19]

Unifying the roles of printer and man of letters like no other figure in the eighteenth century, Franklin expressed the harmony and power —the hegemony—that the Third Realm had achieved three centuries after the invention of printing. His assertion of the moral and intellectual power of the Republic of Letters is integral to its evolvement into world-historical meaning in the Revolution and the founding of the new nation. And yet, like Voltaire, though unlike more exuberant intellectuals such as Condorcet, Franklin sensed the historical finitude of the Third Realm. His advocacy of the politics of literacy always conveys an indeterminate aura of ironic reservation about the quest for social order based on human wisdom—Franklin being constantly aware of the precarious balance between civilizational and barbaric impulses in man. His final statement about the liberty of the press is a pessimistic satire entitled "An Account of the Supremest Court of Judicature in Pennsylvania, Viz. the Court of the Press." In a time when the liberty of the press has become an unquestionable assumption of society, the sole recourse of the individual who is singled out for condemnation by its arbitrary decision may be, Franklin suggests, to take up a cudgel against printer and author. Violation of the civility of freedom by the press, in Franklin's satirical view at any rate, justifies liberty of the bludgeon on the part of the victimized individual. But Franklin was disposed to think that man's capacity to create a literary and intellectual realm of existence expressed an ancient opposition to barbarism as inherent in his nature as the inclination to barbarism. He died believing that the God of the universe had conferred the possibility of "Government by human Wisdom"[20] on mankind, and that this possibility could be realized through the agency of the Third Realm. "God

19 Bernard Bailyn, *The Ideological Origins of the American Revolution* (Cambridge: Belknap Press of Harvard University Press, 1967), 22–54, 160–229. Also, see Peter Gay, *The Enlightenment: An Interpretation* (2 vols.; New York: Alfred A. Knopf, 1969), II, 555–68.
20 "Motion for Prayers in Convention," in *Benjamin Franklin: Representative Selections*, ed. Frank Luther Mott and Chester E. Jorgenson (New York: American Book

grant," he wrote almost at the end, "that not only the love of liberty, but a thorough knowledge of the rights of man, may pervade the nations of the earth, so that a philosopher may set his foot anywhere on its surface, and say, 'This is my country.'"[21]

Company, 1936), 490. Franklin made this motion in the Constitutional Convention, June 28, 1787.
21 Quoted in Nye, "Introduction" to *Autobiography and Other Writings*, xvii–xviii.

2 / The Symbolism of Literary Alienation in the Revolutionary Age

I n *Mind in the Modern World,* Lionel Trilling points out that when Plato "undertook to say what the right conduct of mind should be, he found the paradigm in the just society." But in modern times the procedure has been reversed, and we find "the paradigm of the just society in the right conduct of mind." We evaluate governments in the ideal by "their intentionality, their impulse toward inclusiveness, by their striving toward coherence with due regard for the disparate elements they comprise, by the power of looking before and after."[1] A detailed comment on mind as the model of American society is not Trilling's purpose in *Mind in the Modern World.* But in his discussion he makes an inference of the first importance for our understanding of the general cultural situation, and more particularly of the literary situation, in the age of our Revolution and early nationhood: the reversal of mind and society as paradigms of order was first fully defined in Thomas Jefferson's respect for mind as the model of government. Jefferson's attitude—or the attitude of the Enlightenment that found a cogent focus in Jefferson—had two drastic consequences. One of these is well known to us; we take it for granted as a fact of our existence. I mean the radical displacement of the traditional community centered in Church and State, and in hierarchy, custom, and ritual, as the model of mind in America by the creation of public mind or public opinion as the model of society. In effect this occurrence relocated American society in the subjective realm of consciousness. The second consequence of the

1 *Mind in the Modern World* (New York: Viking Press, 1972), 37–39.

reversal of the paradigms of order in America stems from the first. This is the paradoxical, complex estrangement of American men of letters from the Revolution and the new nation.

Never overt in the Revolutionary expression, this latter phenomenon is disclosed in a subtle and involved symbolism of cultural and literary displacement and alienation. I shall do no more here than attempt a brief examination of this symbolism in several representative works of the Revolutionary age—a period I am thinking of as extending from about the time of the first active agitation against England in the 1760s until the conclusion of the War of 1812, when American independence was finally secured. Within the broad signification of the term *literature* still prevailing in the eighteenth century, all the writings I shall refer to are literary works. They are the Declaration of Independence and *The Federalist;* selected poems of Philip Freneau; a novel, *Modern Chivalry*, by Hugh Henry Brackenridge; and a periodical essay, "The Rhapsodist," and another novel, *Arthur Mervyn*, by Charles Brockden Brown.

The system of symbols governing the modern concept of the literary vocation came into existence with the articulation in Western civilization of the Third Realm. Commonly referred to as the Republic of Letters, the Third Realm comprehended all secular knowledge under the terms *letters, literature*, and *science*, and as I point out in the preceding chapter, inaugurated a comprehensive critique of the society based on the feudal concepts of custom and tradition, hierarchy and monarchy.[2] By the eighteenth century the Great Critique had developed as one powerful, if not entirely conscious, intention the moulding of government to the model of human mind as this had come to be represented by the realm of letters.

Implemented by two crucial responses to mind's quest for power —the technology of printing and the Reformation (dramatically and forcefully joined by the Puritan intellectuals,[3] who were so large an

2 The schematic description of the Third Realm in the chapter on Franklin will, I hope, serve as a general reference for the appearance of this concept here and elsewhere in this volume.

3 See especially Michael Walzer, *The Revolution of the Saints: A Study in the Origins of Radical Politics* (New York: Atheneum, 1968), 124.

influence on the American settlement)—the emerging Third Realm moved toward its historical fulfillment in America with the proclamation of the Declaration of Independence. The work of a congress of colonials led by a group of philosophes, notably Franklin, Jefferson, and John Adams, this document manifests the triumphant identity of the man of letters and his order. When the Declaration was proclaimed, there no longer stood at the center of the world a king, a bishop, and a hierarchical society, but rather the man of letters and his written declaration of mind's assumption of dominion and power. This dominion demanded full allegiance: "To preserve the freedom of the human mind . . . and freedom of the press, every spirit should be ready to devote itself to martyrdom."[4] Jefferson believed his rhetoric to be justified by the immutable truth of mind's authority. But although the Declaration of Independence symbolizes the right conduct of mind as the pattern of a just society, it intimates uncertainty about the authority of the Third Realm; anticipating the development of an ambiguous relation between the man of letters and a political, economic, and social order that he assumes, or wants to assume, is emblematic of the order of rational, lettered minds—between the Republic of Letters and its citizen, the man of letters.

We may refer to the following elements in the Declaration: (1) its suggestion of the psychic expense of estrangement from a community of kindred and the loss of a traditional social order; and (2) its suggestion of the loss of the classical-Christian sense of transcendent truth.

In the form in which it was accepted by the Continental Congress, the Declaration shows a certain inclination toward finding its climax not in the usurpation by the king of the "just powers" conferred on him by the "consent of the governed," but in a stern account of the crimes of a patriarch against the "brethren" of the colonies. In the version of the Declaration before amendment and deletion, this tendency is more obvious. The king is something of a monster, albeit with the complicity of the people of the homeland, who "at this very time" are "permitting their chief magistrate to send over not

---

4 Jefferson to William Green Mumford, June 18, 1789, in Adrienne Koch (ed.), *The American Enlightenment* (New York: George Braziller, 1965), 341.

only soldiers of our common blood, but Scotch & foreign mercenaries to invade & destroy us." It is "these facts" that "have given the last stab to agonizing affection" and that bid the "manly spirit" in us "to renounce forever these unfeeling brethren." In the denunciation of slavery, Jefferson was more explicit in his depiction of the monstrous character of the king, who is said to have "waged war against human nature itself, violating its most sacred rights of life and liberty in the persons of a distant people who never offended him, captivating & carrying them into slavery in another hemisphere. . . . And that this assemblage of horrors might want no fact of distinguished die, he is now exciting those very people to rise in arms among us, and to purchase that liberty of which he has deprived them, by murdering the people on whom he also obtruded them: thus paying off former crimes committed against the LIBERTIES of one people, with crimes which he urges them to commit against the LIVES of another." Although the last section of charges drawn by Jefferson on the whole shapes a contrast (especially in the original version of the Declaration) between the rational and the irrational, depicting a king who, in his violation of the unalienable rights of man, has become a figure of barbarous irrationality, it also suggests a monarch who has disregarded the unreasoning organic affections of kinship. A significant ambivalence of intention in the Declaration is inherent in its emotionality. The plain intention, to be sure, is to assert the right of revolution disclosed by the "laws of nature and of nature's God"; but this clear purpose is haunted by the expression of resentment against the corruption of a community founded not on rational hypothesis, but existing in the ties of blood and the continuum of tradition. The depth of resentment and the anxiety it provoked may have been greater in Jefferson's version of the corruption of community than in the congressional one. In a compelling revision of the conventional exposition of the Declaration, especially of the Jeffersonian draft, Garry Wills holds that Jefferson, an adherent not of Lockean contractualism but of Francis Hutcheson's philosophy of the moral sentiment and the social affections, intended to place the blame for the alienation of the colonials directly on the British people. The people of the homeland, the brethren of the colonials, supported the king and the Parliament, notably the latter, and therefore bear the responsibility for a grievous impairment of the ties binding a community of natural affection.[5]

A sense of anxiety about intentionality in the Declaration, not mere deference to respect for the Deity, may be the reason why the Congress amended the wording of the original version of the Declaration's conclusion *from* "We therefore the representatives of the United States of America in General Congress assembled, *appealing to the supreme judge of the world for the rectitude of our intentions*, do in the name & by the authority of the good people of these united colonies. . ." The appeal "to the supreme judge of the world" to ratify the good intentions of the Revolutionists qualifies the equation between "nature's God" and the sovereignty of the "good people" and, in fact, introduces an unobtrusive but significant element of doubt into the Declaration about the rectitude of the people's intention as self-verifying or transcendently self-evident. Indeed doubt of the existence of transcendent truth is a spectral presence in more than a little of the literature of the American Revolution. The acceptance of rational mind as the ideal model of a just society not only meant the rejection of constructs of perfect order existing in eternity—Plato's Republic, St. Augustine's heavenly city, Dante's community of hierarchy and degree—but meant too the rejection of the tradition of verifying the truth of order through contemplation. Contemplation depends on the acceptance of an infallible ideal of order outside mind. From Descartes on, mind became identified with the introspective, unstructured functions of consciousness—with the processes of cognition. Believing solely in its own existence, mind has no knowledge outside itself and no reference for action outside its own functioning. Consciousness cannot transcend consciousness.[6] Once the im-

5 See Garry Wills, *Inventing America: Jefferson's Declaration of Independence* (New York: Doubleday and Company, Inc., 1978). The text of the Declaration of Independence as it appears in Jefferson's *Autobiography* (with the Congressional excision and substitutions) is conveniently reprinted in Wills, pp. 374–79. Another convenient reprinting is in *The Portable Thomas Jefferson*, ed. Merrill D. Peterson (New York: Viking Press, 1975), 235–41.

6 See Hannah Arendt, *The Human Condition* (New York: Doubleday Anchor Books, 1959), especially 249–97, for a discussion of thought in the modern world to which I am indebted throughout this book. I also have a general indebtedness to Eric Voegelin, especially to *The New Science of Politics* (Chicago: University of Chicago Press, 1952), 107–32.

port of the loss of contemplative truth was realized, the struggle to achieve a new mode of transcendence became central to nineteenth-century romanticism and exercised a fateful influence on modern history. But in the eighteenth century the effective sense of rationality assumed the existence of the Third Realm. If a transcendent republic outside mind did not exist, a public order of rational, lettered mind conceived by mind itself did. This order represented the right conduct of mind as a truth verifiable in history by the man of letters.

In this connection, it is hardly too much to say, the most important fictional representation of the man of letters in the writings of the Revolution and of the early American republic is Publius, the composite mask of the authors of *The Federalist*. I have in mind at this point the character of Publius as he speaks for Hamilton in the first essay in the papers. In authoritative, measured eloquence he presents his reasons for supporting the new Constitution, yet intimates the problematical quality of his support:

> It has frequently been remarked that it seems to have been reserved to the people of this country, by their conduct and example, to decide the important question, whether societies of men are really capable or not of establishing good government from reflection and choice, or whether they are forever destined to depend for their political constitutions on accident and force. If there be any truth in the remark, the crisis at which we are arrived may with propriety be regarded as the era in which that decision is to be made; and a wrong election of the part we shall act, may, in this view, deserve to be considered as the general misfortune of mankind.[7]

It is not to be expected, Publius says, that philanthropy and patriotism will insure a "judicious estimate of our true interests." We expect "passions and prejudices little favorable to the discovery of truth" to arise from those who, secure in positions in the various states, are fearful of a federal establishment, and from those who want to profit from confusion and division. But Publius does not dwell on impediments to truth. He is more concerned with those persons of "upright intentions" who may be "led astray by preconceived jealousies and fears." Proponents of the Constitution may be

---

7 Benjamin Fletcher Wright (ed.), *The Federalist* (Cambridge: Harvard University Press, 1961), 89.

influenced by bad motives, there being no way to prevent political factions involved in a "great national discussion" from letting loose a "torrent of angry and malignant passions." Publius wants to warn his fellow citizens against accepting "any impressions other than those which may result from the evidence of truth." Saying he will offer his impressions frankly and solely on the basis of his own deliberations, Publius enters a significant qualification of the evidence he has to present:

> I will not amuse you with an appearance of deliberation when I have decided. I frankly acknowledge to you my convictions, and I will freely lay before you the reasons on which they are founded. The consciousness of good intentions disdains ambiguity. I shall not, however, multiply professions on this head. My motives must remain in the depository of my own breast. My arguments will be open to all, and may be judged by all. They shall at least be offered in a spirit which will not disgrace the cause of truth.[8]

The reasons of Publius open to all, but the motives for his reasons hidden and locked away—this is the modified Hobbesian outlook that informs the thinking of Hamilton and ramifies here and there throughout "conservative" thought in the early Republic. If, according to Hobbes, man is generically a creature of passions, the objects of the passions are not a subject for philosophical inquiry. In Hobbes's version of society, the motive of individual passions replaces the ordering inspiration of a quest for the *summum bonum*. All that saves Publius from the Hobbesian bleakness is his "consciousness of good intentions." I will not pretend that I have an open mind on the Constitution, he says; I have finished my deliberations upon it and concluded in its favor. My rational intentions in presenting the case for the Constitution put me above the ambiguity of human motives. What is at stake in the question of the approval or disapproval of the Constitution is the representation to the world that by "their conduct and example" the American people embody "reflection and choice" as the proper source of government. The underlying question, according to Publius, is not whether the new nation embodies a unique nationhood, but whether it represents the capacity of indi-

8 *Ibid.*, 90–92.

viduals in their collectivity as public mind or public opinion to act on the basis of good (rational) intentions. Publius symbolizes the constructive intentionality of public mind as a representation of the Third Realm. In Publius, the eighteenth-century man of letters, the Third Realm is identified as the model of the emergent American Republic.

Even so, Publius does not convince us of mind's propensity for good intentions. It is almost as though he is attempting, without success, to assume the sovereignty of good intentions over the truth he knows always to be darkly present in the processes of consciousness: the ambiguous connection between intention and motive. Publius is aware, we might say, of participating in an unprecedented internalization of history. Even as he urges upon Americans their historical opportunity to form a government based on reflection and choice, he implies the fear that public mind, or public opinion, will prove to be an insidious, disorderly power, hiding both its intentions and its motives in the breasts of thousands of persons and, as one young Federalist man of letters said, constantly exercising not a public but a "secret influence."[9] In spite of the fact that the press has become the education of everyman, public opinion, Publius intimates, is not an extension of, but a threat to, the Republic of Letters.

Yet if he anticipates a diminishing role for the man of letters as the representative of mind's authority in the novel American nation-state, Publius is the man of letters as eighteenth-century philosophe and Revolutionary statesman. He takes for granted his existence under the dispensation of the Third Realm, although he implicitly questions its efficacy. When we turn from the American man of letters in the role personified by Publius to his role as poet and story-teller, we detect a more sensitive, and more distinct, awareness of the displacement of the man of letters in the early American nation-state. Freneau, Brackenridge, and Brown not only suggest in their writings that in the disparity between the golden intention of the Revolution—the establishment of a state based on rational, lettered mind—and the equivocal motivation of this purpose in the passions, there is a loss of literary authority. They self-consciously symbolize

9 Joseph Stevens Buckminster, "On the Dangers and Duties of Men of Letters," *Monthly Anthology and Boston Review*, 7 (September, 1809), 148.

this loss in their depiction of the drama of the American poet, essayist, or novelist, who is presumptively engaged in heroically imagining and proclaiming the new age being ushered in by the Revolution yet is basically uncertain of his role, even to the extent of feeling himself somehow to be an outsider to the good intentions of the Revolution.

> Of all the Poets dead and gone,
> I cannot recollect but ONE
>   That throve by writing rhyme—
> If *Pope* from *Homer* gained rewards,
> Remember, statesmen, kings and lords
>   Were poets, in his time.
> A poet where there is no king
>   Is but a disregarded thing
>   An atom on the wheel;
> A second *Iliad* could he write
> His pockets would be very light,
>   And beggarly his meal.[10]

This lament is not that of a distressed American Tory poet. It is a retrospection on his own career by an aged Philip Freneau, a major voice of the American Revolution and in his prime an unrivaled denouncer of monarchy. "*Kings are the choicest curse that man e'er knew!*" Freneau exclaimed in 1778, a conviction he reaffirmed in the 1790s, envisioning liberation from monarchy as the key to the American future:

> COLUMBIA, hail! immortal be thy reign:
> Without a king, we till the smiling plain:
> Without a king, we trace the unbounded sea,
> And traffic round the globe, through each degree.
>
> . . . .
>
> So shall our nation form'd on Virtue's plan,
> Remain the guardian of the Rights of Man,
> A vast Republic famed through every clime,
> Without a king, see the end of time.[11]

---

10 "The City Poet" in Philip Freneau, *Last Poems*, ed. Lewis Leary (New Brunswick: Rutgers University Press, 1945), 31–32.
11 "America Independent; and Her Everlasting Deliverance from British Tyranny and Oppression" in Freneau, *Poems*, ed. Harry Hayden Clark (New York: Hafner Publishing Company, 1929), 25; "On Mr. Paine's Rights of Man," *ibid.*, 125.

Having once held such a view of kingship, how could Freneau, even in satirical jest, allow himself later to conclude that in the destruction of a king lay the destruction of poetry and consequently the sad lapse of his poetic career? The answer undoubtedly lies partly in the neglect and penury Freneau endured in his long old age, but fundamentally it seems to lie in his lifelong suspicion that rationality is not an inherent human capacity—that actually the monster who is the king is born out of the monster in man. This is the theme that emerges in Freneau's remarkable poem "A Picture of the Times, with Occasional Reflections" (1782):

> Cursed be the day, how bright so'er it shined
> That first made kings the masters of mankind;
> And cursed the wretch who first with regal pride
> Their equal rights to equal men denied;
> But cursed, o'er all, who first to slavery broke
> Submissive bowed and owned a monarch's yoke:
> Their servile souls his arrogance adorned
> And basely owned a brother for a lord;
> Hence wrath, and blood, and feuds and wars began,
> And man turned monster to his fellow man.[12]

In contrast, the poet pictures the premonarchical government conducted by "the hoary sage beneath his sylvan shade," who

> Imposed no laws but those which reason made;
> On peace, not war, on good, not ill intent,
> He judged his brethren by their own consent;
> Untaught to spurn those brethren to the dust;
> In virtue firm, and obstinately just[13]

Freneau discovers in the rise of monarchy a dispossession of man from his original abode in a garden of reason and peace. But his attitude toward the nature of this fall of man is uncertain. A king would not seem to be as responsible for the abrogation of the rule of reason as his subjects, who not only submit to a monarch but adore his arrogance. Does a reverence for kingly authority answer to profound, yet elusive, motives in the consciousness—to nameless desires, terrors, and tribulations that reason cannot respond to?

12 *Ibid.*, 85.
13 *Ibid.*, 85–86.

Freneau pursues the problem he suggests in no certain way. In fact, he turns his poem toward a castigation of King George, depicting his mind as disordered by the demon Ambition. Freneau's "Picture of the Times" not only implies that the human mind itself is contradictory and unreasoning, but that an overpowering demonic insurrection against its original faculty of reason has occurred within it. There are positive efforts in Freneau's poetry to represent the American Revolution as a restoration of a premonarchical state of reason, but all of his more complex poems about America indicate a pessimistic, even a despairing, attitude toward this prospect. Consider, for instance, the well-known poem entitled "To An Author." This has often been interpreted simply as a reflection on the transience of literary effort in the sparse cultural environment of a provincial world: "Thrice happy Dryden, who could meet / Some rival bard in every street!"[14] But "To An Author" addresses itself not so much to the fate of the individual poet in the barren American literary situation as to a threatened deformation of the sensibility of reason and to the loss of the poetic vision of America as a culture of reason.

> An age employed in edging steel
> Can no poetic raptures feel;
> No solitude's attracting power
> No leisure of the noon day hour,
> No shaded stream, no quiet grove
> Can this fantastic century move;
>
> The muse of love in no request—
> Go—try your fortune with the rest,
> *One* of the nine you should engage,
> To meet the follies of the age:—
> On *one*, we fear, your choice must fall—
> The least engaging of them all—
> Her visage stern—and angry style—
> A clouded brow—malicious smile—
> A mind on *murdered victims* placed—
> She, only she, can please the taste![15]

America, it would seem, finds in request neither Thalia, the muse of pastoral poetry, nor Erato, the muse of erotic poetry, and summons

14 *Ibid.*, 353.
15 *Ibid.*, 353–54.

only Melpomene, the forbidding muse of tragedy, whose sign is a sword.

But, it is interesting to observe, the release of America from active warfare did not signify to Freneau a larger place in the nation for a poetry of reason. On the contrary, by the end of the eighteenth century Freneau's vision of the role of the poet and of his message in America became more despairing than it is in "To An Author." In "The Americans of the United States," a poem devoted to a characterization of the Republic near the end of its first decade, Freneau finds no muse at all in request by America and sees the American future as an altogether antipoetic age of prose and commonsense:

> To seize some *features* from the faithless past;
> Be this our care—before the century close:
> The colours strong!—for, if we deem aright,
> The *coming age will be an age of prose*:
> When *sordid cares* will break the muses' dream,
> And COMMON SENSE be ranked in seat supreme,
>
> Go, now, dear book; once more expand your wings;
> Still to the cause of man severely true:
> Untaught to flatter *pride*, or fawn on kings.—
> Trogan, or Tyrian, *give them both their due*.—
> *When they are right, the cause of both we plead.*
> *And both will please us well,—if both will read.*[16]

"*If both will read.*" Freneau makes a gesture of resignation toward the lapsing literary authority in America. Although he retains his conviction of the poet's obligation to rebel against kings, he sees in the bourgeois mind the final destruction of the poetry of reason. The American republic will be dominated by "sordid cares," which are equated with "commonsense"—meaning a devotion to the subjective motives of popular self-interest. An age of prose has issued from an age of iron. Freneau recognizes his vision of the poet's guidance in the restoration of an original republic of reason as a poetic dream. When at the last he refers to the isolation of the poet in a society without a king, he confirms the irony of his own experience of rebellion against a king. A minor poet of the Great Critique, an active citizen of the Third Realm, Freneau felt abandoned in a historical situation that he had at once resisted and helped to make.

16 *Ibid.*, 150.

The relationship of the man of letters to the early Republic is explored both more explicitly and at greater length in Hugh Henry Brackenridge's novel *Modern Chivalry* than it is in the writings of Freneau. Loosely imitative of *Don Quixote*, this fulsome, discursive satire relates the adventures of Captain John Farrago and his Irish immigrant servant, Teague O'Regan, as they move about the communities of an American frontier landscape, a world that mirrors western Pennsylvania, Brackenridge's home and the scene of his comparatively small but emblematic career in American politics.

According to the author, the admonitory theme of *Modern Chivalry* (which was written over a period of twenty-five years, about half of the work being published in the 1790s and the whole not until 1815) is the danger in a democratic society of putting unqualified men in positions of trust and responsibility. But the comprehensive theme of the novel is the problematical role of the man of letters in a society which, shaping itself in the protean image of public mind or public opinion, is incapable of defining its aims or recognizing its motives. *Modern Chivalry* describes a society given over to the vanity of equality. On the simplest level the theme of the fate of the man of letters in such a society is expressed in anecdotes about the aggressions of ignorance against letters. In one instance a candidate for office is accused of having been seen with a book in his hand. He protests:

> I am innocent of letters as the child unborn. I am an illiterate man, God be praised, and free from the sin of learning, or any wicked art, as I hope to be saved; but here is a report raised up, that I have dealings in books, that I can read. O! the wickedness of this world! Is there no protection from slander, and bad report? God help me! Here I am, *an honest republican, a good citizen*, and yet it is reported of me that I read books. O! who can stop reproach? I am ruined; I am undone; I shall loose [sic] my election; and the good will of my neighbours, and the confidence of posterity.

Farrago reflects: "The time was, when learning would save a man's neck; but now it endangers it. The neck verse, is reversed. That is the effect of it. For the man that can read goes to the wall; not him that is ignorant. *But such are the revolutions of opinion.*"[17] In another incident that appears in *Modern Chivalry*, a jury convicts a

17 Hugh Henry Brackenridge, *Modern Chivalry*, ed. Claude M. Newlin (New York: American Book Company, 1937), 419–20.

man of insanity because he admits of "being *addicted to books.*" In this instance a superior judge (in *Modern Chivalry*, it is to be noted, the lawyer and the judge often exemplify the man of letters) takes the case under advisement; and although the outcome is not pursued in the novel, it would seem that the verdict will be overturned.

The major representation of Brackenridge's theme in *Modern Chivalry* occurs in Farrago's efforts to keep his illiterate servant from rising above the station that Farrago believes he should occupy in the democratic republic. But Teague's proper status is hard for his master to define. The whole society is pervaded by the vanity of equality, which binds not only the ignorant, but also the well educated to the bogtrotter's limitations. At one point, for instance, Teague is elected to membership in the American Philosophical Society. But the compelling influence of equality is dramatized most effectively in the impact it has on Farrago. His sensitivity to Teague's meaning in American society and the problems and vexations of his superintendence of Teague—a demanding and delicate task that the captain deems necessary to the welfare of the nation—become the substance of whatever plot *Modern Chivalry* has; and if the novel can be said to have a climax, this is reached when Farrago eventually realizes the nature of his vexatious role. He is the man of letters as democratic chevalier.

> Democracy has its strength in strict integrity; in perfect delicacy; in elevation and dignity of mind. It is an unjust imputation, that it is rude in manners, and coarse in expression. This is the characteristic of slaves, in a despotism; not of democrats in a republic. Democracy embraces the idea of standing on virtue alone; unaided by wealth or the power of family. This makes 'the noble of nature' of whom Thomas Payne [*sic*] speaks. Shall this noble not know his nobility, and be behind the noble of aristocracy who piques himself upon his honour, and feels a stain upon his delicacy as he would a bodily wound? The democrat is the true chevalier, who, though he wears not crosses, or the emblazoned arms of heraldry, yet is ready to do right, and justice to everyone. All other are imposters, and do not belong to the order of democracy.[18]

Resisting the vanity of equality, the democratic chevalier invests democracy with a sense of the heroic. "Now the vote of the citizen

18 *Ibid.*, 403–404.

takes the place of the sword of the adventurer," Brackenridge says. "Shall the knight of the Golden Cross be free from stain in his achievements [*sic*]; and shall a republican prostitute his vote, or dishonor his standing in society by bestowing it on the unworthy?"[19]

But if the proper role of the American man of letters is to be a democratic chevalier, Brackenridge does not see this as a self-assured function. Shall the modern chevalier "complain of usurpation; of undue influence; or oppression and tyranny from ambitious persons; and not be jealous, at the same time of *democratic tyranny* in himself, which is the more pernicious, as it brings a slur upon the purest principles?" Brackenridge declares in Volume II, Part II, of *Modern Chivalry* that he "would make it a principal matter" of his novel to "form the heart to a *republican government.*" To this end he discusses the necessity of uprooting from the heart the "poison weed of ambition"—this to be accomplished by translating the "ambition of doing good" into the *"pleasure* of doing good," which is the "greatest possible pleasure to a mind rightly informed."[20] The purification of the motives of the heart would bring rational intention and motive (head and heart) into a consonant relationship. The modern chevalier would make whole the Hamiltonian dichotomy of intention and motive in the American man of letters, and the man of letters would enter into a state of complete democratic sincerity. Yet Brackenridge remains doubtful about an idealistic reconciliation of the discrepancy between the intention of the Republic to be an emblem of rational mind and the motive of this aim. This is seen most graphically in his personal concern about a discrepancy between the overt intention of his authorship of *Modern Chivalry* and his inner motive in writing it. Is he writing primarily out of his hope to form the heart to a republican government? Or does he write out of his own heart's desire to pursue the pleasure and the power that are the artist's? Brackenridge confesses, *"There is a pleasure in writing, which only the man who writes knows."*[21] This, he acknowledges, is not the joy of doing good; it is the pleasure of self-love. And this, Brackenridge indicates, is related to a still deeper motive in writing his

19 *Ibid.*
20 *Ibid.*, 481.
21 *Ibid.*, 492.

novel—the delight he takes in his power to "elevate small matters," to record the "freaks" of ordinary people, and thus to give the form of truth to the world immediately about him.

> That is the very reason I assume this biography of Farrago. Any one can write the campaign of a great prince, because the subject sustains the narrative. But it is a greater praise to give a value to the rambles of private persons, or the dissensions of a borough town. One advantage is, that these transactions being in a narrow compass, the truth can be reached with more certainty, the want of which is a drawback upon histories of greater compass, most of them being little better than the romance of the middle ages, or the modern novel.[22]

In his compounded ironies, including ironic comments on the genre in which he is writing, Brackenridge illuminates the status and meaning of the literary vocation in America by expressing the truth of his own life. *Modern Chivalry* is a highly self-conscious satirical fantasy about American democracy; at the same time it is an autobiographical history (in the guise of a biography of Captain Farrago) of an aspiring American man of letters—at once a revelation and a concealment of the author's own career. Brackenridge began his life as a man of letters in a youthful self-recognition of his literary gifts and demonstrated these in his collaboration with Freneau in a patriotic poem, "The Rising Glory of America"; but, later, suffering like Freneau from a sense of literary dislocation, he longed for the London community of writers. When he satirizes his literary capacities and mocks his ambition in the dissertation on style that introduces Volume III of *Modern Chivalry*, Brackenridge makes his covert conviction of a thwarted career all the more evident:

> The fact is . . . I possess great versatility of stile, and vast compass of sentiment and imagination. Nature intended me for a writer, and it has always been my ambition. How often have I sighed for the garrets of London; when I have read histories, manners, and anecdotes of Otway, Dryden, and others, who have lived in the upper stories of buildings, writing paragraphs, or essays in prose and verse. I have lamented my hard fate that I was not one of these. Was I to go to London, of which I have sometimes thought, my first object would be to visit the aerial mansions of these divine inhabitants. There is not a garret where any of these have dwelt, or

22 *Ibid.*

where any of their descendants now dwell, that I would not rummage to find papers, scraps and remains, of what may still be there. I would at any rate visit most of the present men who live by their wits, and converse with them, indulging that pleasure which one takes in a consimilarity of genius.[23]

But (again like Freneau) Brackenridge does not finally ascribe the frustration of the identity of the man of letters in America to the lack of literary community. In its total implication *Modern Chivalry* attributes this frustration to the intangible dissolution of the public order of letters in the "convulsions of public opinion." The tension in Brackenridge's work between the high purpose of the man of letters—the democratic chevalier of good intentions—and the tyranny of democracy is never resolved one way or the other. But it is evident that if Captain Farrago cannot control Teague O'Regan, neither can his creator. Brackenridge, whose direct role in the novel virtually replaces that of Farrago in the last five hundred pages of the story, is unsuccessful in his advocacy of the principle that the cobbler stick to his last. Teague, the symbol of public opinion, subjects the master to the servant. The ignorant bogtrotter cannot be repudiated by Farrago-Brackenridge, for the author's obligation to democracy is to redeem him. Although in the democratic situation Teague owes nothing to the self-appointed chevalier, the chevalier is bound by the ties of his democratic idealism to the bogtrotter. As the adventures of Farrago-Brackenridge and Teague come to an end in the days of the second war with England, the author is wondering if Teague will become ambassador to England when the hostilities end, and, if this comes to pass, how he will persuade the bogtrotter to dress "according to the customs of the courts of Europe."[24]

Brackenridge likely would have added the European experiences of Farrago and his servant to his mammoth record of their adventures had not death intervened in 1818. But, limited both by his environment and his talent, he had by this time probably exhausted his apprehension of the drama of democracy and letters. While Brackenridge was composing his long, clumsy novel, a gifted and possibly more advantaged writer had created a portrayal of the American man

23 *Ibid.*, 171.
24 *Ibid.*, 808.

of letters that is more complex than either Freneau's or Brackenridge's. In the Philadelphian Charles Brockden Brown's intuition of
his age, we find explicitly suggested the ironic subjection of literary
authority to public opinion that Brackenridge merely intimates.

> I venture to intrude myself upon the public, not in the fond expectation
> of contributing a more than ordinary share of amusement or instruction
> to the common stock. My ambition has already devoted me to the service
> of my country, and the acquisition of true glory, but I am too well ac-
> quainted with my own deficiencies, to hope for fame in this capacity. If
> my continual struggles shall at length raise me to a level with medioc-
> rity, and my readers expect not the eccentric genius of a higher sphere, I
> shall be perfectly satisfied. In the mean time I humbly bespeak their can-
> dour and indulgence to well meant endeavours in their service. Every
> person who commits his writings to the press has by that means volun-
> tarily parted with his ancient liberty and becomes the general vassal; If
> [sic] he brings to his new station spirit and vivacity sufficient to suit
> himself, at all times, and in every change of disposition, to the humours
> and caprice of his lord, he may perhaps, though a slave, enjoy a state of
> splendid vassallage, and reflect with less uneasiness upon the loss of free-
> dom. But if he possess neither abilities to please, nor industry to attempt
> it, he may justly dread the consequences, and it is incumbent upon him,
> as soon as possible, to imprecate the vengeance due to his rashness. I shall
> therefore, on my first appearance, very formally apologise to the good
> company for the intrusion of so worthless a visitant: not that I suppose
> any apology can vindicate dullness or inactivity in the eyes of the public.
> It is a voluntary obligation, which the writer enters into, and it is proper
> that the intire [sic] performance of the condition be completed. Satis-
> fied that the present circumstances of the writer if disclosed, would ren-
> der his most glaring deficiencies excusable, I am content to recommend
> myself as a candidate for future approbation only. An insatiable thirst for
> fame, is by no means incompatible either with a mean capacity or consti-
> tutional indolence. Whenever this heavenly spark is discovered, tho' sur-
> rounded by the wettest rubbish, and smothered in the depth of rudeness,
> and obscurity, it is our duty to recall it into being, to place it in a more
> favourable situation, and at length by care and assiduity to raise it into
> life and action. A genius for poetry and science is little more than an in-
> clination to excell in that particular department. With whatever defects
> of heart or understanding, therefore, it may be accompanied, some indul-
> gence should be allowed to the noblest infirmity of human minds.[25]

25 Charles Brockden Brown, *The Rhapsodist and Other Uncollected Writings*, ed.
Harry R. Warfel (New York: Scholars' Facsimiles and Reprints, 1943), 2–3.

I have quoted from Brown's characterization of the Rhapsodist, the periodical essayist he introduced to the public in 1789. Although the exact relation of Brown to the fiction of the Rhapsodist can be no more than speculative, we are without doubt justified in discerning the image of Brown's sensibility of vocation in his inaugural work. The posture of the Rhapsodist is arresting. He has come to Philadelphia from some remote western spot, where (apparently after military service in the Revolution) he has cultivated the life of the man of letters in solitary independence. But on arriving in the city, he immediately assumes the role of vassal to his "lord," the reading public, voluntarily surrendering his freedom of mind and yet appealing to the lord-public to give whatever spark of genius he may have a chance to burn. Displaying an inverted pride—his gross flattery of his readers hiding his resentment, and perhaps his disdain, of them —the Rhapsodist bows to the author's dependence on the public in the age of printing and democracy. But he counters his obeisance by expressing his self-knowledge of the situation. In his calculated servility the Rhapsodist rules out the possibility of the man of letters as a chevalier in the new American society. Farrago consciously saves what he can of order and decorum, of a past social and literary authority, by self-consciously investing himself in the symbolic role of democratic chevalier. The Rhapsodist, however, has little regard for the role of author as moral preceptor. Proposing to "converse with his reader not as an author but as a man," he wants above all else to demonstrate that he is earnest and sincere.

Elaborating the theme of sincerity in modern literature, Lionel Trilling (in a longer study closely related to the essay on *Mind in the Modern World*) has shown how much the writer's desire for sincerity intensified with his discovery of the self's opposition to the falsity of modern society.[26] In America such a discovery was harder to come by than it was in Europe. Both the conservative consensus of the Federalists (which advocated the authority of social classification) and the liberal consensus of the Jeffersonians (which responded to the imperative of equality) assume a suppression of self to society. The Rhapsodist would seem to be a case in point. Taking on the moral

26 *Sincerity and Authenticity* (Cambridge: Harvard University Press, 1972).

burden of instructing his readers about the ironic corruption of the ideal intentions of society by base motives does not seem to occur to him. To be sincere, he seems to say, is to be fully responsive to society's varied motives and to be the servant of its psychic needs. Pressing hard on Brown's fragmentary conception of his periodical essayist is justifiable because, for all his haste and awkwardness in composition, Brown is the craftiest and cleverest writer of the early Republic. He clearly invites us of the present age, who put so much store in literary subterfuge, to look beneath his surfaces. In the figure of the Rhapsodist, an American author who self-consciously assumes the guise of an ordinary man and subjects himself to the tastes of the private reader, Brown symbolizes the depletion of literary authority in the new nation.

A falling-off from literary dominion is also a covert theme in Brown's best novel, *Arthur Mervyn*. Indeed, it may be the novel's major theme. In the story Mervyn, a country lad (but less your ordinary country boy than the Rhapsodist, as the testimony of Mrs. Althorpe makes plain), takes over as narrator from Dr. Stevens, who, by virtue of the fact that he is a physician, is in the eighteenth-century sense an accredited man of letters. Mervyn employs a self-conscious and artful style which, as William Hedges says, "is all palpitating sensibility embroidered with echoes of Sterne and Shakespeare."[27] How he has acquired this manner—how this child of obscure and ignorant parentage has learned to read, much less to write so well—is a mystery, and it remains so. Mervyn's eccentric behavior before he comes to Philadelphia leads us to assume that he has an artistic disposition and a penchant for letters and learning. But Mrs. Althorpe, who gives Dr. Stevens an account of the youth, cannot tell Stevens whence Mervyn "derived his love of knowledge or his means of acquiring it."[28] The usual course of the aspiring man of letters—study, apprenticeship to the discipline of writing, a developing consciousness of the polity of letters and learning—is lacking in Mervyn's case. Like the Rhapsodist, Mervyn seems to reflect the anomalous literary situation in Brown's America, yet his symbolic import goes

27 "Charles Brockden Brown and the Culture of Contradictions," *Early American Literature*, 9 (Fall, 1974), 129.
28 *Arthur Mervyn or Memoirs of the Year 1793*, ed. Warner Berthoff (New York: Holt, Rinehart and Winston, Inc., 1962), 222–23.

beyond his representation of that irregular state of affairs. Arthur Mervyn (possibly his first name is symbolic) is a fantasy figure of the man of letters, and he tells his personal history in a style that defines his own consciousness as the emblem of the conduct of his society.

The great aim of the modern chevalier in Brackenridge's novel is to employ style, including satire on style, to demonstrate that the good intentions of the rational society must be seen under the realistic aspect of the often perverse motives of the human heart. The duty of the man of letters, then, is to give society a heart shaped by moral knowledge. Although he has intimations of the necessity of moral instruction as the basis of social action, Mervyn employs a rhetoric accommodated to a society that, in the vanity of equality, has begun to rationalize ignorance as innocence and to imagine its history as a fable of innocence—a society of democratic public opinion given to acting on the basis of its thoughtless and hence incorruptible intentionality to do good. In one scene in his adventures, Mervyn goes in quest of the hapless Clemenza Lodi, who has taken refuge in a Philadelphia brothel. At issue in this episode of the novel is, as Mervyn puts it, "the recitude of my intentions." He discusses the question in two or three amazing reflections of his self-assumed mission to invade the brothel. Here is Mervyn after being told by a servant girl that no one is present in the house:

> Once more I reflected on the rectitude of my intentions, on the possibility that the servant girl's assertions might be true, on the benefits of expedition, and of gaining access to the object of my visit without interruption or delay. To these considerations was added a sort of charm, not easily explained, and by no means justifiable, produced by the very temerity and hazardness accompanying this attempt. I thought, with scornful emotions, on the bars and hindrances which pride and caprice, and delusive maxims of decorum, raise in the way of human intercourse. I spurned at these semblances and substitutes of honesty, and delighted to shake such fetters into air, and trample such impediments to dust. I wanted to see an human being, in order to promote her happiness.[29]

Here is Mervyn at the crucial stage of his invasion of the brothel, right before he opens the door upon Clemenza:

29 *Ibid.*, 303.

My behaviour, I well know, was ambiguous and hazardous, and perhaps wanting in discretion, but my motives were unquestionably pure. I aimed at nothing but the rescue of an human creature from distress and dishonour.

Mervyn adds:

I pretend not to the wisdom of experience and age; to the praise of forethought or subtlety. I chuse the obvious path, and pursue it with headlong expedition. Good intentions, unaided by knowledge, will, perhaps, produce more injury than benefit, and therefore, knowledge must be gained, but the acquisition is not momentary; is not bestowed unasked and untoil'd for: meanwhile, we must not be unactive because we are ignorant, whether our knowledge be greater or less.[30]

Is Arthur Mervyn a representation of the American storyteller and man of letters as an "innocent," or is he a representation of the American writer as a pretender to innocence—a freewheeling con man who, in his dedication to life, liberty, and the pursuit of happiness, is always after the main chance; who mirrors the social and moral ambiguities of his society and its language and uses them to his advantage? The evidence pointing toward an answer is uncertain, and we only complicate the uncertainty by trying to resolve it. Brown himself, we conclude, found the evidence to be equivocal. In Mervyn's mind we see the image of a rising, dynamic, egalitarian society that increasingly makes no distinction between intention and motive, ends and means. The ironic symbolic situation in *Arthur Mervyn* suggests that the *man* of letters in American society, divorced from the moral authority of the *realm* of letters, has lost the ideal of his autonomy as a moral agent and has, in fact, become identified with a rationalization of irrational mind, that is, of public mind or public opinion. Far from representing the authority of a structured and refined American intentionality, Arthur Mervyn, his creator suggests, substantiates the cunning and frightening proverb: "The road to hell is paved with good intentions." Indeed, the ironic nuances enveloping Brown's portrayal of Mervyn foreshadows the ominous representation of the man of letters by Nietzsche at the end of the nineteenth century:

30 *Ibid.*, 309.

Don't we stand at the threshold of a period which should be designated negatively, to begin with, as *extra-moral*? After all, we immoralists have the suspicion that the decisive value of an action lies precisely in what is *unintentional* in it, while everything about it that is intentional, everything about it that can be seen, known, "conscious," still belongs to its surface and skin—which, like every skin, betrays something but *conceals* even more. In short, we believe that intention is merely a sign and symptom that still requires interpretation—moreover, a sign that means too much and, therefore, taken by itself alone, almost nothing. We believe that morality in the traditional sense, the morality of intentions, was a prejudice, precipitate and perhaps provisional—something on the order of astrology and alchemy—but in any case something that must be overcome. The overcoming of morality, in a certain sense even the self-overcoming of morality—let this be the name for that long secret work which has been saved up for the finest and most honest, also the most malicious, consciences of today, as living touchstones of the soul.[31]

In the ironies of their self-conscious interpretation of the vocation of the American man of letters, Freneau, Brackenridge, and Brown reveal their discovery that the modern nation-state, divested of kings and priests and founded on the authority of hypothesis, does not truly constitute a moral mechanism like a watch, but, in a direct and total way unknown before the reversal of society and mind as paradigms of order, duplicates the myriad, bewildering processes of human consciousness. The differentiation of the role of the man of letters in the Revolution by Franklin, Jefferson, and John Adams had seemed more or less clearly to announce that the American man of letters would symbolize the inviolable independence of rational, lettered mind—a mind devoted to the integrity of intention—as the image of a new and just society. But as the dimensions of mind rapidly became ambiguous in America, Freneau, Brackenridge, and Brown—uncertain whether they were men of letters endeavoring to be Americans or Americans trying to be men of letters—experienced an increasing ambivalence in their sense of the literary vocation. They became symbols of the strange subjectivity of American, which is to say, of modern, history.

---

31 *Beyond Good and Evil: Prelude to the Philosophy of the Future*, trans. Walter Kaufmann (New York: Vintage Books, 1966), 44–45.

3 / The Fiction of the Real American Revolution

The relationship between the American Revolution and American literature is so compact—so integral—that it is hard to analyze. The difficulty is scarcely diminished if we limit our inquiry to the connection between only one kind of writing and the Revolution—as in the present instance, that between prose fiction and the Revolution. But imposing this particular restriction on our investigation does enable us to find a focus in a significant problem. When dealing with fiction we are always impelled to ask, what is the bearing of a given fiction on reality? Or inversely, what is the bearing of reality on this fiction? Pursued with sufficient curiosity and ardor, these questions lead us toward the remarkable congruence of history and fiction that has resulted in modern times from the disintegration of the assumed norms of reality or, put another way, from the development of subtle but irremovable barriers between appearance and actuality. Applied to the relation between the American Revolution and fiction, these questions force us directly toward the problem first announced, so far as I am aware, by John Adams: the definition of the reality of the Revolution. On this definition a great deal ultimately depends: not only our grasp of the cause of the event in which the nation originated, but also, in a more profound sense, nothing less than our apprehension of both the existential actuality and the metaphysical character of the nation.

I shall not, I hasten to say, attempt to define the reality of America. My purpose is merely to offer a few speculations about defining the problem of defining the American reality. These arise from a consideration of Washington, Jefferson, and Adams (especially of Adams) as precursors of American fiction—I mean as forerunners of

47

the representative American storytellers. But I shall refer chiefly to their connection with a great American storyteller, Nathaniel Hawthorne; and most particularly to Adams' anticipation of Hawthorne's archetypal story of the American origination, "My Kinsman, Major Molineux."

In June, 1783, General Washington addressed a circular letter to "the governors of all the states on the disbanding of the army." It reads in part as follows:

> The citizens of America, placed in the most enviable condition, as the sole lords and proprietors of a vast tract of continent, comprehending all the various soils and climates of the world, and abounding with all the necessaries and conveniences of life, are now, by the late satisfactory pacification, acknowledged to be possessed of absolute freedom and independency. They are from this period, to be considered as the actors on a most conspicuous theatre, which seems to be peculiarly designated by Providence for the display of human greatness and felicity. Here they are not only surrounded with every thing, which can contribute to the completion of private and domestic enjoyment; but Heaven has crowned all its other blessings, by giving a fairer opportunity for political happiness, than any other nation has ever been favored with. Nothing can illustrate these observations more forcibly, than a recollection of the happy conjuncture of times and circumstances, under which our republic assumed its rank among the nations. The foundation of our empire was not laid in the gloomy age of ignorance and superstition; but at an epocha when the rights of mankind were better understood and more clearly defined, than at any former period. The researches of the human mind after social happiness have been carried to a great extent; the treasures of knowledge, acquired by the labors of philosophers, sages, and legislators, through a long succession of years, are laid open for our use, and their collected wisdom may be happily applied in the establishment of our forms of government. The free cultivation of letters, the unbounded extension of commerce, the progressive refinement of manners, the growing liberality of sentiment, and, above all, the pure and benign light of Revelation, have had a meliorating influence on mankind and increased the blessings of society. At this auspicious period, the United States came into existence as a nation; and, if their citizens should not be completely free and happy, the fault will be entirely their own.[1]

1 *The Writings of George Washington*, ed. W. C. Ford (14 vols.; New York: G. P. Putnam's Sons, 1889–93), X, 254–56.

Intended as an appeal for continuing unity among the states of the new nation, Washington's statement to the governors has many interesting implications. An outstanding one is that, although Washington was a man of action who had lately led a disparate, and often desperate, army of rebelling colonials against the British Empire, he discovers no basis for the continuity of America in a military mystique. Furthermore, although he ascribes victory in the Revolution and the future happiness of the victors to Providence, Washington finds no assured destiny for the United States. He declares, in fact, that the people of the new nation must either take upon themselves the historical imperative of fulfilling "the researches of the human mind after happiness" or else (as he puts it in a portion of the letter subsequent to that which I have quoted) assume the responsibility for an unspecified historical disaster and become a "curse" upon the "destiny of unborn millions." Surely never before in history had a military leader of a people placed such an injunctive stress on their rational use of victory. Washington not only asserts that their historical identity is dependent on their employment of rational intelligence, but he also states that the character of world history is subject to their use of mind. In effect he suggests that the nation created by the Revolution exists not in blood, but in mind. All history attendant upon this event will—no, *must*—unfold from mind or from the lack of it. According to Washington, the model of the nation— the very model of history—has become mind.

It is a matter of some irony that, in his vision of the founding of the United States, Washington suggests that Thomas Jefferson's parental role may well be reckoned more significant than his own. Jefferson was the author of the document that founded the nation in mind, the 1776 Declaration by "the Representatives of the United States of America, in General Congress Assembled," commonly called the Declaration of Independence. Jefferson's greatest work— and the central work in American literature and history—this document does not declare an act of war but, before the court of world opinion, declares in force an act of mind, a theory of revolution: "When, in the course of human events, it becomes necessary for one people, to dissolve the political bands which connected them with another, and to assume among the powers of the earth the separate and equal station to which the laws of nature and of nature's God entitle them, a decent respect to the opinions of mankind requires that they should declare the causes which impel them to the separation." These familiar words, which presuppose the concepts of natural law and the contractual origins of government, also presuppose, it is to be noted, that men everywhere possess the same attributes of mind. These assumptions foreshadow the statement of "self-evident" truths that follows: the equal creation of all men and their endowment with "certain unalienable rights," among these being "life, liberty, and the pursuit of happiness." The violation of these truths in sufficient degree justifies the alteration or abolition of a government and the institution of a new one more likely to secure the natural rights of men and to promote their "safety and happiness." At this point the declaration of American independence, and manifesto of world mind, turns to an exact indictment of the present king of Great Britain. As has often been pointed out, the strategy of itemizing the "repeated injuries and usurpations" of the monarch instead of the grievances that the colonists held against Parliament was inspired in part, at least, by the desire to keep those friends that the colonies had in Parliament. But pragmatic politics is a superficial aspect of the Declaration. Its unstated intention is more profound than the overthrow of a monarch, being nothing less than the transference of society and its government out of the dominion of a hierarchical world of custom and tradition into the dominion of independent rational mind. In the unamended version of the Declaration, one must observe, the concluding formal proclamation of separation from Great Britain is wholly secular. Pronouncing independence solely "in the name, and authority of the good people of these states," the proclamation omits the phrases added later by Congress: "appealing to the supreme judge of the world" and "with a firm reliance on the protection of divine providence."[2] Jefferson, it seems, would have preferred to avoid suggesting any symbolic connection between the act of independence and dependence on the suprahuman, not because Jefferson, as his enemies said of him later, was an atheist, but

2 See *The Portable Thomas Jefferson*, ed. Merrill D. Peterson (New York: Viking Press, 1975), 235–41. The Congress anticipated a continuous resistance by Americans to the separation of Church and State.

because to Jefferson, the good Deist, the Declaration not only symbolized the creation of a new nation but incarnated a possibly per-
fectible realm of mind—a realm that he distinguished from either
the Church or the State, but most particularly from the Church.

Indeed, Jefferson's sense of the absolute opposition of politics and
institutional religion may be one reason why the authorship of the
Declaration belongs to Jefferson rather than to John Adams. Adams,
a member of the committee appointed to draft the Declaration, would
no doubt have liked to have had a larger part in its writing than he
did. Knowing the tortuous pride of an Adams, we can find good evidence for this in an account of the making of the Declaration written by Adams in his old age, in which he says that Jefferson took on
the task after he (Adams) had been urged to perform it. The account
sounds as though the elderly New England statesman had transcribed
a tape recording, although it was tw o centuries before the politics of
the tape would appear. When Jefferson proposed that Adams make
the draft, Adams recalled saying that he would not do it.

Jefferson: You shall do it.
Adams: Oh no!
Jefferson: Why will you not? You ought to do it.
Adams: I will not.
Jefferson: Why?
Adams: Reasons enough.
Jefferson: What can be your reasons?
Adams: Reasons 1st. You are a Virginian and a Virginian ought to appear
at the head of this business. Reason 2nd. I am obnoxious, suspected and
unpopular, you are very much otherwise. Reason 3rd. You can write ten
times better than I can.
Jefferson: Well . . . if you are decided I will do as well as I can.
Adams: Very well, when you have drawn it up we will have a meeting.[3]

In the interests of political harmony and of good writing, Adams
recollected, Jefferson became the author of the Declaration. But the
little story is not true. Adams apparently made up his account of Jefferson's deference to him out of whole cloth; the tape of memory in
an old man's head had been altered by Adams' lifetime jealousy of

---

3 *Works of John Adams*, ed. Charles Francis Adams (10 vols.; Boston: Little, Brown
and Co., 1850–56), II, 514. See Carl L. Becker, *The Declaration of Independence: A
Study in the History of Political Ideas* (New York: Vintage Books, 1958), 135–93.

another's social and literary grace. Still, Adams' story has elements of truth in it. One is the superiority of Jefferson's writing skill to that of Adams. Another truth of equal, perhaps of greater, weight in Adams' tale is Jefferson's qualification to write the Declaration because he was a Virginian. Although Adams had reasons of political expediency for thinking this, did he not discern a more important reason? This lay in the fact that Jefferson the Virginian was more conversant with the cosmopolitan mind of the Enlightenment than was Adams. The New Englander Adams was subject to the conditions of the Puritan heritage, distinguished by its continuing expression in religious disputation and doctrinal theology. Jefferson, reared in a colony that early abandoned a commitment to religious mission, was more completely a citizen of that rational polity of mind that in the overall sense is the chief source of the American Revolution—the Republic of Letters, the Third Realm, in its ideal of its own existence as independent of Church and State.[4]

A disclosure from the logos of rationality, the Declaration of Independence is, in the Jeffersonian vision, the originating word of a novel nation. Based on the power of the rational intelligence to establish a historical order of governance, this new nation symbolizes the completion of the historical differentiation of the Third Realm and has become the embodiment of the Third Realm in pragmatic history. During his presidency and in his long retirement after his years of public service, Jefferson had doubts about rationality as the model of political and social order. But in spite of all countervailing evidence—evidence so abundant in the contradictions of his own life, in no way more so than in his continual ownership of and buying and selling of slaves—Jefferson remained convinced that regenerative rationality had revealed itself as the shaping force of history.

John Adams had no such fixed faith in reason. He subscribed heavily to the enlarged possibilities of man's capacity for reason, but he doubted that rationality is the ultimate reality of man and his history. Thus, although he was no less than Washington and Jefferson a citizen of the Republic of Letters and was no less inclined to seek the truth of the American Revolution in a decisive alteration of the rela-

4 See the remarks on the Third Realm in the two preceding chapters.

tion of mind to history, Adams took a more complex view of its origin. It had been caused, he felt, not so much by the persuasion of the colonials to the self-evident rationality of natural law and the rights of man, as by a transformation in the very nature of their attitude toward human community. This view grew on Adams with the years. In 1818 he said in a letter to a correspondent that the Revolution was in "the minds and hearts of the people." For some it was a change in the basis of their social pieties—in "their religious sentiments of their duties and obligations." For others it was an alteration in "certain habitual sentiments of allegiance and loyalty derived from their education." For all it was an alteration "in an habitual affection for England, and their mother country." The colonists, Adams states, had thought of England as "a kind and tender parent." Confronted with a "cruel beldam, willing like Lady Macbeth 'to dash their brains,' it is no wonder," Adams said, "if their filial affections ceased, and were changed into indignation and horror."[5] And yet Adams was not satisfied that a fundamental change in the social pieties of a people could be explained in terms of a cliché like the parent-child relationship. The nature of the American Revolution transcended this image of order. The *"real American Revolution,"* Adams said (in what may be fairly taken as his most comprehensive summation of the character and effects of the Revolution), consisted in a *"radical change in the principles, opinions, sentiments, and affections"* of the people of the colonies. It was "a great and important alteration" in their "religious, moral, political, and social character." The real Revolution, moreover, not only transcended the familial image of the imperial-colonial relation, but also transcended the image of the Revolution as the 1776–1783 hostilities. "But what do we mean by the American Revolution?" Adams asked. "Do we mean the American war? The Revolution was effected before the war commenced."[6]

Insisting that the Revolution was not to be defined as an armed uprising provoked by immediate grievances of the colonials against king and Parliament, Adams came close to interpreting it as the result of the progressive infusion of rational ideology in the colonial

---

5 Adams to H. Niles, February 13, 1818, in *The American Enlightenment*, ed. Adrienne Koch (New York: George Braziller, 1965), 228.
6 *Ibid.*, 228.

mind. But, as can easily be seen, Adams' grasp of the origin of the Revolution was tense and irresolute. He was, one thinks, vexed by the way mind had been made the authority for a separation that formerly would have been altogether a decision of the heart. In his tendency to find the source of the Revolution in changes of sentiment and feeling, he opposed his inclination to find the authority for it in thought and analysis. Underlying all of Adams' thought and feeling about the Revolution was his general conviction of the fallen nature of man. In the very midst of his great excitement over the approval of the resolution of independence by the Continental Congress—"the day of deliverance," he told Abigail, "to be solemnized with pomp and parade, with shows, games, sports, guns, bells, bonfires, and illuminations. . . . from this time forward, forevermore"—Adams said fearfully, "The people will have unbounded power, and the people are extremely addicted to corruption and venality, as well as the great."[7] Adams' view of the Revolution apprehended the paradox of mind and heart in the movement of history. He was always cognizant of the ironies of mind's powers under their subjection to human impulses. In one of his letters to Jefferson, Adams recalled a story about the gods who are sitting around a festive board conversing, when one of them makes the remark that man possesses "a rational nature." Whereupon the "whole board breaks out into a broad ha! ha! ha! that sounded through the vault of heaven, exclaiming, 'Man a rational creature! How could any rational being ever dream that man was a rational creature?'"[8]

Unsatisfied with explanations of the Revolution as the culmination of rationality, curious about what really had happened in this "awful" (by which he meant awesome) event, the elderly John Adams urged "young men of letters" (by "men of letters" he meant not professional historians, but those who were educated in the use of the literary intelligence) to begin collecting records for a documented history of the Revolution.[9] By this time young American literati did

7 Adams to Abigail Adams, July 3, 1776, in *ibid.*, 186. The resolution of independence was passed on July 2, 1776.
8 Adams to Jefferson, May 29, 1818, in *ibid.*, 230.
9 Adams to Niles, in *ibid.*, 227, 228–29.

not need the urging of their elders to study the meaning of the Revolution. The crisis of the second war with England had passed, and a compulsive surge of nationalism was beginning to be felt by Americans. In so far as this took the form of cultural nationalism, it centered in the demand for a national literature that would interpret and shape the destiny of America. In the heady atmosphere of the post-1815 America, this meant a literature founded on the self-evident truth that the Revolution signified not only the victory of the mind's researches after human happiness, but also the triumph of mind as the directing force in civilization. In 1831 William Ellery Channing said in his "Remarks on a National Literature" that the time had come when "all moral and religious truth may be reduced to one great cultural thought, perfection of mind." [10] The premise implied in Channing's declaration—that American writing will represent, if not the perfection, the perfectibility of mind in America—has been a formative influence on our literary expression. But in a strangely negative way. Its force (as Adams may be said to have forecast) is to be estimated in terms of the ironic challenging of it in our letters rather than its literary affirmation. A striking instance of such a challenge is Hawthorne's well-known story "My Kinsman, Major Molineux."

First published in 1832, a year after Channing's "Remarks on a National Literature," Hawthorne's story is set in the Boston of the 1730s or thereabouts. It begins with an authorial comment upon the fate of the royal administration in the Massachusetts colony. The people of the colony, disliking any power "which did not emanate from themselves," had carried out an insurrection against two governors and made life miserable for the others. The hostility of the colonials extended as well to "inferior members of the court party." The particular political event related in "My Kinsman, Major Molineux" begins to unfold with the description of a moonlight summer evening, when the central figure of the story, a country lad of eighteen years named Robin, well built and attractive in spite of his coarse clothing, makes

10 *The Works of William Ellery Channing, D.D.* (Boston: American Unitarian Association, 1877), 127.

the ferry crossing to Boston. Robin has left his home and family—
his father is a country parson—to go to his father's cousin in Boston.
This is Major Molineux, an official of the crown, who, it seems, has
offered to help either Robin or his elder brother become established
in life. Since the elder brother is destined to inherit the family farm,
Robin is sent to take advantage of Major Molineux's generosity. Upon
his entrance into the little colonial metropolis, "with as eager an eye
as if he were entering London," Robin realizes that he has no idea
where his kinsman lives; but assuming that everyone knows Molineux's residence, he courteously yet confidently inquires of the first
person he meets where this may be. The person he addresses is an
old man in a dark suit who makes his way with the striking of his
cane, uttering at intervals "two successive hems, of a peculiarly solemn and sepulchral intention." This elderly gentleman's response
to Robin is surprisingly ill tempered. Not only does he say that he
does not know Molineux, he threatens to use his "authority" to have
Robin put in stocks for disrespect. Robin flees to the accompani-
ment of laughter from the barber shop outside of which he has had
his encounter with the recalcitrant old gentleman. From now on,
Robin's experiences in his search for his kinsman become more and
more enigmatic. When he goes into a noisy and seemingly hospita-
ble tavern to ask of his kinsman's whereabouts, the innkeeper seems
to suspect that Robin is a bound servant on the run and threatens to
have him jailed. Next he finds himself in "a street of mean appearance," where he discovers a pretty maid in a scarlet petticoat waiting behind a half-closed door. She tells him that this is the entrance
to the Major's house, but that the Major has retired and cannot be
disturbed. Then she takes "our hero" by the hand and asks him in.
But at this moment the night watchman comes by, and the pretty
maid hurriedly closes the door on Robin. Having surmised by this
time that she is a trollop, Robin leaves the neighborhood to wander
here and there in the city with increasing desperation. At length he
encounters a man he had seen for a fleeting moment while he had
been in the inn. This man tells Robin that if he will wait where he
is, the Major will presently pass by. As his informant replies, Robin
is startled to see, as he had not seen earlier at the inn, that the man
has a double visage. One side of his face blazes red, while the other

is "black as midnight." It is as if "two individual devils, a fiend of fire and fiend of darkness had united themselves to form this infernal visage."

Waiting for Major Molineux to come by, Robin seats himself on the steps of a church. Becoming aware of a "large, square mansion," with "an elaborate Gothic window" opening upon a balcony, standing nearby, he speculates about the possibility that this is the home of his kinsman. Soon growing restless, he clambers up a windowframe to view the interior of the church. Seeing moonbeams falling upon an open Bible on the pulpit, Robin is struck by a "sensation of loneliness stronger than he had ever felt in the remotest depths of his native woods." He imagines how this "evening of ambiguity and weariness had been spent by his father's household": a prayer service, the patriarchal parson saying "the old thanksgiving for daily mercies" and offering the "old supplications for their continuance." He imagines the family going into the house; then he hears the latch tinkle and realizes that he is excluded. At this point Robin rouses, as still another stranger enters his life—this time a cheerful, intelligent man who perceives a "country youth, apparently homeless and without friends" and asks kindly why the youth is sitting on the church steps and whether or not he may be of service. Robin describes his situation, advising the gentleman that he has come to "profit by his kinsman's generous intentions," believing himself to have the "necessary endowments" to do so. He has, Robin says, "thought it high time to begin the world." Even as he speaks with the kindly stranger, Robin hears the sound of a trumpet and then that of a great discordant commotion. Led by the man of double visage, now on horseback and in military dress and carrying a sword, a "mightly stream of people" approaches. Among this mob are "wild figures in Indian dress, and many fantastic shapes without a model, giving the whole march a visionary air, as if a dream had broken forth from some feverish brain, and were sweeping visibly through the midnight streets." In the midst of all this madness appears an uncovered cart with a figure in it. When the cart comes "where the torches blazed the brightest" and "the moon shouted out like day," Robin perceives sitting in it in tar and feathers none other than his kinsman, Major Molineux.

He was an elderly man, of large and majestic person, and strong, square features, betokening a steady soul; but steady as it was his enemies had found means to shake it. His face was pale as death, and far more ghastly; the broad forehead was contracted in his agony, so that his eyebrows formed one grizzled line; his eyes were red and wild, and the foam hung white upon his quivering lip. His whole frame was agitated by a quick and continual tremor, which his pride strove to quell, even in those circumstances of overwhelming humiliation. But perhaps the bitterest pang of all was when his eyes met those of Robin; for he evidently knew him on the instant, as the youth stood witnessing the foul disgrace of a head grown gray in honor. They stared at each other in silence, and Robin's knees shook, and his hair bristled, with a mixture of pity and terror.

At the same moment Robin experiences a "bewildering excitement," a "sort of mental inebriety." The laughter he had heard earlier in the evening—the laughter of the woman in the scarlet petticoat, that of the innkeeper, that of the old man with the cane—echoes through the streets as one great laugh, "broken in the midst by two sepulchral hems; thus, 'Haw, haw, haw,—hem, hem—haw, haw, haw.'" Robin looks up and sees the old man occupying the balcony with the Gothic window, the distinguishing feature of the mansion that he had earlier decided must be his kinsman's. The laughter swells in volume, and suddenly Robin is laughing, too, louder than anyone else. The mob moves on, "in counterfeited pomp, in senseless uproar, in frenzied merriment, trampling on an old man's heart." Robin grasps a post for support, as though in a state of shock. But he is not too badly off, merely "somewhat pale, and his eye not quite as lively as in the earlier part of the evening." He asks the kindly stranger the way back to the ferry, but the stranger says that he will not answer Robin's "new subject of inquiry" at this time. "Some few days hence, if you wish it, I will speed you on your journey. Or, if you prefer to remain with us, perhaps, as you are a shrewd youth, you may rise in the world without the help of your kinsman, Major Molineux."[11]

11 For convenience I have used the text of "My Kinsman, Major Molineux" as reproduced from the Old Manse Edition of Hawthorne in *American Literature: The Makers and the Making*, ed. Cleanth Brooks, R. W. B. Lewis, and Robert Penn Warren (2 vols.; New York: St. Martin's Press, 1973), I, 506–15. See Warren's accompanying commentary on it, I, 440–44. The initial printing of this essay is "Hawthorne Revisited: Some Remarks on Hellfiredness," *Sewanee Review*, 81 (Winter, 1973), 75–111.

On this enigmatic note Hawthorne's enigmatic tale ends. What are we to make of it? A great deal has been made of it by Hawthorne's numerous explicators, not the least convincing interpretation being that it is a pre-Freudian allegory depicting the search for a father. But the story, I am inclined to think, is not an allegory; it is a symbolic account of the "real American Revolution."[12] Does not the key to Hawthorne's tale lie in the fact that Robin—in his own self-interpretation a shrewd youth—is already prepared before he comes to pre-Revolutionary Boston for all that happens on the night of his kinsman's degradation? He has been brought up in a seemingly simple, God-fearing community of kinship, custom, and tradition, and yet Robin has somehow absorbed the rationalistic attitudes abroad in the larger world. This is the striking point of the scene when he sees that the man he previously encountered at the inn has a frightening double visage. The unexpected reaction of the simple country boy is described in the story as follows: "A few moments were consumed in philosophical speculations upon the species of man who had just left him; but having settled this point shrewdly, rationally, and satisfactorily, he was compelled to look elsewhere for amusement." Robin dismisses an obvious and fearful mystery. Perhaps the man is a prankster. In any event he is an uninteresting irrationality. Why such sophistication, such rationality, in a country lad? The story gives no explicit answer to this question, but Hawthorne suggests that Robin comes out of a backcountry world which, although wearing the aspect of a society of kinship, custom, and tradition, is still the Puritan society of Massachusetts. This society had risen on the basis of an intensely intellectual and, to be sure, rational criticism of the hierarchy, ritual, and mystery of the established Church-State relation. It has sought to purify the establishment in the name of what it considered to be a literal historical interpretation of Christianity. Puritan rationalism may have been, as students of American history have often said, as important in the dynamics of the Ameri-

12 Cf. Q. D. Leavis, "Hawthorne as Poet," *Sewanee Review*, 59 (Spring, 1951), 179–205. This essay suggests that, as Robin becomes not simply a spectator but a participant in the degradation of Molineaux, he anticipates the Revolution. But Hawthorne's imagination of the Revolution was deeper than Leavis suggests. Like Adams, he saw the colonial mind as having become the emblem of history long before the Revolution itself.

can revolutionary ethos as the rationalism of the philosophers was. In broad perspective, both Puritan intellectualism and the secular intellectualism of the Renaissance and the Enlightenment are integral to the Great Critique, which is the total intellectual context of the Revolution. How well aware Hawthorne was of the intellectual situation in New England is conveyed by his dramatization of it in *The Scarlet Letter;* in the relationship of Dimmesdale and Chillingworth, Puritan and secular intellectualism are two sides of the same coin. Robin's exemplification is further stressed when, looking into the deserted church, he experiences a feeling of utter loneliness. The institutional Church, represented by a solid urban edifice, is removed from his range of empathetic response. Peering into its moonlit interior, Robin experiences no sense of identification with the faith; on the contrary, he is chilled by a sense of his immense isolation. Furthermore, when he nostalgically recalls his participation in worship back in the country, he thinks not of public, but of family, obeisance to God. His attachment to religious tradition is one of personal sentiment, the end result of the isolation of the church from the affectional community of liturgy and ritual.

When Robin witnesses a modern political event—the tarring and feathering of an official of the crown, a symbolic regicide committed by ordinary townspeople of the professional and trading classes—he is already an emergent type of the Yankee bourgeois. He has come out of a society founded in opposition to the community of custom and tradition into a more advanced state of the same society. In a society determined to interpret itself according to the will of intellect, Robin will make his way, not by royal preferment and prescription, but by what he regards as his own sovereign calculation of his needs and desires. He will not go back to the country; save as nostalgic illusion, the choice is not open to him. At the moment when he has presumably become free, his dependence on a vestigial patriarchy ended, he has become isolated in and bonded to history. Although he finds himself in a society that expresses a new equality of condition (which is soon going to be officially dedicated to life, liberty, and the pursuit of happiness) Robin's liberation is darkly qualified by the means of that liberation—the fearful passion engendered in the people in the name of their rational rights. Becoming a rational entity, a discrete self, Robin has also irrevocably become identified with public mind or public opinion. The tarrers and featherers, including the prostitute, it is to be carefully observed, are no spontaneous assemblage of people fired by a sudden passion. The mob is an organized citizenry conducting a carefully planned demonstration; led by that consummate rationalist, the archfiend himself, it has been formed to make treason to the crown compulsory on each citizen of Boston. It is a calculated invocation of, in Rousseauistic terminology, the "general will." The roaring laughter in the wake of Molineux's cart echoes the ironic Olympian laughter around the festive board of the gods in the admonitory tale that Adams shared with Jefferson: "Ha! ha! ha! . . . Man a rational creature!"

If the Declaration of Independence climaxes the work of the Great Critique (the transference of history into mind), Rousseau's concept of the general will seals the work, signifying that everything has become subject to the relentless processes of consciousness, including, most of all, history itself, which is no longer to be regarded as a story but as a process or series of processes. The distinction between the outward and active life known to past ages, the life associated with the actions of heroes, and the inward and contemplative life, the life associated with philosophers and mystics, is no longer meaningful. The sense of history as a series of narrative actions involving kings, warriors, and saints recedes, but not into the inwardness of contemplation. Instead, the sense of history becomes identified with the processes of consciousness.[13] The "radical change in the principles, opinions, sentiments, and affections of the people" (to come back to the words of John Adams) constituted the *real* American Revolution. These changes were inextricably connected to the manner of their occurrence. Ideas and affections were taken out of their location in custom and tradition and relocated in the activities of mind. Adams experienced the awesomeness of this interiorization of action but did not have the literary capacity to articulate it. Implicit in his view of the novelty of the American Revolution is the anticipation that, from now on, the rational and scientific mind will leave nothing

13 See Hannah Arendt, The Human Condition (Garden City, N.Y.: Doubleday Anchor Books, 1959), 155–297 passim.

alone; it will engage in making history, or in engineering it, whether this be through an engineering of nature or of man. Nothing will stay the same for a moment; the word *permanence* will be blotted out of the modern dictionary. More profoundly, Adams' understanding of the Revolution implied that rational behavior masks a subjectification of history. With Hobbes and Rousseau, Adams feared that, although man has the opportunity as never before to be a rational creature, he is becoming as never before subject to his emotionality; that having fallen under the illusion that he makes his own history, man is allowing history to become an illusion. Although I am attributing a more graphic understanding of the eighteenth-century situation to Adams than his analysis of his age on the surface may seem to justify, I adduce this from the hidden drama in Adams: a complicated struggle in the Puritan philosophe between his sense of self-sufficiency and his sense of self-inability in history. This drama was to be repeated in each Adams through Henry, who would finally give it definitive literary expression. Obeying the imperative to self-education, Henry Adams would reveal—particularly in his novels, *Democracy* and *Esther*, and in *The Education of Henry Adams*—the Adamses' inner knowledge of the consequence of making mind the model of American history: a remorseless internalization of history in the self and, as the result, the self's desolating loneliness. Disclosing a kind of state secret, Henry Adams betrayed the destiny of America as promised by the researches of the mind after human happiness. This may be why he published *Democracy* anonymously, brought out *Esther* under a pseudonymn, and had the *Education* printed privately. Yet, as Adams of course knew, American storytellers had all along divined and, in one way or another, disclosed the national secret.

I have said that the story of Robin—it is worth mentioning that he is not given the identity conferred by a last name—is the archetypal story of the American Revolution. It is, I mean, the first concentrated symbolic representation and evaluation of the significance of the Revolution in our literature, for it depicts the decisive emergence of the individual, rational person, possessed of all his unalienable natural rights, out of the old community of kinship and custom, tradition and hierarchy, into the society invented by critical analysis and maintained as an ideological construct. That versions of this emergence make up much of American fiction is not in itself exceptionable. They tell the modern story, one told more powerfully by the great European inheritors of the French Revolution—like Mann, Proust, Kafka, and Joyce—than by the American storytellers. But American writers have a unique relation to the modern internalization of history. In this phenomenon, the United States had its unique beginning and has its existence as a nation. In American storytellers —before, during, and after Hawthorne's time—we encounter numerous kinsmen of Robin. Manifold in appearance and personality, they all represent the singular legend of a people who originated in their displacement in mind. Like Robin, they are cut off from any genuine contact with a world of custom and tradition; like Robin, they are in one way or another ironic and admonitory emblems of the increasing isolation of the self and of the ever-growing burden of self-consciousness in a society existing in and constantly being transformed by the cognitive processes of the human mind; like Robin, they symbolize the final evolvement of the individual into a historical creature.

One cousin of Robin, for instance, is Leatherstocking, the hero of Cooper's saga of the years from the imperial struggle in mid-eighteenth-century America to the time of the Lewis and Clark Expedition during the administration of Thomas Jefferson. The ostensible purpose of this expedition, which was one of the major achievements of Jefferson's presidency, was to bring all the land that would become the continental United States under the dominion of the new nation. But its real motive was Jefferson's desire to bring all of the unknown continental area under the dominion of mind. Jefferson called the Lewis and Clark undertaking a "literary"—that is, a scientific, a research—expedition; and he was passionately curious about what the researching of the continent would disclose. When Leatherstocking dies, he is way out West on the hunting grounds of Hardheart and other Pawnee friends. He has fled as far as he can from history, yet he cannot escape what he is. Cooper makes this plain by introducing into the death scene the young soldier-explorer Middleton, an image of Meriwether Lewis. It is highly appropriate that

Thomas Jefferson should be represented at the death and burial of Leatherstocking. A "man of little l'arning" but, Cooper says, "possessed" of the "highest principles" of civilization, ever the man of action in his long career but obsessively conscious of himself (at times, a garrulous braggart), Leatherstocking incarnates the first stage in the incorporation of a nonhistorical land and its people into the processes of history.[14] When Middleton erects a stone over Leatherstocking's grave, the frontiersman's relation to the Indian society of custom and tradition is abrogated, and he emerges fully into the society of analysis and ideology. Other cousins of Robin are Poe's Roderick Usher, Melville's Ishmael, Mark Twain's Huckleberry Finn, Hemingway's Jake Barnes, Faulkner's Quentin Compson III. More radical symbols of displacement in mind than Robin or Leatherstocking, each of these characters is witness to the terrors of consciousness or, as it may be put, to the absolute horrors of the consciousness of consciousness. They are in kinship to the version of Robin that appears in a slightly later story by Hawthorne, "Young Goodman Brown." As does Brown, a youth who goes out of the orderly, rational Puritan community into the wilderness of his consciousness and discovers there all his fellow citizens pledged to the community of hell, they each symbolize an aborted attempt to get out of history. They each repeat the American legend of origination in mind: the displacement of the sacramental community in the planting of the European colonies, the disappearance of the old modes of action and ritual, and the appearance of a hero whose heroism is to be gauged by the intensity of his response to the consciousness of his self-existence. The archetypal American story is, of course, more explicitly rendered in some stories than in others. A more precise version than that in any of the stories I have just alluded to is to be found in Robert Penn Warren's *All the King's Men*. In this novel Jack Burden, a sometime graduate student in history, tries to escape from history by ascribing all motivation to the Great God Twitch. But witnessing the history of Willie Stark and the counterpointed history of the Civil War soldier, Cass Mastern, Burden becomes a witness to his own history. At one point he makes the Leatherstock-

---

14 See the excellent presentation of "Natty Bumppo and His World" in Brooks, Lewis, and Warren (eds.), *American Literature: The Makers and the Making*, I, 290–319.

ing gesture and goes West (to California), but eventually he accepts his intricate involvement in history and decides as far as he can to be responsible toward it. He will fulfill the American imperative: he will "go out of history into history and the awful responsibility of Time." [15]

One supposes that the archetypal American fiction, the story of the real Revolution, reaches toward its ultimate logical ironies in *All the King's Men*. At the end of the novel, Jack Burden is coming into the second act of his life; he is emerging out of history into history. But it would seem that, as he comes into the second act, he is committing himself to a third, in which, having become responsible for Time, he will, with the best of intentions, seek to control history. There is nothing strange in his commitment. Most Americans make it; although in taking on this impossible responsibility, we displace ourselves in abstraction as surely as an Emerson declaring that there is no past. Somewhere Scott Fitzgerald says that there are no second acts in American lives. He was wrong, as his own fiction shows. There are two acts, and the curtain comes up on a third. The first and second acts are inevitable; we go out of history into history. The third act—the act that began for that amazingly shrewd young Jay Gatsby when he saw the green light on Daisy's dock— we never get through.

15 *All the King's Men* (New York: Bantam Books, 1970), 438.

4 / Slavery and Modernism

A controlling assumption among students of twentieth-century southern literature is that, fundamentally, it is a reaction to modernism. If this attitude can be attributed to a single person, he is probably Allen Tate, whose brilliant critical work is so central to the field of southern literary studies that we cannot conceive it without him. I have especially in mind Tate's essay entitled "The Profession of Letters in the South." First published in 1935, this essay, I believe, can be taken as the beginning of the historical study of the literature of the South by the modern literary intelligence.

At the end of Tate's essay, we encounter an explanation of the twentieth-century flowering of writing in the South that has become classic. The efflorescence, Tate says, has been produced by the "peculiarly historical consciousness of the Southern writer," yet, he observes, the "focus of this consciousness is quite temporary," resembling the "curious burst of intelligence that we get at a crossing of the ways, not unlike, on an infinitesimal scale, the outburst of poetic genius at the end of the sixteenth century when commercial England had already begun to crush feudal England."[1] Implicit in this observation is a refinement—a succinct dramatization—of the relationship of the modern southern literary mind to the culture of the Old South that Tate had been endeavoring to formulate for several years. In the excitement of the days leading up to the organization and publication of the Agrarian manifesto, *I'll Take My Stand* (1930), he had written to both Robert Penn Warren and Donald David-

[1] *Essays of Four Decades* (Chicago: Swallow Press, Inc., 1968), 533.

67

son advocating the founding of "an academy of Southern *positive* reactionaries." The academy was to have a signed "philosophical constitution" setting forth "a complete social, philosophical, literary, economic and religious system." Such a program, Tate wrote Davidson from Paris in 1929, "will inevitably draw upon our heritage, but this heritage should be valued, not in what it actually performed, but in its possible perfection. Philosophically we must go the whole hog of reaction, and base our movement less upon the actual old South than upon its prototype—the historical social and religious scheme of Europe. We must be the last Europeans—there being no Europeans in Europe at present."[2] The Academy of Southern Positive Reactionaries did not become a reality, but Tate's concept of the European scheme as a prototype of the South appears after a fashion in *I'll Take My Stand*, notably in the essays contributed by John Crowe Ransom and Tate. In Tate's essay, entitled "Remarks on the Southern Religion," in fact, the idea that Europe is the inspiriting prototype of the South is the basis for the distinction that Tate draws between nineteenth-century New England and the nineteenth-century South.

> The South could be ignorant of Europe because it *was* Europe; that is to say, the South had taken root in a native soil. And the South could remain simple-minded because it had no use for the intellectual agility required to define its position. Its position was self-sufficient and self-evident; it was European where the New England position was self-conscious and colonial. The Southern mind was simple, not top-heavy with learning it had no need of, unintellectual, and composed; it was personal and dramatic, rather than abstract and metaphysical; and it was sensuous because it lived close to a natural scene of great variety and interest.[3]

Tate continues:

> Because it lived by images, not highly organized, it is true, as Dogma, but rather more loosely gathered from the past, the South was a profoundly traditional European community. . . . The old Southerners were highly

2 *The Literary Correspondence of Donald Davidson and Allen Tate*, ed. John Tyree Fain and Thomas Daniel Young (Athens: University of Georgia Press, 1974), 229–30.
3 Twelve Southerners, *I'll Take My Stand: The South and the Agrarian Tradition* (Baton Rouge: Louisiana State University Press, 1977), 171–72.

critical of the kinds of work to be done. They planted no corn that they could not enjoy; they grew no cotton that did not directly contribute to the upkeep of a rich private life; and they knew no history for the sake of knowing it, but simply for the sake of contemplating it and seeing in it an image of themselves. And aware of the treachery of nature, as all agrarians are, they tended to like stories, very simple stories with a moral.[4]

Five years later, when he published "The Profession of Letters in the South," Tate's conception of the history of the South had become more complex. But if he had become somewhat less certain about the simplicity of the Old South, he still interpreted it as a European community. In this essay the interpretation bears upon the problem of why the Old South failed to develop a literary profession, or even a literary tradition. Tate finds his answer in the aristocratic rule of a planter class who had no real use for literature. The New England plutocracy, he observes, had none either, although in and around Boston a marginal literary life did produce a few distinctive writers.

But it is a sadder story still in the South. We had no Hawthorne, no Melville, no Emily Dickinson. We had William Gilmore Simms. We made it impossible for Poe to live south of the Potomac. Aristocracy drove him out. Plutocracy, in the East, starved him to death. I prefer the procedure of the South; it knew its own mind, knew what kind of society it wanted ... It must be confessed that the Southern tradition has left no cultural landmark so conspicuous that the people may be reminded by it constantly of what they are. We lack a tradition in the arts; more to the point,we lack a literary tradition. We lack even a literature. We have just enough literary remains from the old régime to prove to us that, had a great literature risen, it would have been unique in modern times.
The South was settled by the same European strains as originally settled the North. Yet, in spite of war, reconstruction, and industrialism, the South to this day finds its most perfect contrast in the North. In religious and social feeling I should stake everything on the greater resemblance to France. The South clings blindly to forms of European feeling and conduct that were crushed by the French Revolution and that, in England at any rate, are barely memories.[5]

Both in "Remarks on Religion in the South" and in "The Profession of Letters in the South," as we can see, Tate takes the attitude

4 *Ibid.*, 172–73.
5 Tate, *Essays*, 520–21.

that the Old South is the only part of America that has an experiential knowledge of the life of an organic communal world as this life has been known in Western civilization. Elaborating on the implication of Tate's notion, we may say that the southern writer in the 1920s and 1930s, who consciously realized his inheritance, found himself in a world that had not only known but had lived genuinely old values. Among these are (to make use of a convenient list supplied by the distinguished historical sociologist, Robert A. Nisbet, in *Tradition and Revolt*): "hierarchy, community, tradition, authority, and the sacred sense of life." The New England scene in contrast had been dominated by modernist values: "equalitarianism, individualism, secularism, positive rights, and rationalist modes of organization" (to make use of another list from Nisbet). The "peculiarly historical consciousness" of the southern writer at the "crossing of the ways" in the third and fourth decades of the present century consisted, Tate argues implicitly, in the knowledge that he descends from the "old regime." He has the feudal age in his bones.

In asserting a southern feudalism, Tate's motive is by no means to confine the southern writer to a provincial status. Instead, he intends to place him in the cosmopolitan mainstream of the modern literary sensibility. The modern southern writer has an intimate connection with the very source of the great modern Western literary renaissance; he is connected to the inspiriting motive of Yeats, Joyce, Eliot, Valéry, and Mann. This is to say, he is a voice in that dialectic of modernist and traditionalist values which, generated and regenerated in successive waves of the traditionalist reaction to modernism in the aftermath of the French Revolution, is the substance of modern art and letters. Tate as a modern writer—as a writer educated in the literary world in which a reactionary poem like *The Waste Land* had become the major cultural symbol—needed to believe in the legend of the South as a traditional European community. The need grew out of the literary drama in which he was involved; it was a requirement of the poetry of his role as a man of letters in the modern world.

Interpreters of the South and its literature, I would suggest, need to move to a perspective different from that provided by the struggle between modernism and traditionalism. Ironically, Tate seems to have felt this need even as he wrote his early essays on the South. In the total complexity of these writings, he places a heavy emphasis on the failure of the Old South as a feudal society. The South, he points out, did not have a feudal religion; it had Protestantism. It was a "semi-feudal society." The Old South did not have a labor system that related the aristocracy to the soil as serfdom did; it had chattel slavery, and the chattels were black and out of cultural origins completely alien to those of the masters. The Old South did not have a stable politics; it was "hag-ridden by politics" and thus always in a state of crisis. The Old South, Tate virtually says, could not under the circumstances of its actual existence have had an organic society in the feudal sense. What Tate did not see—we suspect, I think, that he did not quite want to see it, for he comes so close upon it—is simply that, although southerners appealed to the feudal image, it was because, save for the Greek and Roman worlds, they did not know what other historical image to appeal to. Since they did not have any possibility of living by what Tate calls "the higher myth of religion," they actually lived by what he calls the "lower myth of history." Endeavoring to adapt the life of European traditionalism to their situation, they imitated forms of feeling and emotion that had become historical and so succeeded only in being ornamental and meretricious. The southern feudal artifice rang as hollow as an empty suit of armor.

What the southerners were really trying to be was something else—something essentially not Grecian, not Roman, not feudal. They were never able adequately to express their aspiration, although they came close to it in some ways in the works of George Fitzhugh of Port Royal, Virginia, most expressly so in his *Sociology for the South* and in his *Cannibals All!* The South wanted a world in which chattel slavery was established beyond all doubt as the right and proper principle of the social relation, a world in which society was built securely, permanently, unqualifiedly on the right of men to hold property in other men. The struggle of the Old South was not between a traditionalism rooted in European forms of feeling and emotion and an outside (or an inside) insurgent modernism. Under the historical circumstances that it faced—under the historical nature of its existence—the South's struggle was between the rise of a unique slave society and the forces of modernism.

Tate observes that, had the antebellum South had a literature, it would have been unique in representing "the old regime" in modern times. Employing the term *literature* in the sense of a society's expression in letters, we may more correctly say that the Old South *had* a literature, but we understand its nature and importance only when we grasp its inner irony—I mean, when we see that it represents the novelty of the southern reaction to modernism. One of the most significant essays on southern culture between the time of the Civil War and Tate's "The Profession of Letters in the South" is to be found in the chapters on Richmond, Charleston, and Florida in Henry James's *The American Scene* (1907). Central to James's concept of the South is the way in which the southern self-interpretation conceive a "world rearranged" to accommodate the "interest of slave-produced Cotton."

> The solidity and comfort [of the South] were to involve not only the wide extension, but the complete intellectual, moral and economic reconsecration of slavery, an enlarged and glorified, quite beatified, application of its principle. The light of experience, round about, and every finger-post of history, of political and spiritual science with which the scene of civilization seemed to bristle, had, when questioned, but one warning to give, and appeared to give it with an effect of huge derision: whereby was laid on the Southern genius the necessity of getting rid of these discords and substituting for the ironic face of the world an entirely new harmony, or in other words a different scheme of criticism. Since nothing in the Slave-scheme could be said to conform—conform, that is, to the reality of things—it was the plan of Christendom and the wisdom of the ages that would have to be altered. History, the history of everything, would be rewritten *ad usum Delphini*—the Dauphin being in this case the budding Southern mind.[6]

James depicts the Old South as having reacted to modernity (that is, to the "reality of things," by which he meant nineteenth-century liberal humanism and the grand doctrine of the "century of hope," the "Progress of Civilization") not by any return to a medieval tra-

6 *The American Scene*, ed. W. H. Auden (New York: Charles Scribner's Sons, 1946), 373–74.

ditionalism, but by proposing to establish itself on the basis of "an entirely new harmony," on a "different scheme of criticism." The South sought not to root the rationale of its difference from the modern world in the deep places of an old mind, but, on the contrary, to found its existence and establish its difference from modernity on a new mind. The mind of the Old South was a "budding mind." What would this new world that the southerners wished to fashion have been like if the southerners had succeeded in making it? James does not pursue this question. He devotes himself to the barren cultural situation that was created in the South by the effort to make the new mind. The pursuit of the "Confederate dream" meant a drastic repudiation of the artistic and literary tradition of Western civilization. It "meant a general and permanent" intellectual quarantine, James declares; "meant the eternal bowdlerization of books and journals; meant in fine all literature and all art on an expurgatory index." James continues:

> It meant, still further, an active and ardent propaganda; the reorganization of the school, the college, the university, in the interest of the new criticism. The testimony to that thesis offered by documents of the time, by State legislation, local eloquence, political speeches, the "tone of the press," strikes us to-day as beyond measure queer and quaint and benighted —innocent above all; stamped with the inalienable Southern sign, the inimitable *rococo* note. We talk of the provincial, but the provinciality projected by the Confederate dream, and in which it proposed to steep the whole helpless social mass, looks to our eyes as artlessly perverse, as untouched by any intellectual tradition of beauty or wit, as some exhibited array of the odd utensils or divinities of lone and primitive islanders. It came over one that they *were* there, in the air they had breathed, precisely, lone—even the very best of the old Southerners; and, looking at them over the threshold of the approach that poor Richard seemed to form, the real key to one's sense of their native scene was in that very idea of their solitude and isolation. Thus they affected one as such passive, such pathetic victims of fate, as so played upon and betrayed, so beaten and bruised, by the old burden of their condition, that I found myself conscious, on their behalf, of a sort of ingenuity of tenderness.[7]

Although in his remarks James becomes patronizing, and at the same time somewhat sentimental, about the meaning of the south-

7 *Ibid.,* 374–75.

ern quest for an independent intellect, he suggests graphically that
the drama of the quest lay in its openness to historical novelty and
in the resulting isolation of the South in modern history. The Jamesian suggestion is unintentionally buttressed by the interpretation of
the Old South offered by the remarkable Marxist historian, Eugene D.
Genovese. In two compelling works—*The Political Economy of
Slavery* and a sequel, *The World the Slaveholders Made*—Genovese
argues cogently that the southern slaveholders conceived, and to
some extent actually created, a unique historical community. He
presents a South that sought to realize itself, not in the "institutional inheritance" of the old European regime, but in a "patriarchal
and paternalistic ethos" stemming from the rule of a "resident planter
for whom the plantation was a home and the entire population part
of his extended family." Contrasting this regime with its counterpart in South America, Genovese points to several critical aspects of
the plantation regime in the southern United States. One was the
ending of the foreign slave trade at the moment the cotton South
came into being. The slaveholding class was forced to rely primarily
upon the development of a Creole slave population. However strong
the purely exploitative motive in their use, southern slaves were
thus necessarily accorded paternalistic treatment. They responded
by being the only slave class in the New World to reproduce itself.

> The initial motivation to provide the slaves with adequate food, shelter,
> clothing, and leisure was of course economic, and the economic pressures
> for good treatment if anything grew stronger over time. It is nonetheless
> naive to leave matters there and to see economic interests and morals as
> discrete categories. Once extended over a generation or two, the appropri-
> ate standards of treatment became internalized and part of the accepted
> standard of decency for the ruling class. The growth of a creole slave pop-
> ulation narrowed the cultural gap between the classes and races and pre-
> pared the way for those feelings of affection and intimacy which had to
> exist if paternalism was to have substance.[8]

Another crucial aspect of the history of slavery in the American
South, as Genovese interprets it, was the liberation of the southern
slaveholding class from England by the American Revolution. "If

8 *The World the Slaveholders Made: Two Essays in Interpretation* (New York: Pantheon Books, 1969), 99.

separation from England liberated a national capitalist régime in the North," Genovese contends, "it simultaneously liberated a plantation slave régime in the South." The result was that the southern ruling class, constrained by no power save a fairly weak central government in Washington, was invited to assume autonomous power over the region of the new nation in which slavery was a primary institution. Such an invitation was not to be neglected. The southern slaveholders soon moved toward another critical turning point in their history. This was "the formulation of the positive-good proslavery argument." Signaling "the maturation of the ruling class and its achievement of self-consciousness," this argument was no mere apology for slavery. On the contrary, "it represented the formulation of a world view that authentically reflected the position, aspirations, and ethos of the slaveholders as a class." In its "final formulation" this view, as presented by the writer whom Genovese regards as the greatest southern theorist, George Fitzhugh, set forth slavery as "the proper relationship of all labor to capital." In Genovese's opinion, such a conception of the link between slave labor and capital "had no counterpart in the Caribbean or in Latin America."

Its development would have been especially difficult in Latin America since the Catholic tradition . . . recognized slavery but declared it to be unnatural. Paradoxically, it was precisely the most originally bourgeois of the slaveholding countries that produced a coherent defense of slavery as a mode of production in its social, political, ideological, and moral aspects. The paternalism at the core of the slaveholder's ideology rested primarily on the master-slave relationship but extended itself outward to encompass the white lower classes. As the régime developed, the plantations became increasingly self-sufficient and more enclosed as productive-consuming units. In the slave states as a whole . . . there was considerable progress toward regional self-sufficiency. Locally, this development meant the dependence of yeomen and poorer whites on the plantation market. . . . For the most part . . . planters do not appear to have exploited their economic opportunities with anything like ruthlessness but to have considered them part of a wider social responsibility. Many of the yeomen and even poor whites (that is, largely declassed freemen) were related to the planters. The local records of Black Belt counties make it clear that members of the same family occupied positions in all classes and income groups within the same county. The distinctly Southern sense of extended family cannot be understood apart from the social structure at the center of which stood the plantation, and it provided a powerful impetus for social cohesion, ruling-class hegemony, and the growth of a paternalistic spirit that far transcended master-slave and white-black relationships. There were undoubtedly powerful counterpressures, especially those associated with the egalitarian ethos, which would have to be given due weight in a full account. It is nonetheless clear that much of the political power of the planters and much of that oft-noted loyalty of the nonslaveholders to the régime derived from these semi-paternalistic relationships. . . . The slaveholders of the Old South . . . had inherited no hierarchical political principle to draw upon and had to develop this extended paternalism carefully, with full account of the contrary democratic and egalitarian attitudes residing deep in the lower classes. Southern paternalism developed in a contradictory, sometimes even hypocritical way, but the existence and force of the tendency among so egalitarian-minded a people tells us a great deal about the character and power of the plantation system.[9]

Reaching to fulfill its destiny, Genovese says, the southern slaveholding class came eventually to the final turning point in its history. It was impelled to secede from the nation-state that it had joined following the American Revolution and to stake everything on its capacity to set up its own nation-state. But it was too late in history for this effort to be successful, for by this time the economic and political goals of the southern slaveholding world were obsolete. A world marketplace had become the center of the economic life of Western civilization and the principle of the sovereignty of the people the center of its political life. The master class of the South had no way effectively to cut the South off from the world marketplace —and could not envision doing so except in the austere logic of a George Fitzhugh. Nor could the southern master class perform—or envision performing save in a Fitzhugh's vision—the logically necessary act of unifying the southern slave system by enslaving the lower-class southern whites. In theory, the master class was not restrained by the unity of the white race from converting all the available labor supply in the South—lower-class white as well as free Negro—to the slavery system. Racism in the Old South was strong, but it was a result of special circumstances and not an inherent part of the logic of the slave South. Slavery remained always basically a class and not a racial ideology. In the case of the lower-class whites,

9 *Ibid.*, 100–101.

the master class confronted a segment of a southern populace that had attained to an autonomous class position and was potentially powerful enough to rise against the master class and destroy it.

In summation, and I apologize for giving what is no doubt an over-simplified resumé of his concepts, Genovese tells us that antebellum southern society "is to be understood, not as a form of capitalism, much less as a form of feudalism," but as a slave society structured by class, although "deformed by internal and external ties to the capitalist world and profoundly flawed by racial caste."

If we accept Genovese's view of Old South history as being within the realm of a possible interpretation of a complicated and paradoxical epoch in modern history, we are led to consider its conceivable bearing on the interpretation of southern literature. I refer particularly to the problem of interpretation with which we commenced: defining the reactionary nature of modern southern literature.

When we look at the Old South as a singular slave society, we realize the extent to which its literary expression in its entirety—that is to say, the history of its literary life and the character of its literary expression in the varied forms of poetry, fiction, oratory, and the social and political essay—constitutes both the explicit and the implicit record of the Old South's experience of its struggle for uniqueness in history. In contrast to the traditionalist intellectual of the post-French Revolution stamp, a Joseph de Maistre or an Edmund Burke, the nineteenth-century southern man of letters sought, not to restore the sensibility of a European traditionalism, but to encourage the building in the midst of modern history of an autonomous slave society. Had it come to fruition, we may speculate, this society would have been neither feudal (Tate) nor prebourgeois (Genovese) but a world of its own inner determining. At the same time, it would have been a society accommodated to finance capitalism, industrialism, and a world market.[10] In the final phase of the Old

10 In *Politics and Power in a Slave Society, 1800–1860* (Baton Rouge: Louisiana State University Press, 1977), J. Mills Thornton III presents a striking case for discovering the shaping reality of the South in the southern interpretation of the Jacksonian imperatives: "The essence of Jacksonian society was the worship of the idols Liberty and Equality. Southerners, because of their daily contact with genuine slavery, were even more fanatically devoted to the Jacksonian cult than were most Americans." Thornton regards his perception of southern reality as antithetical to the perceptions of either Ulrich B. Phillips or Genovese.

South, Henry Timrod, poet laureate of the Confederacy, dreamed in "Ethnogenesis" that the Cotton Kingdom would become a salvational world power, bringing global peace and prosperity and redeeming the laborers of all nations from poverty:

> But let our fears—if fears we have—be still,
> And turn us to the future! Could we climb
> Some mighty Alp, and view the coming time,
>   The rapturous sight would fill
>   Our eyes with happy tears!
> Not for the glories which a hundred years
> Shall bring us; not for lands from sea to sea,
> And wealth, and power, and peace, though these shall be;
> But for the distant peoples we shall bless,
> And the hushed murmur of a world's distress;
>   For, to give labor to the poor,
>   The whole sad planet o'er,
> And save from want and crime the humblest door,
> Is one among the many ends for which
>   God makes us great and rich!
> The hour perchance is not yet wholly ripe
> When all shall own it, but the type
> Whereby we shall be known in every land
> Is that vast gulf which laves our Southern strand,
> And through the cold, untempered ocean pours
> Its genial streams, that far off Arctic shores
> May sometimes catch upon the softened breeze
> Strange tropic warmth and hints of summer seas![11]

No work more graphically conveys the singular divorcement of the Old South from modern history than Timrod's proclamation of the new southern nation. Far from assuming that the literature of the Confederacy is continuous with the expression of a traditionalist society, Timrod implies that the mission of the southern poet is to help a society under great historical stress to make an image of itself and of its meaning in history.

When we regard southern writings from the standpoint of the southern struggle for historical realization, we see how important it is to

11 *Literature of the South*, ed. Richard Croom Beatty, Floyd C. Watkins, and Thomas Daniel Young (Chicago: Scott, Foresman and Company, 1952), 323–24.

study all the literary expression in the South and not simply its novels and poems. We see how fundamental—in an age when the use of letters was still the primary assimilating civilizational power—literary expression was in the Old South. And in this expression—from William Byrd II, through Thomas Jefferson, through Edmund Ruffin, who fired the first shot on Fort Sumter—we see the man of letters trying to make himself at home as a master in a slave society (not as feudal lord, but as plantation patriarch). But the cost of making the man of letters into the *southern* man of letters was the loss of contact with the shape and substance of modern literary history: the great drama involving the reaction of traditionalism against modernism that commenced in the early nineteenth century. The writer of the Old South, after the age of Jefferson at any rate, lacked the sense of past and present in conflict, of European tradition and American modernity. Such a sense was vividly present in the New England writer. "There are always two parties, the party of the Past and the party of the Future; the Establishment and the Movement," Emerson said in defining his age. "At times the resistance is reanimated, the schism runs under the world and appears in Literature, Church, State, and social customs."[12] No such vision of the mid-nineteenth century was available to Emerson's southern contemporary. As I have said elsewhere, in the Old South the realm of the State, in the interest of developing the ideology of slavery, virtually assimilated the realm of the Church and the realm of Letters. It has been in the Republic of Letters that the debate between traditionalism and modernism has effectively taken place. The Old South literati—not deliberately, not even consciously—withdrew from this polity for the sake of affiliating with a vision of a historically singular social, political, and economic order. Their legacy to the South was largely barren until Tate and others, rejoining the literary polity of Western high culture, the intellectual homeland of Thomas Jefferson, began a poetic reassimilation of the Old South to this dominion. In Tate's phrase, they defined the "crossing of the ways" in the South, reinterpreting the history of southern literature and placing it in the dialectic between traditionalism and modernism. In so do-

12 "Historic Notes of Life and Letters in New England," in *The Portable Emerson*, ed. Mark Van Doren (New York: Viking Press, 1946), 514.

ing they at once fostered the legend of a traditionalism rooted in Europe as the integrating force in Western culture and obscured the assimilating power of the defense of the "peculiar institution" in the Old South world.

But if we accept the peculiar institution as the center of the world view of the Old South, we may well conclude that its influence on the southern mind was more responsible for the "peculiarly historical consciousness" that Tate observed in the southern writer at the "crossing of the ways" than any world view derived from a European traditionalism. Understanding this, we are possibly able to understand that the twentieth-century southern writer in a special way inherited from the Old South the chief issue in the dialectic between traditionalism and modernism—the nature of man in relation to community. Are we inescapably creatures of community, expressing ourselves properly and truly as men solely through a community of blood, myth, and ritual; or are we truly ourselves as men only when liberated from the bonds of "organic" community? In the Old South this issue did not take the form it did under European, or New England, or general American conditions. It took the uniquely intense historical form of the South's effort to reconcile freedom and community through the development of a modern society founded on chattel slavery. This effort to bring forth a modern slave society sent the Old South to the wall and destroyed it. Although the commitment to slavery was gravely questioned by many southerners, and even rebelled against by some, there was ultimately no southern willingness to compromise on the part of those who held power in the South. The world the plantation regime made realized the meaning of its own mind, all right—realized it better than some of those who represented it in roles of leadership. Towards the end of the Civil War, as Robert F. Durden shows in his striking compilation of documents concerning the Confederate debate on emancipation, both Jefferson Davis and Robert E. Lee were eager to accept slaves into the Confederate armed forces on condition of their freedom.[13] If enough Confederate troops could have been mustered in this man-

13 *The Gray and the Black: The Confederate Debate on Emancipation* (Baton Rouge: Louisiana State University Press, 1972).

ner, the South might have had a chance for a negotiated settlement of the Civil War. But the Old South society preferred to go down as it was. And unless we grasp the intensity of its preoccupation with its vision of itself as a modern order, constituting at once a community of masters and slaves and a political and moral economy, I doubt if we can understand the presence of the Old South in the twentieth-century southern literary imagination. I am not necessarily saying with Quentin Compson, "You would have to be born there." (Eugene Genovese was born and raised in Brooklyn, incidentally.) I am saying that you have to know something about the special history of the American South to grasp the inheritance of the southern writer from "old slavery times."

From the complex frustration and defeat of the Old South's attempt to become a unique slave society, the modern southern writer inherited, as did no other American writer of his age, a compelling drama of man and community. There was available to the southern writer in story, in the silent artifacts of unspoken memory, and in the very silence of the South on some matters—in the gesture and style of the life around him—the experience of a people who had deeply lived the tensions of the modern aspiration to community. They had lived it not only in the manners and conventions, ceremonies and rituals, amenities and conflicts of the outward society, but also in the goodness and evil, the nobility and depravity of the inner worlds of the individuals in it. They had lived it in the terrors and horrors of human nature and in the resistance to these and, moreover, in the recognition that the intricate bonds of human community may be composed as much of hate as of love. The South had experienced the life of community lived, as Faulkner puts it, out of "the heart's driving complexity." This experience is obviously present in the powerful imagination of community that we know in Faulkner, Tate, Warren, Eudora Welty, Richard Wright, Flannery O'Connor, William Styron, Walker Percy, Ralph Ellison, Ernest Gaines, and Alice Walker. But how this imagination is rooted in the deeper levels of the southern life is scarcely yet understood. I have been thinking since first seeing it in Eugene Genovese's review essay on George P. Rawick's study, *From Sundown to Sunup: The Making of the Black Community* (the book that serves as the introduction to *The Ameri-*

can Slave: A Composite Autobiography, the amazing compilation
of narratives by ex-slaves collected by the WPA in the 1930s), that
the imagination of community in the southern expression is nowhere
more strikingly evidenced than in the recollection of William Colbert, born a slave in Georgia in 1844.[14] Colbert tells a story of master
and slave that cannot be told other than in his own words:

> Nawsuh, he warn't good to none of de niggers. All de niggers 'roun' hated
> to be bought by him kaze he wuz so mean. When he wuz too tired to whip
> us he had de overseer do it; and de overseer wuz meaner dan de massa.
> But, mister, de peoples wuz de same as dey is now. Dere wuz good uns
> and bad uns. I jus' happened to belong to a bad un. One day I remembers
> my brother, January, wuz cotched over seein' a gal on de next plantation.
> He had a pass but de time on it done gib out. Well suh, when de massa
> found out dat he wuz a hour late, he got as mad as a hive of bees. So when
> brother January he come home, de massa took down his long mule skinner
> and tied him wid a rope to a pine tree. He strip' his shirt off and said: "Now,
> Nigger, I'm goin' to teach you some sense." Wid dat he started layin' on
> de lashes. January was a big, fine lookin' nigger, de finest I ever seed. He
> wuz jus' four years older dan me, an' when de massa begin a beatin' him,
> January never said a word. De massa got madder and madder kaze he
> couldn't make January holla.
> "What's de matter wid you, nigger?" he say. "Don't it hurt?"
> January, he never said nothin', and de massa keep a beatin' till little
> streams of blood started flowin' down January's chest, but he never holler.
> His lips was a quiverin' and his body wuz a shakin', but his moutf it neber
> open; and all de while I sat on my mammy's and pappy's steps a cryin'.
> De niggers wuz all gathered about and some uv 'em couldn't stand it; dey
> hadda go inside dere cabins. Atter while, January, he couldn't stand it no
> longer hisself, and he say in a hoarse, loud whisper:
> "Massa! Massa! have mercy on dis poor nigger. . . ."
> Den . . . de war came. De Yankees come in and dey pulled de fruit off de
> trees and et it. Dey et de hams and cawn, but dey neber burned de houses.
> Seem to me lak dey jes' stay aroun' long enough to git plenty somp'n t'eat,
> kaze dey lef' in two or three days, an' we neber seed 'em since. De massa
> had three boys to go to war, but dere wuzn't one to come home. All the
> chillun he had wuz killed. Massa, he los' all his money and doe house
> soon begin droppin' away to nothin'. Us niggers one by one lef' de ole
> place and de las' time I seed de home plantation I wuz a standin' on a hill.
> I looked back on it for de las' time through a patch of scrub pines and it

14 *From Sundown to Sunup: The Making of the Black Community* (Westport, Conn.:
Greenwood Publishing Company, 1972).

look' so lonely. Dere warn't but one person in sight, de massa. He was a-settin'; in a wicker chair in de yard lookin' out ober a small field of cotton and cawn. Dere wuz fo' crosses in de graveyard in de side lawn where he wuz a'settin'. De fo'th one wuz his wife. I lost my ole woman too 37 years ago, and all dis time, I's ben a carrin' on like de massa—all alone.[15]

In his study on the significance of the WPA narratives, Rawick presses hard upon the thesis that the African blacks enslaved in the Old South became an Afro-American people with their own community and culture. They became so by heroic resistance to the masters and to the white racism pervasive in the South. In revising our conception of the Old South to emphasize its character as a slave society, certainly we cannot fail to take into account the rise of the black community. But does the poetic tragedy of the quest for community in the South lie any more purely in the black experience of the slave society than in the white experience of it? It is of the utmost interest to all of us, black or white, who are students of southern literature, that William Colbert of Georgia perceived that it did not. He perceived this as clearly as William Faulkner of Mississippi or Allen Tate of Tennessee. Probably he perceived this more surely than they did. It may be that, in some underlying process of carrying knowledge to the heart (to echo Tate's key phrase in "Ode to the Confederate Dead"), William Colbert taught them this.

15 *Ibid.*, 104–105.

CODA / The Act of Thought
in Virginia

"History, Stephen said, is a nightmare from which
I am trying to awake."
—James Joyce, *Ulysses*

Since the publication of Richard Beale Davis' *Intellectual Life in Jefferson's Virginia, 1780–1830* (1964), no one has accepted Henry Adams' oversimplified concept of the Virginian mind in the era of the early Republic: "Law and politics were the only objects of Virginia thought."[1] Approaching his subject through a variety of categories—formal education, reading and libraries, religion, agrarian theory and practice, science, fine arts, belles lettres, oratory, law, politics, and economics—Davis marshalls documentary evidence indicating a vigorous diversity of mental effort in Virginia during the first four decades of the Republic. "Perhaps beyond any of their American contemporaries," he suggests, "they exemplified the best qualities of the Enlightenment which was just then disappearing in Europe, combining with it a sense of national destiny and necessity."[2] But although *Intellectual Life in Jefferson's Virginia* establishes the range and remarkable quality of thought in the age of the third American president, its full implication has become evident only with the publication of Davis' magisterial *Intellectual Life in the Colonial South, 1585–1763*: the flowering of intellect

---

1 Henry Adams, *History of the United States*, I, quoted in Richard Beale Davis, *Intellectual Life in Jefferson's Virginia, 1790–1830* (Chapel Hill: University of North Carolina Press, 1964), 1. In a briefer version, the above essay was presented at the meeting of the Division on American Literature to 1800, Modern Language Association, on December 30, 1978. In the present revised and expanded form, it was presented at the thirty-ninth Conference of the Institute of Early American History and Culture, University of Tennessee, April 28, 1979. This Conference honored Richard Beale Davis. It is presented here as a kind of coda to the themes developed in the first three chapters.
2 Davis, *Intellectual Life in Jefferson's Virginia*, 4.

in Jefferson's world was the fulfillment of a lengthy indigenous development.

Pursuing the general thesis in his culminating work that, as he puts it, "rationalism was a dominant quality of the southern mind . . . from Captain John Smith and the early witchcraft trials [the southern trials, that is] straight through to Thomas Jefferson," Davis not only documents and describes the large interest in secular letters and learning in the intellectual center of the planting colonies, Virginia, but also shows that this was an evolving interest.[3] Taken together, *Intellectual Life in the Colonial South* and *Intellectual Life in Jefferson's Virginia* open the prospect that, under sufficient interpretative pressure, the life of the intellect in the Virginia of colonial times and in the Virginia of the early Republic will reveal not only an outer but also an inner pattern of secular rationality. As a pioneering scholar in the life of the mind in the South, in other words, Davis challenges us to trace and elaborate a Virginian—an essentially southern—cast of mind from its inauguration in the Elizabethan adventurer-historian who founded Jamestown to its complex embodiment in Jefferson, world-historical revolutionist and matchless writer, who not only composed *A Summary View of the Rights of the British Colonists*, the Declaration of Independence, and the *Notes on the State of Virginia*, but who at the same time set down a massive and unrivaled body of epistolary writing on every topic of interest to the Enlightenment, including the nature of the human mind. In taking up such an endeavor, can we hope to discover what historians have so far largely doubted: a Virginian mind as definitive as that of Massachusetts; or more broadly, a mind of the early South as distinctive and coherent as that of early New England?

The pursuit of the challenge presented by Davis ultimately involves attention to the many wholly neglected or even unknown specimens of the colonial southern intellect that he recovers in his exhaustive inquiry. Let us be directly concerned here only with determining how—or, to be sure, whether or not—various prominent writings within the scope of Davis' studies illustrate the colonial South's commitment to modern secular culture.

3 Davis, *Intellectual Life in the Colonial South* (3 vols.; Knoxville: University of Tennessee Press, 1978), I, xxx.

As an exemplification of secularity, for instance, John Smith's *Generall Historie of Virginia, New-England and the Summer Isles* arrests us in its very first words—the author's self-conscious dedication to his patroness, "the most illustrious and most noble Princess, the Lady Francis, Duchess of Richmond and Lenox." Of his work Smith says:

> This History, as for the raritie and varietie of the subject, so much more for the judicious *Eyes* it is like to vndergoe, and most of all for that great *Name*, whereof it dareth implore Protection, might and ought to haue beene clad in better robes then my rude military hand can cut out in Paper Ornaments. But, because of the most things therein, I am no Compiler by hearsay, but haue a propertie in them: and therefore haue been bold to challenge them to come vnder the reach of my owne rough Pen. That, which hath beene indured and passed through with hardship and danger, is thereby sweetened to the *Actor*, when he becometh the *Relator*. I haue deeply hazarded my selfe in doing and suffering, and why should I sticke to hazard my reputation in Recording? He that acteth two parts is the more borne withall if he come short, or fayle in one of them.[4]

Smith's anxious approach to the composition of his *Generall Historie of Virginia* conveys the extent to which, in the first quarter of the seventeenth century, the ever-increasing secularity of letters is attended by a self-consciousness of history and how this makes for a union of self, letters, and secular history. Such an intimacy of these elements is unanticipated in secular texts, save perhaps in some of the writings of later Roman times. We realize how small a precedent lies in the most obvious and expected source, the heroic literature, when we regard how strangely John Smith qualifies the heroic style, saying "That which hath been indured and passed through with hardship and danger is thereby sweetened to the *Actor* when he becometh the *Relator*." Instead of emulating the actor as bard, responding to a firmly established concept of the actor-relator defined by his community, Smith is closer to assuming the modern character of the actor-relator, a mutant creature who appears as the technological achievement of printing begins to become definitive in Western culture. As the author of a printed book—a manufactured object, available in multiple copies, made to be held in many hands yet in the

4 *Travels and Works of Captain John Smith*, ed. Edward Arber (2 vols.; Edinburgh, J. Grant, 1910), I, 275–76.

hands of only one person—Smith expresses the relation between author and reader as a part of the experience of individuation accompanying the development of secular history as the mode of existence.
This experience is particularly intense for the author; for his book,
an embodiment of himself brought forth into time, lives only in the
favoring response of the reader. The writer imagines a close familiarity—a sweetness of association—with an audience that, whether
composed of one person or many, is not merely his patron, but also
the necessity of his being. Smith's sense of his connection with the
Lady Francis, it may be noted, has somewhat exotic sexual connota-
tions. Referring to the "honorable and vertuous ladies" who "even in
forraine parts" have "offred me rescue and protection in my greatest dangers," including "in the vtmost of many extremities, that
blessed Pokahontas," Smith says: "And so verily these my adventures haue tasted the same *influence* from your *Gratious hand*, which
hath given birth to the publication of this *Narration*. If therefore
your Grace shall daign to cast your eye on this poore Booke, view I
pray you rather your owne *Bountie* (without which it had dyed in
the wombe) than my *imperfections*, which haue no helpe but the
shrine of your *glorious Name* to be sheltered from censorious condemnation."[5]

Smith's metaphorical appeal to his patroness—in which he recognizes her as mother, midwife, critic, and heroic protectoress of his
book—suggests that by his day the printer's screw (if I may be allowed a certain crudity of explicative conjecture) has become a submerged metaphor for a phenomenon that I have elsewhere (in a different though not unrelated context) termed the sexuality of modern
history. The printing press has become identified with the fecundity
of the womb of time—of, more precisely, the womb of modern history. Issuing endlessly from the press to an ever-growing number of
readers (themselves the veritable offspring of the press), the printed
word, as never the spoken or the manuscript word, has become not
only a carrier of history but integral with it. In the historical account,
in the novel, in the biography—most directly in the autobiography
(and Smith's *General History*, it has been said, is close to being an

5 *Ibid.*, I, 276–77.

autobiography)—writer, patron, and reader come together in an intimate historical transaction. They are joined in a generative union of
history and the technological instrumentation of the human mind
as the model of history.

This union signifies both its cause and its effect: a progressive
subjectification of history in the individual consciousness. Such an
internalization, which may well be reckoned the major characteristic of modern secularity—of modernity itself—was forecast when
the rational mind began to project its own operations as a model of
nature—and not only this, but also to conceive of mechanical instruments (among them, the magnetic compass, the spring clock,
the telescope, and the printing press) as demonstrations that the
world of time and space is modeled on cognitive processes. The interiorization of time and space effected by compass, clock, telescope,
and printing press repudiated the assumed complete relation between
consciousness and basic sensory perception. In the subsequent loss
of the equation between appearance and reality, the Western society
joined in blood and cosmic mystery, and made real in image and
icon—the sacramental, hierarchical, corporate, prescriptive community of Christendom, a society of myth and tradition—was displaced as the model of consciousness. The new model of consciousness is an integral expression of consciousness itself. Comprehending
as it does the shifting of man, nature, society, and (ultimately) God
into secular mind, this process of internalization is the self-conscious
subject of John Donne. In a poem like "Anatomy of the World," he
marks the poet's severance from the old community of bards and
heroes. Whether he wants to do so or not, the poet modifies his role
as actor-relator, taking on the guise of the modern man of letters and
attaching himself to the emerging realm of cosmopolitan secular
mind. The actor-relator may even be transformed into the complete
secularist like Francis Bacon, the scientist, moralist, historian, and
literary stylist, who gives expression to his age when he says flatly,
"Knowledge is power." Incarnating the Republic of Letters, or the
Third Realm, in Solomon's House and portraying the man of letters
as the Father of this dominion, Bacon proclaims in the *New Atlan-
tis*: "The End of our Foundation is the Knowledge of Causes, and secret motions of things; and the enlarging of the bounds of Human

Empire, to the affecting of all things possible."[6]

The most direct trans-Atlantic transmission of the Baconian sense of the empire of secular mind was not to New England, but to Virginia. It may be, as Perry Miller once argued, that the intention in the settlement of Virginia was the establishment of an order that would preserve and extend a sacramental society of God and King.[7] But this aim did not hold. Seizing on the coincidence of climate and soil and the newly created market for tobacco, the Virginia colonists made a life for themselves based on time and chance. The opportunistic quality of the Virginia enterprise was heightened when, by the late seventeenth century, the colonists embraced the historical contingency of African slavery to solve their labor problem. At a point when the New England consciousness had not yet experienced the displacement of the theocratic society (which in a sense is the "purified" version of the medieval sacramental existence) and had scarcely begun to modify its pervasive religiosity, the Virginian consciousness was preparing the way for the society modeled on rationality and controlled by a secular morality, the society of Thomas Jefferson.

The writings of Captain John Smith constitute an element in this preparation. In Smith's literary endeavors, the actor-turned-relator is a figure on the margins of the heroic age. He apes the heroic gesture, but the path that the heroic adventurer beats across the frontiers of the world leads, in Smith's case, to the world marketplace and the world-historical printing shop. Self-serving, always a bit ridiculous, Smith wears the aura of Don Quixote; and his account of his adventures is at the same time an unintentional parody of the heroic manner and an expression of the ineffable sweetness of discovering his identity in his personal experience of (to quote the evocative, wholly secular, and truly post-Gutenberg definition of history that Davis extracts from Smith's *Advertisements for Unexperienced Planters*) "the memory of time, the life of the dead, and the happiness of the living."[8]

In his patient and thorough documentation of intellectual activity

6 *The Works of Francis Bacon*, ed. James Spedding, Robert L. Ellis, and Douglas D. Heath (15 vols.; Boston: Houghton Mifflin and Company, n.d.), V, 398.
7 See Miller, *Errand into the Wilderness* (New York: Harper's, 1956), 99–140.
8 Quoted in Davis, *Intellectual Life in the Colonial South*, I, 73.

in the colonial South—of, as he puts it, the southern "cerebration"
—Davis provides the possibility of our discovering a deeper continuity from Smith to Jefferson than has been known or even suspected.
The possibility basically lies in tracing in southern colonial culture
what Hegel describes in his *Philosophy of History* as the essential
cultural consequence of the modern subjectifying of history: a secularization of the spiritual, which issues in a spiritualizing of the
secular.

Hegel speaks of this phenomenon occurring at a point when the
modern man finds that *"secular pursuits are a spiritual vocation."*[9]
Even though seventeenth-century New England writers—the actors
in history and relators of history like Bradford, Higginson, Johnson,
and Cotton Mather—believed (as John Cotton said) that God "pre-
senteth every age with a new stage of acts and actors," they assigned
all history to (as Cotton said) the "wise and strong and good providence of God." Whether the "womb of truth" be barren or fruitful,
Thomas Hooker observed, depended "meerly upon Gods good pleasure," who opens and shuts it "from bearing . . . , according to the
counsell of his own will."[10] The shift in New England thought and
emotion from a governing reliance on providential direction to a humanistic self-reliance (which at the extreme of its inclination rendered the divine consciousness immanent) affords a long, intricate,
yet coherent drama of the closure of modern existence in secular
history. Still, the drama of the spiritualization of the secular in New
England is not as fundamental in shaping the motives of the emerging American nation-state as the more intangible and less coherent
drama of the secularization of spirituality in the planting colonies.
Heralded by Smith, this drama reaches a definitive stage in Robert
Beverley and, more complexly, in William Byrd II, yet they are but
anticipations of its crucial culmination in Thomas Jefferson, author
of the American Declaration of Independence. A climactic representation of the interiorization of history and the institution of mind
as the model of society, this document is one of the supreme spiri-

---

9 Georg Wilhelm Friedrich Hegel, *The Philosophy of History*, trans. J. Sibree (New
York: Willey Book Company, 1944), 365.
10 *The Puritans*, ed. Perry Miller and Thomas H. Johnson (New York: American
Book Company, 1938), 85.

tual texts of modern secularism. I am not prepared to say categorically that the Declaration could have been written only by a southern colonial, but I think it likely that this is so. At any rate, only in Virginia was the transformation of the actor-relator into the modern man of letters fulfilled in an intellect consummately attuned to the historical movement of man out of the society of myth and tradition into mind.

Yet even the most ardent Revolutionist was aware that the Declaration hardly described the relationship of mind to the historical society in which its author lived. In fact, although it conclusively implies the great political and sociological alteration announced by the Puritan Rebellion and ratified by the Glorious Revolution—the vanquishing of the monarchical sociality of blood by the rationale of society and government discovered by mind (whether this be mind as represented by John Locke, the Scottish Common Sense philosophers, or "intellectual middlemen" like John Trenchard and Thomas Gordon)—the Declaration is almost devoid of any suggestion as to mind's relation to the reality of the society it presumed to declare independent of British rule. The actual society was a disparate one, in which chattel slavery, evolving from historical fortuity into a primary institution in the southern colonies, had become crucial to the future of whatever order the thirteen colonial entities might attain after they achieved independence. The Declaration refers to slavery only once: in the charge, somewhat obliquely stated, accusing the king of committing an atrocity of war by "exciting domestic insurrection amongst us." The specific historical event behind the accusation was the appeal in 1775 by Lord Dunmore, governor of Virginia, for slaves to rise against their masters. Jefferson's struggle to generalize the horror of Lord Dunmore's act resulted in a lengthy, convoluted denunciation of the king for having "waged cruel war against human nature itself" by enslaving unoffending Africans, trafficking in them, and then encouraging them to turn on their masters, "thus paying off former crimes committed against the LIBERTIES of one people, with crimes which he urges them to commit against the LIVES of another." [11] Setting up an unresolvable tension between

11 *The Portable Thomas Jefferson*, ed. Merrill D. Peterson (New York: Viking Press, 1975), 235–41. Garry Wills, *Inventing America: Jefferson's Declaration of Inde-*

the values of liberty and life, Jefferson points to the irrationality of the king who would loose slaves upon their masters, yet in so doing he suggests the more fundamental irrationality of slavery itself. Reducing Jefferson's involved, ambivalent rehearsal of the king's fomentation of a slave uprising, the Congressional version of the Declaration implies not only the general sanction of slavery by the revolting colonies (which some members of the Congress from the southern, and no doubt some from the northern, colonies wished to affirm), but also an accommodation of mind (its model) to the institution of slavery. Failing to disavow slavery, the Declaration ironically associates the perpetuation of the order of masters and slaves in America with the man of letters and the literary order. The fatefulness of this association was revealed in the 1830s, when another kind of actor-relator as American man of letters appeared on the scene, this one wearing the guise of the abolitionist. The American man of letters as abolitionist (committed to a total antithesis between slavery and mind) and the American man of letters as slavery advocate became world-historical literary figures. But even before this, the American slave master and man of letters like Jefferson who could question and even oppose slavery while he assented to its peculiar appropriateness under certain conditions—the Jefferson who penned the Declaration of Independence—had disappeared. Keeping to a course on the slavery issue which, although directed toward emancipation through colonization, held in view slavery's regional distinctiveness in the American Republic, Jefferson tacitly accepted the institution as necessary to the South, and to him personally. He attempted to avoid the dire underlying meaning of his position—to wit, that a slave society demanded the conformance of mind (and of consciousness and conscience) to its needs.

The threat of slavery to mind nonetheless remained a constant tensional element in Jefferson's thought. In *Notes on the State of Virginia*, it is evident in the part stressing the mental inferiority of Africans. It is more evident in the fierce outcry against slavery in Query 18, in which Jefferson depicts the institution as such a de-

---

pendence (New York: Doubleday and Company, Inc., 1978) bears generally on my discussion.

struction of the morals and industry of the masters and such a desecration of the humanity of the slaves that God in His wrath might
decree the overturning of the social order by the slaves. This unexpected denunciation of slavery was provoked, we surmise, neither
by Jefferson's simple moral aversion to slavery nor by his fear of slave
insurrection. The outcry measures the degree to which the historical dilemma of African chattel slavery had become subjectified in
his consciousness. In the midst of a book intended to present Virginia as a promising instance of a society developing on the model of
mind, the author (the Virginia philosophe, Jefferson, addressing answers to the queries propounded by a fellow French philosophe) implies that slavery may hold—almost surely does hold—dominion
over mind in Virginia. In his singular awareness of the opposition
between the dominion of mind and the historical particularity of his
world—a world imprisoned in fortuity and contingency—Jefferson
is the first American man of letters to assume southern history as a
psychic burden. Our appreciation of the character of this burden is
enhanced by the argument in Edmund S. Morgan's *American Slavery/
American Freedom: The Ordeal of Colonial Virginia*. Morgan describes how the Virginian lords in the later seventeenth and early
eighteenth centuries, fearing an increase in the poor resulting from
the use of indentured white laborers and being unable in a postfeudal
(or prebourgeois) historical situation to enslave the poor of their
own color, turned to African slavery. This expediency averted the
problem of an insurgency on the part of the landless white poor by
replacing them with laborers whose status as human beings was
considered to be so inferior that their enslavement required no justification. By means of this expediency, and with no deliberate intent,
the Virginians created a society in which large and small landown-
ers, freed of the fear of potential mob violence, could unite in the
Enlightenment idealism of liberty and equality—or, as I would have
it, in a society modeled on mind. Without acknowledging it, without even knowing it in any overt way, the Virginians stood on African slavery as the pragmatic historical condition of American independence from King and Church.

We can imagine that Jefferson might have relieved himself from the
burden of history by admitting, in the private recesses of his under-

standing, that the commitment of a Virginia man of letters to freedom ironically demanded his support of slavery. Or we can conceive that Jefferson might have lifted the burden of history entirely by quietly making an even more devastating admission: the contingencies of history constitute the inescapable shaping force of both mind and society. But Jefferson himself hardly entertained either notion. He balanced the burden of history with his conviction, reasserted to the end, that the Revolution was an act of mind freed from traditionalism and transcendent over the accidents of history. The revolutionary situation "presented to us an album on which we were free to write what we pleased," he said in 1824. "We had no occasion to search into musty records, to hunt up royal parchments, or to investigate the laws and institutions of a semi-barbarous ancestry."[12]

Jefferson's conviction of the efficacy of rational mind rested in his faith in the eighteenth-century materialist psychology. He conceived the index to existence to be feeling and "*thought* to be an action of a particular organization of matter." Endowed by the Creator with the capacity for thought, the substance that is the mind is continuous in Jefferson's view with the substance that is the body and perishes with it. Epitomizing the Enlightenment secularization of consciousness, the materialist psychology affords the basis of the Jeffersonian notion that each generation is historically discrete. Essentially its own creation, a generation is self-sufficient.

> Can one generation bind another, and all others, in succession forever? I think not. The Creator has made the earth for the living, not the dead. Rights and powers can only belong to persons, not to things, nor to mere matter, unendowed with will. The dead are not even things. The particles of matter which composed their bodies, make part now of the bodies of other animals, vegetables, or minerals, of a thousand forms. To what then are attached the rights and powers they held while in the form of men? A generation may bind itself as long as its majority continues in life; when that has disappeared, another majority is in place, holds all the rights and powers their predecessors once held, and may change their laws and institutions to suit themselves. Nothing then is unchangeable but the inherent and unalienable rights of man.[13]

12 Jefferson to John Adams, August 15, 1820, *The Writings of Thomas Jefferson*, ed. Andrew A. Lipscomb and Albert E. Bergh (20 vols.; Washington, D.C.: Thomas Jefferson Memorial Association, 1905), XV, 274.
13 Jefferson to Major John Cartwright, June 5, 1824, *ibid.*, XVI, 44.

In his idea of generational autonomy, Jefferson does not deny the relevancy of the past. But envisaging the past as a reservoir of facts about human experience, to be used for whatever they may be worth in improving the present, he radically accentuates the internalization of history. Ignoring all but the third element in the formulation of history as expressed by Captain John Smith ("the memory of time, the life of the dead, and the happiness of the living"), Jefferson fragments the psychic continuity of history. To be sure, he virtually suggests the logical consequence of generational autonomy, the isolation of history in the individual psyche.

Save in certain chilling moments (such as that recorded in the eighteenth Query of the *Notes on Virginia*), Jefferson experienced no terror in this; for he subscribed to the spirit of an age that, as Hegel says somewhere, believed that "thought ought to govern spiritual reality." Indeed, Jefferson saw historical reality as defined by and subject to the moral activity of secular thought. Five years before he wrote the Declaration, for instance, Jefferson advised a correspondent against yielding to moral strictures on fiction. Referring to one of the episodes at the beginning of Laurence Sterne's *A Sentimental Journey*, Jefferson says that it makes no difference whether Sterne's story of being unkind to a Franciscan friar and then repenting of his act is true or fictitious.

> In either case we equally are sorrowful at the rebuke and secretly resolve *we* will never do so: we are pleased with the subsequent atonement, and view with emulation a soul candidly acknowledging its fault and making a just reparation. Considering history as a moral exercise, her lessons would be too infrequent if confined to real life. Of those recorded by historians few incidents have been attended by such circumstances as to excite in any high degree this sympathetic emotion of virtue. We are, therefore, wisely framed to be as warmly interested for a fictitious as for a real personage.[14]

Commenting on Hegel's sense of history, Lionel Trilling in *The Opposing Self* observes how Hegel recognized a "new category of judgment" in the moral life of the later eighteenth century. No longer judged solely by its conformance to principle, the deed had become subject to review for the quality—the moral style—of its perfor-

14 Jefferson to Robert Skipwith, August 3, 1771, *ibid.*, IV, 238–39.

mance. This is why, Trilling says, Hegel dwelled at length on the difference between "character" and "personality," seeing personality as a response to the need for expressing the "manner and style of a moral action."[15] Reading Trilling on Hegel as a gloss on Jefferson on Sterne, we are struck by the completeness of Jefferson's interiorization of history. Conceiving the proper model of history to be the exercise of the self-conscious faculty of rational sympathy and benevolence, Jefferson implies that secular history—unfolding out of the moral imagination of the individual—embraces every act, whether real or contrived. History embraces consciousness. And not only this. The further implication is that history is modeled, not simply on the moral principle involved in an act, but also on the quality of the performance of the act—on, Trilling points out in *The Opposing Self*, whether the act is genuinely "sincere" or not. Modern history is not only consciousness, it is conscience—that terrible faculty which, developing in the course of the secularization of the spiritual, commands, no, impels, us to act rightly and then imperiously judges whether or not the rightness of the act is ratified by the manner and style of its execution. The burden of history is assumed by the self. Its driving motive, as Trilling says, becomes the demonstration of the "purity" of our secular spirituality, and its constant anxiety the discovery of "signs" of admission to "the secular-spiritual elect." The motive of the self as historical creature differentiates "personality" (formed by reference to inward imperatives) from character (formed by reference to transcendent principles).[16]

The extent to which Jefferson's experience of individuation—of conformance to the demands of "personality"—informs the Declaration of Independence is no doubt impossible to determine. In his later years (as I have observed earlier in these studies) an aged John Adams made up a story about assigning the task of writing the Declaration to Jefferson because he (Adams) was "obnoxious," and, besides, Jefferson could write better.[17] In a way, Adams probably knew that his little fiction told the essential truth; for although he had a

15 Trilling, *The Opposing Self: Nine Essays in Criticism* (New York: Viking Press, 1959), 228–30.
16 *Ibid.*
17 See Carl L. Becker, *The Declaration of Independence: A Study in the History of Political Ideas* (New York: Vintage Books, 1958), 135–36.

hair-trigger personal sensitivity to his own implication in history—and not only this, but also a distinct sense of mind as the model of history—as a post-Puritan New Englander Adams referred history to moral principle in the abstract and his own role as a historical actor-relator to the transcendence of character. Somehow he knew that he was always out of harmony with the fundamental tone and temper of history in his age; and Jefferson, ever in accord with it. Perhaps he even understood that Jefferson's participation in the modern internalization of history is fulfilled in the Declaration; that embedded in this document is not only a sense of the shaping force of the personal moral act in history, but also a sense of the style and manner of personal moral action as intrinsic to meaning in history.

In a deep way, the Declaration came from the hand of an actor-relator who understood that his own personal being and the being of each and every person in a "candid" and expanding world of letters (created by an expanding technology of literacy) was becoming committed to a self-evident, self-reflective, and self-fulfilling interpretation of history. As a sacred text of secular history, the Declaration promises all who believe in it a place among the secular-spiritual elect. It announces—what was no doubt implicitly prophesied by John Smith a century and a half earlier—a historical purification of everything hostile to the interests of individuation, to the complete fulfillment of self-consciousness. It also announces a civilizational crisis, the crux of which is a repudiation of society as the model of history in deference to the promise that the person—the existential self—is at once the creature of history and its autonomous source and end. It is instructive to see this crisis emerging in the civilizational microcosm of Virginia, producing astounding results in Jefferson's time, coming to compose the complex center of the tragedy of a modern slave society, and assuming, in the present century, still more complicated dimensions.

Returning specifically to the writings of Richard Beale Davis, let me attempt to remark in conclusion upon one of several fruitful suggestions he makes in *Intellectual Life in Jefferson's Virginia* about possible continuities between the Jeffersonian age and that immediately succeeding. Not all post-Revolutionary men of letters, Davis observes, shared Jefferson's assurance that psychic reality is securely controlled by the rational intellect. John Randolph did not, nor did John Marshall. And still less did some of those younger men of letters who, as Davis points out, were falling under the spell of the movement that may be regarded as one of the major indices to the modern civilizational crisis, literary romanticism. Among the young literary figures was Edgar Allan Poe, whose "earliest known critical writing," Davis says, "is a sort of symbolic link between . . . the Jeffersonians and the writings of the American Flowering" [the mid-nineteenth-century era]. Davis also indicates a possible connection between the Jeffersonians and Poe's imaginative writing. In 1809, he points out, there appeared in an abortive little magazine venture in Richmond an essay bearing features of Edgar Allan Poe's "The Fall of the House of Usher" (and of the poem that is an integral part of the story, "The Haunted Palace"). It is at least within the realm of probability, Davis conjectures, that Poe's childhood perusal of a file of *The Visitor* in John Allan's library is a source of the most famous of his stories.[18] Extending Davis' assertion that Poe's early critical work suggests a tie between the Jeffersonians and the work of the American Renaissance, we may, I believe, envision his most famous story, "The Fall of the House of Usher," as fully emblematic of the connection.

Significantly, the symbolism in Poe's tale is developed without reference to the "peculiar institution." Yet coming out of the depths of a literary imagination thoroughly empathetic with Jeffersonian and post-Jeffersonian Virginia, the story of Roderick Usher in a profound sense concerns enslavement. Involving two actor-relators, two men of letters, the nameless narrator and Roderick, "The Fall of the House of Usher" tells what happens subsequent to the displacement of the society of myth and tradition by the society of mind—a development completed in Virginia (and, for that matter, in all parts of the older seaboard South) by 1830. Placing Poe's story in a broad frame of symbolic reference, we may say that it occurs after the rational mind, under the burden of its interiorization of history, has collapsed as the model of history. Through an observer-narrator's depiction of Usher's consciousness, rational mind, so to speak, re-

18 Davis, *Intellectual Life in Jefferson's Virginia*, 288, 265–66.

calls its own destruction. (The observer-narrator, it should be said, may be quite unreliable and may, in fact, be telling a story that is a symbolic reference to the collapse of his own mind.) The song that the poet and lutist Roderick sings to the narrator describes "a fair and stately palace" that had stood in "the greenest of our valleys"— this being the "monarch Thought's dominion." But Thought's imperial power and autonomy have been destroyed by invading demonic forces, "evil things in robes of sorrow."

> And travelers now within that valley
>   Through the red-litten windows see
> Vast forms that move fantastically
>   To a discordant melody;
> While like a ghastly rapid river,
>   Through the pale door,
> A hideous throng rush out forever,
>   And laugh—but smile no more.

Usher's metaphorical description of hysteria leads to a discussion with the narrator in which Usher—climaxing a series of symbolic connections in the story between the physical substance of his ancient house and his mind—fervently maintains that the stones of the mansion possess sentience. Attributing feeling to what Jefferson called "mere matter," Usher disavows the "particular organization of matter" that Jefferson says constitutes the human mind. Trespassing, as the narrator says, on the "kingdom of inorganization," Usher identifies mind, not with its rational ordering of phenomena, but with its experience of the self's will to autonomy. Usher confirms the suggestion in his song that the monarch Thought's dominion is at one with the dominion of the self. A kind of grotesque parody of the eighteenth-century materialist psychology, the gloomy story of the House of Usher is a history of the overthrow of mind by the very capacity on which Jefferson erected the "fabric of all the certainties we have or need"—*i.e.*, mind's response to, its sensation of, matter and motion.[19] Poe's tale repudiates the notion held by

19 Jefferson to John Adams, August 15, 1820, *Writings of Jefferson*, ed. Lipscomb and Bergh, XV, 274. For all his declaration of psychic assurance, Jefferson was aware that he erected the fabric of certainty close to the edge of the abyss. Consider the tension implied in the following comment in the letter to Adams: "Rejecting all organs of information, therefore, but my senses, I rid myself of the

Captain John Smith, and endorsed by Thomas Jefferson, that history may be shaped by an act of thought on the part of a novelist and rendered as a self-conscious moral exercise in achieving the "happiness of the living." But at the same time, and in a terrifying way, it enhances those elements of Smith's definition of history that Jefferson rejects. Presenting the memory of time and the life of the dead as existing in the unremitting sensation of the self's consciousness of self, it suggests an unmitigable subjectification of history—an identification of history with a self beyond social structure, a self ("personality") so dedicated to the will to be a self that it rules conscience out of consciousness and closes society and history in its absoluteness.

An actor in and a relator of the history of the House of Usher, the poet-historian Roderick Usher, whose favorite reading is an esoteric volume called the *Vigiliae Mortuorum secundum Chorum Ecclesiae Maguntinae* ("The Watches of the Dead According to the Choir of the Church of Mayence"), embodies a ludicrously melodramatic yet darkly foreboding and compelling interpretation of the rationality represented by a slave-holding secular-spiritual elect who endorsed the Declaration of Independence. In Poe's age, Virginians at times tried to deny their descent from a secular company of philosophes like Jefferson and to believe that they descended from a feudal world of masters and servants; that whatever mentality they needed was ordered by its reference to a hierarchical society—immaterial, transcendent, and far removed from the drives of the secularized, individualized, isolated modern consciousness. Poe knew better. He understood that the world he had been reared in was the result of an effort to model history on the Jeffersonian "creed of materialism"—on matter endowed with the "mode of action called thinking." And Poe understood more than this. In the inner reaches of his symbolic imagination, this homeless scion of the master class comprehended

---

pyrrhonisms with which an indulgence in speculations hyperphysical and antiphysical, so uselessly occupy and disquiet the mind. A single sense may indeed be sometimes deceived, but rarely; and never all our senses together, with their faculty of reasoning. They evidence realities, and there are enough of these for all the purposes of life, without plunging into the fathomless abyss of dreams and phantasms." (*Ibid.*, XV, 275–76.) On Poe's psychology, see especially two essays by Allen Tate: "Our Cousin Mr. Poe" and "The Angelic Imagination: Poe as God," in *Essays of Four Decades* (Chicago: Swallow Press, 1959), 385–423.

that he and his fellow Virginians lived in the first slave society in history to assume as its origin and model the act of thought by the free and rational mind. In "The Fall of the House of Usher," he creates a dreamlike, nightmarish formulation of the irony of such an assumption, dramatizing how the faculties of intellect and feeling are enslaved to the inherent and unalienable will of the self, the all-possessive dominion of existence. Obliquely yet trenchantly, Poe's story suggests that in modern history—as it reveals itself in the Virginia microcosm—the model of a perfect society, its necessary condition, is the will of a master self, perfected in the knowledge that self-will is God immanent in history and that slavery to self-will is freedom. That Usher is a fiction of the actor-relator only contributes to the moral meaning of Poe's story. Like fictitious dreamers from Hamlet through Stephen Dedalus, he is a symbol of the condition of the real dreamers in modern history, from Cromwell through Hitler. No more than any of these dreamers—and this is his horror—does he desire to awaken from the nightmare of the power that the modern self bestows on the self.

5 / The Civil War and the Failure of Literary Mind in America

W alt Whitman said of the American Civil War that "the real war will never get in the books" (meaning except his own); Sherwood Anderson said that "no real sense" of the conflict "has yet crept into the pages of a printed book." Both affirm a major irony of American literature: the failure of our literary imagination, early and late, to encompass the most critical war in the history of the national existence. By and large, however, American writers, and not less historians of our writing, either have been insensitive to this ironic shortcoming in the national letters or, what may be more likely, have, whether intentionally or unintentionally, hidden it from themselves.

Daniel Aaron, in *The Unwritten War: American Writers and the Civil War*, fulfills a singular need in our education. Developing his fundamental subject, the unwritten Civil War, he brilliantly assimilates and describes the written war. Although the process is selective, it nonetheless provides us with the first adequate analytical survey of the large body of writings about the war from Hawthorne and Melville to Faulkner, Robert Penn Warren, and Edmund Wilson. The survey is accomplished chiefly through a series of essays on individual authors, these being presented in the context of a series of historical interpretations and generalizations. The latter involve the differentiation of periods and discussions of minor figures and of recurrent themes and motives, as, for example, the sectional war of words from the 1850s to the 1930s. The overall organization of *The Unwritten War*, we must conclude, is complex yet comprehensive, reflecting a diligent scholar's magisterial familiarity with and grasp of various and numerous materials. But the admirable command that Aaron assumes over his materials derives, it would seem, not so much from his persevering and skillful scholarship as from a spiritual fervor which, although not overwhelming, suffuses his book. He is a literary historian who is interested, to use one of his own terms, in "literary justice." In the French sense of the term, he is engaged with his subject, and his subject is fundamentally the deficiency of the moral will of American writers in their treatments of the Civil War. Concerned with the compelling way in which the conflict "touched and engaged a number of writers" of the past century, Aaron is convinced that it never engaged them sufficiently. Save for a few to whom he gives at least a partial exemption from insufficient engagement, he sees American writers—past or recent, northern or southern—as having failed to achieve a transcendent moral vision either of the fratricidal (Edmund Wilson calls it "incestuous") conflict of the 1860s or of its aftermath. Evading the war, dodging its challenge to reveal its meaning, if not its causes, our writers have never got at its reality—its essential truth. Admitting that to do so distorts Aaron's objective recognition of the forces of cultural determinism on the writers he discusses, we may with some justification find in *The Unwritten War* a suggestion of an American version of *le trahison des clercs*.

The suggestion emerges in several ways. One of them is in the ascription of "malingering" to Henry Adams, Henry James, William Dean Howells, and Mark Twain. The term is qualified by quotation marks. Still, its pejorative accent quietly asserts itself, and it is underscored in comments (much later in the book) about the failure of writers to do "literary justice" to "companies of men, North and South, who purchased their immunity from military service." A bought immunity, as he makes clear, was not literally the case with Adams, James, Howells, or Mark Twain. Adams spent the war years abroad as a secretary to his father in the American embassy in London; James suffered a mysterious hurt, either real or psychic, and considered himself disqualified from service; Howells went to Italy on a diplomatic appointment; and Mark Twain, after a brief and unheroic experience in a remote, improvised, frontier Confederate company known as the Marion Rangers, said his farewell to arms and went West. But in each of the four instances, there was a failure of moral nerve: "Not one of the four writers ever condemned the American War openly or disparaged the contestants, but each covertly resented the demands of the War on his mind and body and felt guilt of some sort about this failure to meet them." Possibly the charge of covert malingering is directed most harshly against Howells:

> Howells's almost unseemly haste at this time to escape his military obligations, his self-solicitude, and his irritation with a war that threatened to derange "all my literary plans" are hardly endearing. Here was a young man, reared like James and Adams in an antislavery home, who as a journalist in the 1850s had found it "undeniably amusing" to play the game of "firing the Southern heart." He had celebrated John Brown in verse . . . , and he had written a campaign biography of Abraham Lincoln. But even before the shooting began, the circumspect reporter had second thoughts and changed from partisan to observer.[1]

Aaron attaches a good deal of importance to an unacknowledged sense of guilt that may have pursued Howells throughout his career as a result of his "escape" from military duty, even attributing Howells' lonely and highly unpopular defense of the Chicago anarchists in 1887, not to a transcendent moral creed, but to "an unconscious desire to cancel out his unvalorous withdrawal in 1861."[2]

It is mildly ironic that, when Aaron comes to consider John W. De Forest, he quotes as an epigraph Howells' declaration that *Miss Ravenel's Conversion* is worthy to be placed beside *War and Peace*. De Forest is presented as the writer who came closest to writing truly about the Civil War, before Faulkner at any rate. Thirty-five when it came, almost too old to campaign, "unmilitary and bookish" and "a bit hypochondriacal," married and a father, De Forest "had more reason for staying out of the War than most of his younger literary contemporaries." But he became a captain in a Federal volunteer regiment and did his part in the fighting. His descriptions both of battlefield scenes and of civilian life are beyond question among the best in the literature of the Civil War. Whether or not De Forest's depiction of the struggle comes close to meeting the grand specification of General Grant for a "truthful history" of it—one doing "full

1 *The Unwritten War: American Writers in the Civil War* (New York: Alfred A. Knopf, 1973), 122.
2 *Ibid.*, 132.

credit to the courage, endurance and soldierly ability of the American citizen, no matter what section of the country he hailed from or in what ranks he fought"—may well be doubted; unless, that is, we are willing to disassociate De Forest from the Heaven vs. Hell interpretation of the war offered by one of his characters, Dr. Ravenel, and to make generous allowance for the various evidences of arrogance and snobbery that have repulsed some students of his work.

Considering southern writing of the Civil War and the postwar age, Aaron explores the difference between the idea that a southern writer ought to have written a great war epic or novel and the actual achievement of southern writers. Southern writers of the Civil War epoch had definite advantages in being close to the action, and after the war they had all the advantages of knowing a disaster from the inside. A great subject was immediately at hand: "the fall of the Confederacy seems emblematic of the human tragedy—an outraged, self-deceived, vainglorious, brave people (not without fear and apprehension) tilted against the ever replenished armies of the North and against impersonal forces that organized and equipped them."[3] But we see this in retrospect. What kind of southern author would have been required in the years of Reconstruction and beyond to imagine the possibilities of the human tragedy symbolized by the South and its people? *The Unwritten War* offers an ideal construct: "a man old enough to have fought in some of the campaigns; an insider, yet sufficiently unbeguiled by Southern preconceptions of caste and race and culture to appraise the parochialism of his section; a humorist and ironist gauging without cynicism the comic disproportion between Southern claims and performance; a student of human behavior who relishes the variety of types that flourished in the eleven 'countries' of the Confederacy and records with Chekovian nostalgia the passing of a way of life."[4] Needless to say, Aaron finds no southern writer in the pre-World War I age who measures up to this ideal. He does find a few writers, in the period of the war and after, who have "some detachment and insight." If unequal to a De Forest, they are worth our appreciation: Henry Timrod, Mary Chesnut, and George Washington Cable. Of the three, Mary Chesnut is judged to

3 *Ibid.*, 227.
4 *Ibid.*, 227–28.

be the most attractive; her *Diary* (unpublished in the author's lifetime) is "more genuinely literary than most Civil War fiction" and reads like a great novel—in places "breezy and scandalous, and irreverent," and in other places "nostalgic, sad, bitter," filled with characters pulsating with life. When he finally turns to the literature of the South in the 1920s and subsequent decades, Aaron suggests that William Faulkner comes closest to representing the ideal construct of the southern Civil War novelist. Faulkner "belonged to no literary party and remained uncaptivated by stylish myths. He was steeped in the Southern past . . . but he contemplated it without benefit of ideology and contrived a special language (in which mockery and piety, blasphemy and belief curiously commingled) to evoke it."

> Faulkner's War is multidimensional. He sees it as historical event, as a mirror reflecting personal and sectional character, and finally, and most important, as a buried experience that must be unearthed before it can be understood. Yet it defies exhumation because the reality is inseparable from the myth. Never a shrill partisan, he acts as the chronicler of a clan, not the historian looking for causes or the moralist dispensing praise and blame. He stands aside and comments, pours into his story vast amounts of random misinformation and legend, enters sympathetically into the minds of the self-deluded and deceived—the unconscious myth-makers. No one character speaks for him, and it is never unmistakably clear whether the authorial voice or community opinion is being heard. Perhaps the author is best described as a one-man chorus, challenging, raising questions, identifying himself with the myth-makers at some points (for he, too, is filled with Southern ghosts), yet withdrawing at other times and refusing to side with the emotionalists. As a privileged insider, he is entitled by virtue of his origins and his bardic role to say things no outsider would be permitted to say.[5]

This passage might well be glued on the wall of every student of Faulkner, for it conveys the quality and range of his imagination more succinctly, eloquently, and accurately than most of the book-length inquiries into the creator of Yoknapatawpha County do. With such a grasp of Faulkner's mode and method of imagination, Aaron is able within the scope of a few pages to present a commentary on Faulkner's "elegiac and ironic" depiction of the Civil War—in *Sartoris, The Unvanquished*, and elsewhere—that may well be the best discussion of this subject yet made.

5 *Ibid.*, 315.

And yet in spite of his conclusion that Faulkner "extracted from a welter of fact and fantasy and myth about a ruined land, a brave but fallible people, and an outraged race" the "ultimate essence" of the Civil War, Aaron cannot conclude that Faulkner captured "the real sense." He implies that in Faulkner—as in Whitman, Melville, Hawthorne, Mark Twain, and all the other writers who appear in *The Unwritten War*, including De Forest—there is a failure to confront the Civil War in its full reality. This failure may have occurred in some writers because they were "not sufficiently haunted" by the war or "outraged enough" by it, so that it did not penetrate their feelings. But by and large, American writers felt deeply enough about the war. They simply never confronted it. "The War was not so much unfelt as unfaced." In a span of a hundred years, no writer "emerged to provide a comprehensive inspection of the War or to piece out an intelligent design from its myriad disconnected fragments."

What has blocked the literary intelligence, the rational literary perception, from penetrating and organizing the meaning of the Civil War? This seems to be finally the general shape of the deepest question *The Unwritten War* has to ask about the literature of the Civil War. It is asked in several ways but with no final reply. The answer that would seem to be the most attractive to Aaron is formulated in his Introduction:

> One would expect writers, the "antennae of the race," to say something revealing about the meaning, if not the causes, of the War. This book argues implicitly throughout that, with a few notable exceptions, they did not . . . "The shrewdest people," Freud once observed, "will all of a sudden behave without insight, like imbeciles, as soon as the necessary insight is confronted by emotional resistance." . . . The "emotional resistance" blurring literary insight, I suspect, has been race. Without the long presence of chattel slavery, Americans would not have allowed the usual animosities springing from cultural differences to boil up into murderous hatreds. Without the Negro, there would have been no Civil War, yet he figured only peripherally in the War literature. Often presented sympathetically (which ordinarily meant sentimentally and patronizingly), he remained even in the midst of literary well-wishers an object of contempt or dread, or an uncomfortable reminder of abandoned obligations, or a pestiferous shadow, emblematic of guilt and retribution.[6]

6 *Ibid.*, xviii.

Although this is not a position that *The Unwritten War* consistently supports, it is the most firmly stated theory the book has to offer about the failure of American writers to confront the Civil War. From Whitman and Melville (Whitman who absolutely opposed slavery but believed that blacks "in the mass" have "about as much intellect and calibre" as "so many baboons," Melville who came to regard the war as "a white man's tragedy") through Henry Adams (who, like his father, looked upon the Negro as a strategic propaganda weapon in the war), Howells (who was a "benign" racist), and Mark Twain (who feared Negro supremacy), on into Cable and Faulkner (who, like Melville and Mark Twain, "were haunted by racial nightmares"), Aaron finds evidence of the racial inhibitions of the American writers who have portrayed the Civil War. In spite of the fact that "black slavery" was its "root cause," few writers, except for an occasional Whittier, either before or after 1865 appreciated the Negro's literal and symbolic role in the war. Northern writers "shared the prevailing liberal sentiment on slavery." It was "a social evil . . . and an embarrassing anachronism that exposed the United States to European slurs." The war was only secondarily "a crusade to free the slave." It was "the long-suffering North's reply to Southern bullies"; or it was "an ordeal devised by God to purge the Americans of their materialism"; or it was "a struggle to make the Union what the South had prevented it from becoming—a nation in the European sense of the word, a country to be proud of." As for southern writers: "They glossed over the exploitation of human flesh (which most of them had no relish for anyway) with such euphemisms as 'Southern Rights' or 'Southern Independence' or the 'Southern Way of Life,' and like their Northern counterparts allowed the Negro no more than a supernumerary part in what they chose to see as a white man's war." For writers, as well as for the generality of Americans, Aaron holds that before the Civil War Negroes "had formed an unassimilable foreign body; a dangerous necessity in slave territory, an unwholesome and unwelcome excrescence elsewhere." In the war's aftermath the popular image of the Negro was modified, but the literary evidence shows that the image of the Negro "as a docile child or putative rapist" held its dominance all over America. "It is tempting," Aaron says, largely on the basis of the literary references he offers, "to read into the fury of the intersectional war a redirected or displaced aggression against blacks—outcasts before, during, and after the War."[7]

Prudent and discriminating in his outlook throughout *The Unwritten War*, Aaron does not yield fully to the possibility of this psychic reading of postbellum American literary history. He nevertheless establishes a broad historical implication: confronted with the moral problem of an alien black race that had been forcibly imported and made into a slave race in their country, white Americans—as a result of mixed but powerful guilt feelings—bloodily disputed the nature of the national Union; after the great bloodletting, which established the illegality of chattel slavery, they engaged in a general rejection of the aliens who had caused the disastrous struggle. Participating in this rejection, American writers have impaired, if not in effect rejected, their role as the detached or alienated, the most sensitive perceivers of the moral meaning of history, and the chief prophets and moral instructors of modern America.

I would like to raise a somewhat contrary possibility. This would hold that a genuine experience of guilt about the plight of the Negro among white American writers has been very limited. At the same time, it would hold that many writers have nevertheless experienced deep feelings of alienation from American society because of their moral perception of the nature of the Civil War. The Negro, we have to remember, was until very recently largely outside the Western humanistic and literary sensibility. When writers began in the early post-Christian times (the nineteenth century) to become self-conscious moral "antennae" of society and to assume the ethos and guise of alienation from society's purposes as expressed in dynamic nationalism and in scientific and industrial materialism, they identified themselves as a highly literate opposition to the power structure of modernity. Their sense of their role as moral critics of their society has not called compellingly for white American writers, northern or southern, to associate themselves with the alienation of the Negro. They have been, in several cases, attracted rather toward making a connection between their feelings of alienation from a

7 *Ibid.*, 333.

machine and money culture and the fate of the South. Hawthorne (though he died before the Civil War ended), Melville, Adams, James, Mark Twain, Allen Tate and the Fugitive-Agrarian group, and Edmund Wilson all, in some degree, relate their estrangement from the modern nationalized, bureaucratic power state (as this has manifested itself in America) to the historical fate of the South. In an arresting interpretation of *A Connecticut Yankee in King Arthur's Court*, Aaron points out that Mark Twain's account of civil war in Arthur's England between the old and the new orders—which ends with Hank Morgan, "the Promethean capitalist" engaged in "bringing intellectual light and technological power to a backward people," blowing up everything—may be an oblique depiction of the American Civil War. Although the catastrophic denouement of *A Connecticut Yankee* brought about by the forces of modernity cannot be taken, I would say, as an implied approval of the South by Mark Twain, it would seem that in his love-hate relationship with the South the affectionate side of the affair increased as he grew older.

In a captivating essay in his *The Writer in the South* (entitled "Mark Twain and the Postwar Scene"), Louis D. Rubin, Jr., records an instance when affection may have momentarily become triumphant. Introducing Colonel Henry Watterson at a celebration of Lincoln's birthday in Carnegie Hall in 1901, Mark Twain declared that "we of the South are not ashamed" of opposing the Union, having done "our bravest best, against despairing odds, for the cause that was precious to us and which our conscience approved." We of the South, he said, "are proud of the record we made in those mighty collisions in the fields."[8] Associating himself not only with the Confederacy, but also with the great battles of the war, Mark Twain—whose actual role in the war was so negligible—deliberately told one of the greatest "stretchers" of his life. Rubin doubts that Mark Twain himself knew why he did this. Maybe he was being somewhat grotesquely ironic, but a safer conjecture seems to be that he was symbolizing his mood of alienation from the expansionist power state that had recently instigated the Spanish-American War. It was one way of proclaiming the inner secession from the United States

8 *The Writer in the South: Studies in a Literary Community* (Athens: University of Georgia Press, 1972), 81.

that Mark Twain kept making, or trying to make, throughout his later years, if not throughout most of his life.

Mark Twain's mood can be compared to that of Edmund Wilson in *Patriotic Gore*, the well-known volume of essays on the literature of the Civil War that Aaron reads variously as a "gothic drama," a "dramatic monologue," a "homily," and a "remarkable literary synthesis." In the notorious introductory essay to *Patriotic Gore*, Wilson dwells on the irrepressible "power drive" of nations as the key to the history of the United States. Dismissing secession and slavery as "pseudo-moral issues," he asserts that "the North's determination to preserve the Union" in the 1860s "was simply the form the power drive now took." Lincoln responded fully to the imperative of history. He was—like Bismarck and Lenin—an idealist, a solitary man living with a "concentration of purpose," the founder of a great state, an "uncompromising dictator." In his essay on Alexander H Stephens, vice-president of the Confederacy, Wilson makes a forceful comparison between Stephens and Lincoln. Stephens was an impossibilist. He believed so strongly in the individual as opposed to the organized state that he stood against some of the Confederacy's desperate moves to save itself, opposing the suspension in 1864 of the right of habeas corpus and even military conscription. "The Cause of the South is the Cause of us all!" Stephens exclaims at the end of *A Constitutional View of the Late War Between the States*. He believed, genuinely believed, that the cause of the South was civil liberty and not slavery. Recognizing that we all have some of the benevolent despot in us, Wilson suggests that most of us have "an unreconstructed Southerner" in us as well. In studying the drama of Stephens' career, Wilson discovers in it an intransigent defense of individual liberty and, doing so, relates this to the cause of freedom for the twentieth-century American, who is "more and more hampered by the exactions of centralized bureaucracies of both the state and federal authorities." Wilson wonders "whether or not it may not be true, as Stephens said, that the cause of the South is the cause of us all."

Although Wilson found the real sense of the Civil War in the emergence in America of the triumphant ideology of the power state which represents the force of science and technology assimilated to political force, *Patriotic Gore* is not (as the appeal to Stephens indicates) a consistent statement of this deterministic thesis. Wilson displays a highly charged emotional resistance to his own conception of the reality of American history. It is a kind of resistance to accepting the American reality that has paradoxically been most strongly nurtured by the alienation, not the conformity, of American writers; for it is when they have felt most disaffected from America that they have most wanted to believe that American history, seen in its true aspect, is modeled on rational independence of intellect and spirit. Has the need to believe in such a concept of our history—to believe in it lest the lettered mind abrogate its meaning—blocked the literary imagination from an encompassing treatment of the meaning of the Civil War more fundamentally than the race issue? In inquiring into the literary imagination and the war, we should perhaps distinguish between black slavery as an occasion of the conflict and the war's relation to mind. Another impossibilist, Henry David Thoreau, made this kind of distinction some ten years before the national division broke out in full-scale warfare in his essay on "Resistance to Civil Government." The occasion of this pronouncement was his refusal to pay a tax to a government that supported slavery. The meaning of the occasion was the discrepancy that the author saw between the moral intelligence of an educated and perceptive "few" and the power of the State. The complexities involved in discriminating between occasion and principle increased rapidly in antebellum America. When the actual fighting began, Thoreau was probably no longer capable of making such a discrimination. Nor surely was his mentor, Ralph Waldo Emerson, smelling the gunsmoke and, as he said, liking it. By the 1860s, no more than the smallest handful of American intellectuals still possessed the capacity to transcend the dire immediacy of the civil conflict. But these included Hawthorne and Melville—by virtue of their ironic sense of the Civil War's repudiation of the nation's establishment on the model of rational principles—and (in the sense that, as I have indicated, Wilson understands him) Alexander H. Stephens.

Wilson veritably makes Stephens into an American saint. He assigns to Stephens' *Recollections* the character of a great American book and, while admitting its virtual unreadability, declares that *A*

Constitutional View of the Late War Between the States is an indispensable view of American history. Following Stephens in the years after the Civil War, he pictures the emaciated former vice-president of the Confederacy sitting in a wheelchair in the House of Representatives of the reunited nation. Here, where he served for ten years as the representative from Georgia following his release from prison and the removal of his civil disabilities, Stephens appeared to be a man "shrunk to pure principle, abstract, incandescent, indestructible."

> He resigned in 1883, but immediately ran for Governor of Georgia and won. He was now seventy years old, and the duties of the office killed him. He died in March of the following year. In the mutterings of a final stupor, he said suddenly very clearly: "But I carried it individually by six hundred majority," and these were his last words. It was the death of the old political South—the South of Jefferson and Madison, of Randolph, Calhoun and Clay; of the landowners' and merchants' republic, of the balance of power in Congress, of the great collaboration and the great debates.[9]

It was also, as Wilson so deeply comprehended, the death of the republic of the patrician clerisy and its conception of a nation formed on the literate, rational mind. In an important sense, the historical event Wilson is concerned with in *Patriotic Gore*—at a level just below that of articulation—is not the Civil War, but what this catastrophe so clearly signifies: the historical failure of the community of the lettered in America. For Wilson, the meaning of this failure lay, not only in its bearing on the professional identity of the writer in America, but in its impact on his personal, his innermost, sense of being.

---

9 *Patriotic Gore: Studies in the Literature of the American Civil War* (New York: Oxford University Press, 1962), 437.

6 / The Southern Exodus from Arcadia

As we know it in Western literature, the pastoral mode originated in the self-conscious recognition by the poetic mind that it represented a differentiation from an integral, or cosmic, existence. In his sophisticated awareness of displacement from the cosmological mode, the Western poet sought to describe the relationship between two experiences: the experience, lost and not to be repeated, but recorded in the continuum of consciousness, of an exile from the cosmic homeland; and the experience of the disparate, eventful historical mode of existence. An endeavor to recover the pastoral mode is dramatized in Theocritean pastoral of the third century B.C., in which a primordial sensibility—a compact or unmediated perception of existence—is quite deliberately assumed as the basis of poetry. This assumption, although stylized and symbolic, seems credible in so far as the poet ignores his awareness of historical existence. As a city dweller living in history, Theocritus imagines, and perhaps even successfully suggests, that the poet may return to Arcadia and directly encounter the cosmological world. In his *Eclogues* (37 B.C.), Virgil, citizen of the first world city and the first world-historical poet (who later made his historical consciousness transparently clear in the *Aeneid*), takes the recovery of the cosmological sensibility in Theocritus as his model; but in the ironic complexities of his poem, he implies that a self-conscious recovery of the cosmic apprehension of existence is incredible. The order of reality, Virgil tacitly acknowledges, is empirical history. The poetic capacity is governed by the historical situation of the poet. In her study of the *Eclogues*, Eleanor Winsor Leach says:

The variety of nature is the basis for the complexities of the *Eclogues*. The poems have no consistent landscape. No one image stands out as typically pastoral. Their world is created as a microcosm of nature, offering the contrasts that nature offers to the eye. But in creating his varied landscapes, Virgil is also conscious of their symbolic potential, of parallels between nature and man. Like the faces of nature, the emotions of men are varied and inconsistent. The four modes of landscape in the poems have associations with patterns of conduct and thought; the farm with man's desire for order, the rustic world with his anxieties and uncertainties, the wilderness with his uncontrolled passions, and the *locus amoenus* with his fantasies and his urge for withdrawal. The cultivated field, the wilderness, and paradise are territories of the human mind. In the midst of his varied landscapes, the poet explores man's nature as an emotional and a historical being, and traces the conflicts of order and disorder that beset his affairs to their deep beginnings in human thought.[1]

The landscape in the *Eclogues* becomes a literary artifice; poetic wit renders it as a symbol of the differentiated consciousness. Made into territories of the mind—reduced to the elements of the "wilderness" and the *locus amoenus* ("paradise")—the cosmological landscape becomes a representation of the historical awareness of the polarities of order and disorder and the need to reconcile them. Deliberately reversing the role of the primordial landscape in the poetic consciousness, Virgil implies that, instead of imaging a unified sensibility, it represents the fragmentation of an original poetic comprehensiveness. The poet is conscious of a dissociation of sensibility, a dispossession of the organic imagination by history.

In the long and persistent devotion to the pastoral mode, the possibility of the repossession of organic perception—of an interven-

1 *Virgil's Eclogues: Landscapes of Experience* (Ithaca and London: Cornell University Press, 1974), 112. Insisting on the specifically Roman context of the *Eclogues*, Professor Leach illuminates Virgil's implied recognition of the differentiation of history from a prehistorical mode of existence. I adapt her remarks to my own argument, I trust not willfully so. The present essay affords a commentary on certain aspects of my study entitled *The Dispossessed Garden: Pastoral and History in Southern Literature* (Athens: University of Georgia Press, 1975). More particularly, it offers a refinement and enlargement of the focus on southern historicism in my article entitled "Faulkner and the Southern Symbolism of Pastoral," *Mississippi Quarterly*, 28 (Fall, 1975), 401–15. References to some of the same illustrative materials are essential to the revisionary intention. I acknowledge a general indebtedness to Eric Voegelin, *Order and History* (4 vols.; Baton Rouge: Louisiana State University Press, 1954–75), especially Volumes I and IV.

tion of the primordial sensibility in the historically conditioned con-sciousness—has been a tantalizing yet always incredible motive. Indeed, the submerged Virgilian conceit of the poetic consciousness as a cosmic garden dispossessed by history has, it is not too much to say, largely governed the relationship between poetry and history in Western literature. The pastoral imperative has been, not to recover a verifiable sensibility, but its sophisticated symbol, the land of Arcadia.

Only at one point in the lengthy attraction to the Greco-Roman pastoral mode has the recovery of the cosmological sensibility seemed credible to the historically conditioned literary imagination. This is in the time of the English settlement of the New World and in the subsequent age of the rise of what is now the United States of Amer-ica. The reason for this is to be found, not in a reduction of historical awareness in the poet's mind at this moment in history, but in the greater complexity of this awareness. What may be referred to as a second stage in the differentiation of history had been reached. The unified sensibility afforded by the Christian myth—which had suc-ceeded the evolvement of Roman history and the Roman world view and had reunified perception (not in a cosmological but in a hierar-chical existence)—was yielding to the developing modern sense of history. The modern differentiation (marking the fifteenth through the eighteenth centuries) embraced the coincidental recovery of the classical world and the discovery of a world (America) still existing in the cosmological age. Imbued with classical paganism, the Re-naissance mind was susceptible to the notion that its contact with the New World constituted the direct intervention of a transforming primordial sense. Juxtaposed between the sense of a lost cosmic mode of existence and the recognition of the historical mode, America, in other words, offered to become an embodiment of a pastoral reversal of historical consciousness. The permutations of the image of Amer-ica as an explicit recovery of Arcadia are well known, having been brilliantly analyzed in Henry Nash Smith's *Virgin Land* and Leo Marx's *The Machine in the Garden*. Smith and Marx emphasize how, in the emergence of an American literary vision out of the Euro-pean pastoral vision of America, a pagan literary cosmos becomes the credible basis of an American pastoral ideology that envisions the

American destiny as the progressive transformation of the continent into the Garden of the World—a "well-bordered green garden" dotted with self-sufficient farms and villages," a "chaste uncomplicated land of rural virtue."[2]

It follows from their emphasis on the American receptiveness to a literary allusion that both Marx and Smith should be concerned about its adverse influence on American culture: the harmful political and social consequences of a pastoral distortion of the sense of historical reality in America. One can hardly dispute this concern. It does tend, however, to obscure the presence in the American literary imagination of a motive counter to the notion of America as a pastoral intervention in history: an impulse, both pragmatic and ironic, to recognize the modern differentiation of history as more decisive than that known to Virgil. Occurring primarily in the southern literary mind, this impulse manifests itself in writers from Robert Beverley to William Faulkner, who represents its culmination and, in all probability, its effective conclusion. This is not to say that the impulse to historical determinism is recorded only in writers of the South. Its presence in New England writers is striking, but, in contrast to its early implication in the southern literary vision, its appearance, in Henry Adams and Robert Frost and others, is late. For nearly three centuries, America as an image of pastoral recovery was associated in the New England mind with the revealed mission of a spiritual elect. Whether this mission had in view an America that was a "pleasure garden of the Lord God of Hosts"—or, in the aftermath of the Puritan vision, a transcendental cosmos (Thoreau's *Walden*)—it assumed that consciousness embodies an ideal world of mind or spirit. "In the end," Leo Marx comments, "Thoreau restores the pastoral hope to its traditional location. He removes it from history, where it is manifestly unrealizable, and relocates it in literature, . . . in his own consciousness, in his craft in *Walden*."[3] Thoreau in a sense dealt with empirical history in the Virgilian way, but

2 Marx, *The Machine in the Garden: Technology and the Pastoral Ideal in America* (New York: Oxford University Press, 1965), 141. See Smith, *Virgin Land: The American West as Symbol and Myth* (Cambridge: Harvard University Press, 1950. Reissued with a new preface, 1970), especially 123–88.
3 Marx, *The Machine in the Garden*, 265.

in a deeper sense he dealt with it in the New England way: he referred it to the immanentization of the Kingdom of God. To the extent that New England was the education of the nation—and this was to a considerable extent—the New England tendency in the nineteenth century to a millennialistic, or gnostic, projection of its mission was embraced in the image of America as the Garden of the World.

But, by and large, the southern literary mind did not envision a coalescence of the Kingdom of God and the Garden of the World as a way of substituting for the loss of a revealed history. In fact, in so far as the southern imagination has its origins in the first southern settlement, the Virginian, it begins with the acceptance of this loss as a necessity of Virginia's involvement in the empirical development of the modern marketplace economy. When Massachusetts was still being settled as a Holy Commonwealth, Perry Miller has pointed out, Virginia had assumed that its role in history was to propagate, not the gospel, but tobacco.[4] Thus the literary response to the meaning of colonial Virginia was more open to the Arcadian impulse than to the messianic pastoralism associated with Massachusetts. But the response to Virginia was also more open to the force of modern historical interpretation. The literary possibilities of this situation were forecast in Michael Drayton's celebration of Virginia in "To the Virginian Voyage" (1606). Drayton describes Virginia as the recovery of "Earth's only paradise / . . . To whom the Golden Age / Still nature's laws doth give," yet he makes the recovery of paradise the fulfillment of heroic imperialism.

> Whenas the luscious smell
> Of that delicious land,
>   Above the seas that flows
>   The clear wind throws,
> Your hearts to swell
> Approaching the dear strand,
>
> In kenning of the shore,
> (Thanks to God first given,)
>   O you, the happi'st men,

---

4 Miller, "Religion and Society in the Early Literature of Virginia," in *Errand into the Wilderness* (New York: Harper Torchbook, 1964), 99–140.

Be frolic then,
Let cannons roar,
Frighting the wide heaven.

And in regions far
Such heroes bring ye forth
    As those from whom we came,
    And plant our name
Under that star
Not known unto our north.

And as there plenty grows
Of laurel everywhere
    Apollo's sacred tree,
    You may it see
A poet's brows
To crown, that may sing there.[5]

In Drayton's poem, the image of Virginia as a pastoral realm fails to intervene in the poet's consciousness of the colony as a symbol of Britain's historical destiny. "To the Virginian Voyage" implies, furthermore, that the image of a pastoral paradise is no more than a convention, in itself a historical phenomenon. A century later, the tension between the Arcadian recovery and the commitment to the historical view is dramatized in the consciousness of Robert Beverley, whose *History and Present State of Virginia* (1705) is a remarkable embodiment of the drama of the literary mind in colonial Virginia. Beverley assumes three distinguishable voices in his book. One is the admonitory voice of the master of Beverley Park, the man of letters and the law, who aspires to make Virginia a pastoral autonomy. Another voice is that of Beverley the "Indian," declaring (in the Preface): "I am an *Indian*, and I don't pretend to be exact in my Language: But I hope the Plainness of my Dress, will give . . . the kinder Impressions of my Honesty, which is what I pretend to."[6] A third voice in Beverley's *History*—composed perhaps of some combination of the voice of Beverley the man of letters on his pastoral plantation and the voice of Beverley the honest Indian—speaks with

5 *Oxford Anthology of English Poetry*, ed. Howard Foster Lowry and Willard Thorp (New York: Oxford University Press, 1956), 233–34.
6 Beverley, *The History and Present State of Virginia*, ed. Louis B. Wright (Chapel Hill: University of North Carolina Press, 1947), 9.

the intonation of the poet of broad historical awareness. Describing a Virginia sadly altered but not improved by the English settlers (who have destroyed the Indian cosmos, lost the communal life they had known in England, and begun to degenerate into an economy of wastrels), this voice gives the impression of a possibly complete differentiation of the history of Virginia from the sense of cosmic unity. Intimating that early eighteenth-century Virginia belongs to an unfolding historical process, it represents the inception of agrarian capitalism in a world marketplace society. In his later years, Beverley attempted to make his own personal existence a representation of Virginia as a pastoral cosmos. Decrying the Virginian dependence on tobacco, he cultivated grapes as an alternate crop and imitated the Indians in the spartan economy he maintained at Beverley Park.

The rapid growth of chattel slavery in the eighteenth century widened the distance between the plantation as a pastoral dominion and as a historical actuality, the plantation being increasingly dependent, not only on the imperial commodity market, but also on the world slave market. It was, I surmise, in response to his own terrifying vision of Virginia's historical involvement in chattel slavery in the eighteenth query in the *Notes on the State of Virginia* that Jefferson in the nineteenth query envisions American yeoman farmers as the chosen people of God, and the economically independent and spiritually self-fulfilling farm as Arcadia incarnate in America. Jefferson interposes in his imagination of the grim historical destiny of the slave society a paradigmatic image of American pastoral. The appeal to this image, one fundamentally opposed to the idealization of the South's dominant institution, the slave plantation, illustrates how greatly the historicity of slavery inhibited the literary imagination in the South. Although confused attempts to make the plantation the symbol of a pastoral intervention in history do not represent the whole of the effort to write fiction about the plantation, they indicate the frustration of William Gilmore Simms and others in the pursuit of the Arcadian imperative.

In one crucial direction, the awareness of the South's subjection to history fostered literary power. Consider the writings of the southern humorists, especially the works of the greatest ones, George Washington Harris and Mark Twain, in whose writings the subversion of the pastoral motive by the historical becomes a consummate subject in our literature.

The Sut Lovingood stories by Harris are an elaborate parody of the pastoral opposition to history. An inversion of the American bucolic nobleman, the Jeffersonian farmer, in another, more significant, if less definite, dimension, Sut is a parodic figure of Pan, the goat god of cosmic pastoral. We take delight in the vivid poetic movement of Sut's language as the narrator of his own stories, seeming as it does to display an absolute reintegration of sensibility, not only in a minute faithfulness to the vernacular of Sut's society, but through a violent destruction of conventional language. Yet, in the Sut Lovingood stories, not only does a genteel narrator's surrender of the storytelling to a vernacular narrator dramatize the historical character of language, but Sut's self-conscious figuration of his role as an "orthur" (he writes both a "Preface" and a "Dedicatory" to his book) defines his storytelling as a part of cultural history.[7] In the historicity of his speech and function, Sut mocks the possibility of a cosmological reintegration of word and thing. His stories record no renaissance of a pastoral cosmos in America—no deconstruction of history, no reunification of religion, law, and sexuality under the aspect of a transcending myth. On the contrary, even under the crude conditions of a world on the margins of settled society, conformist attitudes toward religion and sex repress Sut's outlaw urge to renew the cosmic unity of nature and spirit. His opponents, like Parson Bullen and Sicily Burns (whose first name satirically echoes Theocritean pastoral), are instrumentalities of a historical society. Locked in the brutalizing life of the southern semifrontier, Sut embodies the consciousness of a community that is post-Enlightenment yet, unlike the society of New England or the genteel South, has no romantic coloration. As he rebels against his society, Sut both defines and accepts himself as a creature of history.

So does Huckleberry Finn in his conflict with society. Much has been made of that episode on the raft when Huck commits his soul to hell in order to save Jim. It has been taken as a moment when a transcendent natural, or pastoral, virtue intervenes in Huck's bond-

7 Harris, *Sut Lovingood's Yarns*, ed. M. Thomas Inge (New Haven: College & University Press, 1966), 25–30.

age to history. But immediately after he comes close to experiencing a revelation of historical society as a tissue of lies, Huck lapses into the comfortable historicity of his moral condition. He will "go to work and steal Jim out of slavery again," for it is just the kind of thing he ought to do, being "brung up" to wickedness.[8] Huck cannot sustain the freedom entailed in making a moral choice. He cannot breathe on the level of suprahistorical moral deliberation. The historical society governed by its self-serving conventions of right and wrong is his home. Like Sut a self-conscious vernacular author, Huck is not a victim of history; rather, as the unwittingly ironic historian of the inner history of his world, he is the creature of history. He lives in the historicism of consciousness. Even as he says that he will light out for the territory to escape civilization, he knows the futility of the gesture. The irony of making it confirms the incredibility of an American Arcadia. Restoration of faith in Arcadia is beyond the power of the American literary imagination.

And yet the drama of the redemption of the American literary consciousness from historicism through the intervention of a recovered pastoral mode of feeling was still to reach its apogee. This happens in the spacious, entangled work of William Faulkner, which begins with his vision of the poet as a dispossessed, introverted faun in *The Marble Faun* and comes to its climax in two stories based on the southern differentiation of the modern historical sensibility from the dream of an American incarnation of the pastoral cosmos, *The Hamlet* and *Go Down, Moses*. The dominant voice in these works, comparable in power to the voice of Virgil, is that of Faulkner the poet of historical vision. In the latter work, Ike McCaslin relinquishes his patrimony in the belief that a relic of the cosmic garden, Sam Fathers, has set him free from history, when in fact Sam is bound to modern history as firmly as his black forebears were bound to chattel slavery, and Ike's very illusion of freedom is his prison. But *Go Down, Moses*, often considered a series of stories instead of a novel, is a loosely constructed work, and its thematic development is diffuse. *The Hamlet* is a more powerful work; in fact, it is the most concentrated evocation of the drama of pastoral and history in American

8 Huck's debate with himself about Jim occurs in the thirty-first chapter of *Adventures of Huckleberry Finn*.

literature. Bringing spirits dispossessed from Pan's garden—Will Varner, Eula Varner, Ike Snopes, and others—into various relationships with Flem Snopes, the rank product of the modern society of history (a creature of history who epitomizes the death of poetic consciousness, which is to say, the death of the soul), *The Hamlet* focuses on an amazingly intricate contrast between the pastoral and historical modes of existence. An exquisitely elegiac yet carefully calculated parody of the pastoral novel, devoted among other things to the subject of cow diddling, it sets forth the ultimate absurdity of a pastoral interposition in the modern historical consciousness. In the final scene, the impotent Flem departs from Frenchman's Bend with his bride, Eula, the fertility goddess herself. They are on their way to Jefferson and the promised land of the New South and their immutable destinies as creatures of history.

As we know, Faulkner rebelled against his impulsion to the historical nature of community and the historicism of the individual consciousness, and in subsequent episodes of the Snopes trilogy he confers on Flem the grace of the literary artist (hardly the same as the grace of God) and gives him a soul. In the killing of Flem by his brother Mink, the great historical poet who narrates the trilogy encompasses Flem in the poetry of humanity. Flem, it would seem, has done what he had to do, not as a societal automaton, but as a human being with a heart subject to the driving pressures of history. Although Faulkner also tried to make Eula represent the human heart under such pressures, he could not make her credible as a citizen of Jefferson. He could really do nothing for a goddess displaced in history. In a frustration that she did not comprehend and that Faulkner could not resolve, Eula kills herself. Her self-inflicted death wound bleeds across the pages of the southern literary expression, which records the story, not of a historical exile from a cosmic garden, but of an unwilling yet willed exodus out of Arcadia into history—out of a place created by the historical consciousness itself as a refuge against the psychic depredations of history.

PART II

We are open to the possibility that meaning and significance arise only in man and in his history.

—Wilhelm Dilthey, *Meaning in History:*
Wilhelm Dilthey's Thoughts on History and Society,
translated and edited by H. Rickman (1961)

Certain accomplished novelists have a habit of giving themselves away which must often bring tears to the eyes of the people who take their fiction seriously. I was lately struck, in reading over the pages of Anthony Trollope, with his want of discretion in this particular. In . . . an aside, he . . . admits that the events he narrates have not really happened, and that he can give his narrative any turn the reader may like best. Such a betrayal of a sacred office seems to me, I confess, a terrible crime; . . . it shocks me every whit as much in Trollope as it would have shocked me in Gibbon or Macaulay.

—Henry James, "The Art of Fiction" (1884)

But the guilt of outliving those you love is justly to be borne, she thought. Outliving is something we do to them. The fantasies of dying could be no stranger than the fantasies of living. Surviving is perhaps the strangest fantasy of them all.

—Eudora Welty, *The Optimist's Daughter* (1972)

7 / The Will to Art in Postbellum America

For a long time, Kate Chopin was almost lost to American literary history; her recognition as a significant American storyteller has come only in recent years. During her brief, semiprofessional literary career—which occupied the last fifteen years of a relatively brief life (1851–1904)—the only appreciable notice she received was as a local colorist, particularly during a period around 1899 following the publication of a novel entitled *The Awakening*. The taste of the age condemned this story, which deals frankly with a woman's sexuality, as virtually obscene. Fifty years later, *The Awakening* was acknowledged as an important addition to the canon of American fiction. And among the writings of nineteenth-century American feminine authors (there was no dearth of them), the story about Edna Pontellier's rebellion against society now holds a place of preeminence. Indeed, it may be that no novel by a woman writer in nineteenth-century America matches the power of *The Awakening*, unless it is Harriet Beecher Stowe's *Uncle Tom's Cabin*, published a half century earlier (serially in 1851 and as a book in 1852).

There are interesting connections between Mrs. Chopin and Mrs. Stowe. One lies in the story of Robert McAlpin, who in a time before the Civil War was the lonely, brutal master of Place-du-Bois Plantation on the Cane River in northwestern Louisiana. He is supposed to be the original of Simon Legree in *Uncle Tom's Cabin* and to have numbered among his chattels a Negro who suggested the character of Uncle Tom to Harriet Beecher Stowe, the information about Place-du-Bois having been conveyed to the New England writer by a brother who had been in Louisiana. In her first novel, *At Fault*, published in 1890, Kate Chopin recalls the legend of the cruel dominion ruled by

McAlpin when she has two lovers visit his grave, a place feared by all and from which the lovers retreat with due trepidation. Kate Chopin's sense of the story of Place-du-Bois was heightened, not only by the fact that her husband's father had acquired it after McAlpin's ownership—and had, possibly because he was largely an absentee master, allowed its reputation for cruelty to remain unredeemed—but also by the fact that it remained in the possession of the Chopin family and that she eventually came to know it personally in its post-Civil War state. Moving to Louisiana from her native St. Louis after her marriage in 1870 to a Louisiana Creole, Oscar Chopin, Kate Chopin first came to know New Orleans and its environs, her husband being a cotton factor in the Crescent City. When Oscar Chopin failed in the cotton business, she and her several children went to live in the village of Cloutierville in Natchitoches Parish, center of the Cane River country. The Chopins lived in Cloutierville for some four years while Oscar Chopin managed a part of the family holdings. After her husband's death in 1883, Kate Chopin stayed in Louisiana for a year, then moved her family to St. Louis.

The return to her native city, where she first began to write her stories, no doubt helped to give Mrs. Chopin a perspective on the Louisiana society she had known for nearly two decades. In some of its outstanding characteristics, this society was a special version of the society of the American South, the population of Louisiana representing an unusual mingling of Spanish, French, Negro, and (as a distinct minority for a long time) Anglo-Saxon elements, nowhere so much so as in the two exotic areas in which Kate Chopin had lived. But for all its differences, Louisiana was a part of the South. Like all of the former Confederate States of America, it was a world haunted by its past as a slave society and by the memory of a catastrophic defeat in a ravaging war, and at the same time conscious of its existence under the pressures of the dynamic historical imperatives of a revolutionary modernity. These pressures, to be sure, had been present in the South before the war, the South's dream of an isolation from modernity having been just that, a dream.

One of the keys to Louisiana society, as Harriet Beecher Stowe clearly saw, was a key to American society as a whole by the 1850s: the sublimation of the decreasing functional identity of the family by the development of a singularly American piety of family. This insight—and it constitutes another link between Mrs. Stowe and Mrs. Chopin—underlies Mrs. Stowe's shrewd discernment of the condition of Augustine St. Clare and his family. The sensitive, poetic, and neurotic Augustine, his neurasthenic wife, and the strange child Little Eva, who wants above all for people to love one another, fail markedly to fulfill the requirements of the patriarchical family, which was supposed to be the basis of authority in southern society. Nor do the St. Clares represent the kind of family ideal that historically supplanted that of the patriarchical group, that is, the family based on idealized conjugal love. St. Clare, who is an oblique representation of the suffering artist, is the victim, not only of an uncertain relation to a slave society, which he can neither affirm nor deny, but also of a psychically destructive family situation to which he is bound by an insidious sentimentality, including a compulsive worship of his dead mother. Mrs. Stowe, emotionally enmeshed in the American worship of home and fireside, surely did not intend in *Uncle Tom's Cabin* to intimate as much about the nature and consequences of the piety of family as she does; in doing so, she shows the artist's capacity for comprehending the inner truth of a situation not explicitly grasped by the intellect.

Two or three decades removed from Harriet Beecher Stowe, Kate Chopin came into a more profound awareness than the New Englander of the depletion of the identity of the family and of the attendant liberation of individuals from family roles once assumed without question. Although she faithfully adhered to the roles of wife and mother, she apparently experienced a convincing inner vision of release from the bondage of matrimony and maternity. The inspiriting motive of this experience—the how and why of it—is not altogether clear. But its overall context was a consciousness essentially larger than Mrs. Stowe ever came into—an awareness experienced in one way or another by Poe, Melville, Hawthorne, Emerson, Thoreau, and, most decisively, by Whitman—of the vacuous condition following upon the loss of a transcendent meaning for human existence or, as it may be more dramatically rendered, following upon the death of God. The ironic drama of the post-Christian apprehension of the loss of the sense of religious transcendence—and of the compensating search for the Absolute in art, philosophy, and history that so strongly compelled the Western mind in the last century, and still compels it—entered into Kate Chopin's vision through her reading in various modern writers. Among these were theorists of modern man like Darwin, Huxley, and Spencer. But the shaping influence on her vision, as Per Seyersted suggests, was the poetic and dramatic projection of her age in the art of writers like Whitman, Ibsen, Zola, and Maupassant. Kate Chopin—who made no attempt to renew the sense of the Absolute through the Roman Catholic faith in which she had been reared—found in the works of these rebels that the discipline of art is a way of revealing the disorders of the soul in a world divested of traditional forms of authority. She found, moreover, that the discipline of art is at once a liberation from the repressive bourgeois pieties and an imposition of meaning on the seeming meaninglessness of the individual existence. In his study of Kate Chopin, Robert Arner points to a crucial statement about Maupassant in one of Mrs. Chopin's essays: "Here was a man who had escaped from tradition and authority, who had entered into himself and looked upon life through his own being and with his own eyes; and who, in a direct and simple way, told us what he saw."[1] Kate Chopin did not mean that Maupassant's achievement consisted of an introverted withdrawal of the self from the world; she meant that Maupassant had succeeded in centering his vision of the world in art. His success provided an illumination of her own struggle, and in this luminosity she made the achievement of art her career, which Arner sees as a development "from local colorist to realist of theme and subject matter to psychological realist."[2]

There is a good deal of the psychological realist in George Washington Cable in his most artful stories, as in *The Grandissimes*; there is a great deal of the psychological realist in the fictional art of Mark Twain at his best, as in *Adventures of Huckleberry Finn*; and, for that matter, in some of his worst art, as in *Pudd'nhead Wilson*. But Kate Chopin is the first writer to focus with artistic intensity on the theme of the sexual identity of the family and the individual in south-

1 "Kate Chopin," *Louisiana Studies: An Interdisciplinary Journal of the South,* XIV (Spring, 1975), 17.
2 *Ibid.,* 19.

ern settings. In fact, save for Whitman and Dreiser in their different ways, she is the first American writer to achieve a precise focus on the vexing and often agonizing relationship between sexual and social identity in American society. She was able to do this because, at least by the time she wrote *The Awakening*, she had come fully into an awareness of the Nietzschean knowledge of the modern "destruction of the *moral* interpretation of the world" and of the nihilism that results from it. She was aware, as Nietzsche was aware, that "the goal is lacking; the answer is lacking to our 'Why?'" Mark Twain also grasped this lack of meaning in modern life, increasingly as he grew older. In his efforts to achieve a vision of despair—to bring despair under the contol of art—he wrote finally a kind of dream vision called *The Mysterious Stranger*. Kate Chopin, endeavoring to cope with the same nihilistic mood that inspired *The Mysterious Stranger*, wrote *The Awakening*, at first called "A Solitary Soul." Mark Twain never finished his novel. The reasons for his failure to do so are various, but surely a paramount one is that he failed to achieve—as he had in his one truly great story, *Adventures of Huckleberry Finn*, in which Huck's mind takes over—the detachment of the modern literary artist. This consists in attaining the perspective of the controlled response to a subject, no matter how passionately apprehended. Kate Chopin attained such a perspective. Speaking of the moralistic reaction against *The Awakening*, she said: "Having a group of people at my disposal, I thought it might be entertaining (to myself) to throw them together and see what would happen. I never dreamed Mrs. Pontellier making such a mess of things and working out her own damnation as she did. If I had had the slightest intimation of such a thing I would have excluded her from the company." Quoting this remark in his essay on Kate Chopin in *Patriotic Gore*, Edmund Wilson says that "in its ironic insouciance" it is characteristic of her, which would appear to be an apt enough evaluation.[3] It is doubtful, however, if Wilson is correct in attributing to Kate Chopin a "serene amoralism." The measure of her detachment—of her will to art—in *The Awakening* is that she meant what she said about Edna Pontellier's damnation of herself. In the detachment of

---

3 *Patriotic Gore: Studies in the Literature of the American Civil War* (New York: Oxford University Press, 1962), 591.

her method, in the resources of her growing art, Mrs. Chopin was enabled to create a self-creating character—one who, like Huckleberry Finn or, on a smaller scale, Augustine St. Clare, has a life larger than the confines of the story in which the character appears. But Mrs. Chopin is detached from her creation; she is not Edna Pontellier. Edna, refusing the role of artist (which is held up to her by the example of Mademoiselle Reisz) as well as the role of wife and mother, surrenders to a fascination with the self as the supreme entity—to an existential agony and ecstasy—and drowns herself.

Out of the southern world that she came into contact with in Louisiana, Kate Chopin in her short career as a writer of fiction began the creation of a dramatic dialectic that developed out of the imagination of an opposition, occurring within the consciousness of the individual, between the demands of self and those of society. The promise of what she began was greater than the time that she had available for its fulfillment. Perhaps after the rejection of *The Awakening*, it was greater than she had the strength to fulfill. Had she known a few other writers like herself, she might have found a sustaining will in community with them. But she worked in loneliness, lacking a community with the contemporaries of her spirit.

Now she has a community with her successors—ironically, not one through direct influence, for being displaced in literary history, she has had little direct influence on them, but a community of motive and theme. In her fiction, notably in *The Awakening*, Kate Chopin offers a dramatization of the psychic expense of the destruction of the moral order: the process of self-damnation through self-salvation. This has been a powerful motive in the art of the writers of the twentieth century, in none more so than those associated with the Southern Renaissance; and of these, in none more so than the most famous and substantial of them all, William Faulkner. It is unlikely that Faulkner knew the writings of Kate Chopin. For this reason, it is a still greater tribute to her insight into the anguished sensibility of modern times that we may see, for instance, a relationship between Edna Pontellier, who drowned herself in the Gulf of Mexico in the 1890s, and Quentin Compson III of *The Sound and the Fury*, who drowned himself in the Charles River at Cambridge, Massachusetts, in 1910. Both were involved in a fundamental confounding of the sexual relationship, and both experienced a suicidal intensification of self-awareness.

Shakespeare, of course, had forecast them both and (as Faulkner knew) all of modernity, in the art of *King Lear, Hamlet,* and *Macbeth.* Life "is a tale / Told by an idiot, full of sound and fury / Signifying nothing," Macbeth says when informed of the suicide of Lady Macbeth, who had disordered a world at the expense of refusing her role as a woman. (Shakespeare himself lived in a time when a queen brought an empire into being at such a cost.) The first great post-Christian writer in Western civilization, Shakespeare in his unparalleled prescience prophesies what must happen to the storytellers of a people who, for over a thousand years, lived a faith that slowly found its focus in an image of perfect motherhood and who, with the faltering of the faith, are doomed to live its death for another thousand years or more, while their storytellers seek the art to enact the stages in the life of this death. The stories of Kate Chopin focus on an attempted conquest of the meaning of modernity by an American imagination. Like Hawthorne's tales a generation earlier, they represent an awakening to the modern literary art.

8 / The Spectatorial Attitude

In *A Second Flowering: Works and Days of the Lost Generation*, Malcolm Cowley makes a pointed distinction between Thornton Wilder and the other American novelists of the generation of the 1920s: the others "are all in some way historians." Wilder (Cowley observers in the chapter entitled "Time Abolished") spent some of his early years as a student of archeology in Rome, where he "learned to look backward and forward through a long vista of years." Such a perspective encouraged the development of a literary vision that not only "denies the importance of time," but—in spite of Wilder's devotion to neoclassic standards—declares the moral autonomy and transcendent worth of the individual in accordance with the Emersonian tradition. Wilder "deals with the relation of one to one, or of anyone to the All, the Everywhere, the Always." In *A Second Flowering*, Cowley also makes a distinction between E. E. Cummings and writers of the twenties who predicate their vision on the historical quality of life. He refers particularly to the way in which the later Cummings wrote in the "romantic, mystical, anarchistic" vein of the New England Transcendentalist. Cummings dismisses history as "supremely unimportant," in contrast to the timeless moment of "wonderful one times one." But Wolfe, Hemingway, Faulkner, Dos Passos, and Fitzgerald, Cowley says, conform their works to a historical perspective, depicting a "living community in a process of continual and irreversible change."

> Their basic perception was of the changes in their own time, from peace to war, from stability to instability, from a fixed code of behavior to the feeling that "It's all right if you can get away with it." For them the Great War was a true event, in the sense that afterward nothing was the same. All of them were "haunted fatally by the sense of time," as Wolfe says of

his autobiographical hero. His second novel was *Of Time and the River.* Hemingway's first book was *In Our Time* and he let it be understood, ". . . as in no other time." Faulkner saw his time in the South as one of violent decay. When Dos Passos tried to put thirty years of American life into one big novel, he invented a device called the Newsreel, intended to convey the local color of each particular year. Fitzgerald put the same sort of material into the body of his stories; he wrote as if with an eye on the calendar. *The Great Gatsby* belongs definitely to the year 1923, when the Fitzgeralds were living in Great Neck, Long Island, and *Tender Is The Night* could have ended only in 1930; no other year on the Riviera had quite the same atmosphere of things going to pieces. Both books are historical novels about his own time, so accurately observed, so honestly felt, that the books are permanent.

In other words, Wolfe, Hemingway, Faulkner, Dos Passos, and Fitzgerald—a predominance of the major literary artists of the twenties —regarded the historical condition of man as the basis of their art. In their very sense of its historicity—in their complete fidelity to the specifics of an age—these storytellers, or, speaking broadly, these poets, imposed the order of art on a particular time and gave it lasting meaning.

Although in his assessment of the writers of the Lost Generation Cowley emphasizes their dominant regard for art as a rendering of the historical moment—in contrast to the "unsocial and antihistorical" motive of the mavericks Wilder and Cummings—he is drawn finally and perhaps more forcefully toward the view that "almost all" the writers of the twenties were "great spinners and weavers of legend." They created legendary heroes: the young man in Hemingway (an "Indian brave"), the "Fitzgerald young man who believed in the green light," and the "Thomas Wolfe young man bent on devouring the world." But more than this, they placed their heroes in "larger patterns of myth." Hemingway and Faulkner notably, though others as well, seemed to want to give their stories a dimension of depth in a far past: "to recover a prehistoric and prelogical fashion of looking at the world." They had an underlying epic impulse and wanted to make a "cycle of myths for a new century which—so they had felt from the beginning—was to be partly a creation of their own."

Thus Cowley concludes his second book on the Lost Generation. (We may reckon it to be his third, considering that in its totality, with its revisions and additions, the second edition of *Exile's Return* published in 1951 is almost a different book from the first edition of 1934.) *A Second Flowering* leaves us with an affirmative impression of the work of the Lost—or, as Cowley thinks we should now call it, the "lucky"—Generation. It also leaves us with the impression that the writers of the 1920s constituted a community of artists standing at the center of a cycle of creative myths that they discovered in their experience of America; and, more than this, it suggests to us that these writers constitute a legend of an heroic elite: "The good writers regarded themselves as an elite, a word that later came to be a sneer. They were an elite not by birth or money or education, not even by acclaim—though they would have it later—but rather by such inner qualities as energy, independence, vision, rigor, an original way of combining words (a style, a 'voice'), and utter commitment to a dream. Those qualities they grouped together as their 'talent,' about which they spoke as if it were something precariously in their possession, a blooded animal, perhaps, to be fed, trained, guarded carefully, and worked to the limit of its power, but not beyond." Though Thomas Wolfe must be judged as not quite up to fully appreciating the mystique of the elite, he "always dreamed of becoming a hero, and that is how he impresses us now; perhaps not as a hero of the literary art on a level with Faulkner and Hemingway and Fitzgerald, but as *Homo scribens* and *Vir scribentissimus*, a tragic hero of the act of writing."

Heroes of the literary art, greater or lesser, but heroes—Cowley celebrates his contemporaries as literary worthies comparable to those of the first flowering of American literature in Emerson's day. They were a second—a midsummer—flowering of the American garden. This was not because they sprang up in direct response to Emerson's "American Scholar" or other cultural declarations issued by the nineteenth-century writers. They knew little enough about Emerson and his fellows but were instead responding to a repetition of the general Emersonian imperative. Issued by literary spokesmen as widely different from Emerson as Pound, Eliot, and Joyce, the urgent challenge was yet the same: the individual writer's responsibility for fulfilling the "unlimited possibility" of literature in the present age.

Among writers of the twenties, Cowley demonstrates, the possession and husbanding of talent was assumed as a heavy and serious burden. Often it became an inhibiting burden. Most of Cowley's contemporaries suffered grievously at some point from the lonely self-knowledge of declining talent. This happened usually before the writer reached his mid-forties; it happened to Hart Crane before he was thirty. Long, steady, uninterrupted achievement was unknown to writers of the 1920s. Furthermore, as Cowley observes, his generation wrote few works of truly unquestionable greatness. He does not quite say that these stand alone as isolated monuments to unsustained genius, testifying to the destructive isolation of their creators. But surely the most graphic images of writers in *A Second Flowering* are those of loneliness: of Crane—all used up and virtually finished as a poet—hurrying toward a taxi stand outside Grand Central Station, his destination probably the waterfront and a compliant sailor, and Cowley—who had a most affectionate compassion for Crane—watching him and thinking of his friend as "being on a furlough from the dead," existing in the grip of "the iron laws of another country than ours"; of the paranoiac Hemingway during his last years, his "aggressiveness and his killer instinct" turning "against himself, the last of his possible trophies"; of Cummings, "One Man Alone," a person of great courage but drawing back from the larger work he might well have done, writing in his apartness poems that at times turned out to be "gimcrack and wasted" inventions.

On one side, the image of the writer in *A Second Flowering* is that of a member of a productive generational community; on the other, it is that of the writer as a solitary self, often imbued with a tendency toward his own destruction. Although a prominent motive in Cowley's compelling and indispensable book is a mellow desire to remove any lingering doubt about the Lost Generation's full return to the homeland and its corporate contribution to American literature and American culture, this is countered to a considerable extent by the depiction of the individual writer as isolated—exiled—in modern history.

In a sense, *A Second Flowering* represents part of a long struggle on Cowley's part to redeem the American writer from his condition of alienation. It would be misleading to say that this struggle has dominated Cowley's wide-ranging work as a literary critic. It is hardly too much to say that it provides a strong unifying theme in his complex and varied achievement. But in the same breath we must observe that it is a struggle that Cowley has never intended to win. When we add to his criticism Cowley's small but important body of poetry, we see running through the whole range of his work as a twentieth-century poet, critic, and literary and cultural historian a basic motive of alienation. As both a creator and an interpreter of the literature of the Lost Generation, Cowley is a contributor to one of its leading aspects: a myth or a legend of creativity that is definable as a poetics of exile. He apprehended first the American writer's exile from childhood, second his exile from society, and finally his exile from what may be termed the sense of being in the wholeness of the self. The first two revelations are stated in Cowley's best-known book, *Exile's Return;* the third—of which the first two are stages—is nowhere explicitly formulated by Cowley. Implied in the first edition of *Exile's Return*, it would seem to be significantly modified in the second edition, as it is also in an essay entitled "A Natural History of the American Writer." But it is strong in Cowley's critical essays on leading American writers, including his commentaries on Frost, Whitman, Hemingway, and, more notably, those on Hawthorne and Faulkner. The most substantial treatment of the exile from the self in Cowley, however, is to be discerned in his own creative works, his poems. Most of these appear in *Blue Juniata: Collected Poems* (1968).[1]

In "Privatation and Publication: A Memoir of the Year 1934" (*Sewanee Review*, Winter, 1975), Cowley points out that *Exile's Return*, a book dealing "in large part with friendships and joint activities," was "written in more than the usual isolation . . . on lonely weekends in the New England countryside, and in a Tennessee farmhouse two miles from a telephone, and later in the empty inn at Riverton," its sentences first being "tramped out . . . on walks in the

1 This volume is to be distinguished from the *Blue Juniata* published in 1929. In effect it is an independent work. See *Malcolm Cowley: A Checklist of His Writings, 1963–1973*, ed. Diane U. Eisenberg (Carbondale: Southern Illinois University Press, 1975).

woods or along farm lanes, as a sort of dialogue between the inner poet or maker and the inner critic or listener." At the same moment Cowley was a tribally inclined person, engaged with other writers and intellectuals in New York and serving as literary editor of the *New Republic*. He had "that almost universal but also specifically American weakness, the craving to be liked—not loved, not followed, but simply accepted as one of the right guys." When the initial critical response to *Exile's Return* came—as Cowley explains, a generally harsh one—he felt that his inner being had been violated. He was "like a timid nocturnal animal suddenly exposed to blinding sunlight, while shapes loomed over me and voices argued about whether to cage me and put me on display or let me scuttle back under the weeds." In his memoir, Cowley does not explore the theme of privatation beyond this depiction of his wounded feelings. But he nonetheless informs us about the nature of the inspiration that made *Exile's Return*: how little the book derives from his experience of a return to America, how much it comes out of his experience of the isolation of the self in America.

It could be that the critics who passionately disparaged *Exile's Return* were moved not so much by Cowley's ostensible dedication to the socialist revolution against capitalism as by his native and more basic revolutionary motive: a disposition to exalt the autonomous sacramental self. A logical romantic extension of the value that the American Revolution placed on the individual, this is the chief doctrine of American literary idealism, assuming its most radical form in the socially destructive doctrine of Emerson, which his disciple Thoreau suggested one might actually practice. American literati like Bernard De Voto, peculiarly sensitive to the doctrine of the "imperial self" (as one recent critic calls it) and all of the nuances of the "egotistical sublime," react vigorously against Thoreaus who would disturb the ideal by trying to make it real. Instinctively guided by the pragmatic individualism that Americans accept as the functional mode of the self, they don't want things thrown out of balance by extreme attacks on American materialism as the death of the self.

And that death is the informing notion of the first edition of *Exile's Return: A Narrative of Ideas*, for Cowley means by ideas the forces "that half-consciously guided people's actions, the ones they

lived and wrote by."² Influenced markedly by the early Van Wyck
Brooks, Cowley begins *Exile's Return* by positing a deracination of
the American self represented by the literary generation born in the
later nineteenth century. The most dramatic evidence of this condition he finds in the exile of this group of writers from the fundamental aspect of reality in America, childhood. It was not a normal separation of childhood from adulthood. The country of childhood cast
them out, though surviving in their minds as their "most essential
baggage," and each exile carried with him an urn containing a de-
posit of his native soil, as Cowley puts it in the poem concluding the
first chapter of *Exile's Return*. The deracination of the lost generation of American writers was, he indicates, inherent in the condition of American society: in its transformations of itself through the
technological conquest of nature and in its consequent separation
of experience and learning in its educational institutions. Having
learned nothing but literature in the abstract in either their early
schooling or in college, future American writers—notably those
who, impatient to get into the "Big Show," volunteered as ambulance drivers before April, 1917—underwent "a still further separation from reality" in the experience of war. They developed what
was for young men an unusual detachment from life—a "spectatorial
attitude." After the war the writers, or would-be writers, returned to
America, where they ended up in that great conglomeration of the
uprooted, New York City. Living in cold-water flats in Greenwich
Village, they grasped at the illusion that reality is to be found in art.
Later, becoming convinced that America was a place of "hypocrisy
and repression" in which reality would never be allowed to emerge,
they went back to Europe, principally to Paris; here they submitted
themselves to the symbolist discipline (or indiscipline) in which the
intensification of self-consciousness presumably leads to the truth
of pure consciousness—to the higher reality of the "religion of art."
Although they often protested against America and thought that
they might never return, these young writers ironically remained

2 The subtitle of the second edition of *Exile's Return* is *A Literary Odyssey of the
1920s*. It might be argued that the first edition is more truly cast as an odyssey
and the second as an exploration of ideas. The element of retrospective explication is at any rate a prominent feature of the second edition.

dependent on their homeland, not only for subsistence money, but for a sustaining sense of identity. From abroad they argued the virtues, at least the possible virtues, of America with contemporaries who had not yet managed to escape to Europe. When they returned, they faced the problem of making a living in a society from which they felt alienated, but which they still believed somehow held the possibility of their spiritual fulfillment. Living the life of the writer in the last years of the booming twenties—and many of them tried to make a living out of writing—they became more sensitive than ever before to the enclosure of the individual in the civilization of industrial capitalism. A system capable of satisfying the physical needs of the individual, but one that "could never satisfy the needs of the individual spirit," American society seemed to be a trap from which there was no escape.

The story of Harry Crosby could be taken as a case in point. He was a young writer who could find no home save death and who committed the ultimate act of self-identity by killing himself in New York in the fateful autumn of 1929. In Crosby's case, the separation from reality that had begun in the exile from childhood had been so confirmed by his further detachment from life during his service in the war that he assumed the literal truth of the doctrines of the surrealistic manifesto issued in *transition* in June, 1929: the absolute autonomy of the literary creator; his dedication to "pure poetry" and expression "through the rhythmic 'hallucination of the word'"; his "right to disintegrate the primal matter of words"; and his right to abolish the tyranny of time. Absurd as they are, these ultimate doctrines of the religion of art represented to Crosby the justification of his suicide. But the over-all context of his act was the "madness of his class and age." Thus "at the end he was becoming a symbol of the bourgeois society from which he had fled: he was at the height of his strength and was moving toward his own destruction; he was like a swimmer who, after battling the current, turns and swims with it in a magnificent burst of speed and vigor, each of his strokes being multiplied three times by the power of the stream, congratulating himself, moving faster, till at last the cataract."

The same autumn of his death, the madness that Crosby exemplified came to an end in the Wall Street crash. Following the crash, Cowley indicates in *Exile's Return*, there was a new revelation. Writers began to see that they must become workers in a social revolution. Comprehending that "their real exile was from society itself, from any society with purposes they could share, toward which they could honestly contribute and from which they could draw new strength," they envisioned their mission to be the transformation of American society into an expression of the reality of the spirit. Or it may be more accurate to say that they envisioned their task to be the fulfillment of the socialist promise of the American society to which they now returned. Freed from the writer's burden of self— from the introspection and loneliness of the interior monologue demanded by the religion of art—they would be the spokesmen of a larger and brighter world to be realized in America.

The extent to which Cowley believed that the writer of the Lost Generation could return to America and be at home can be measured in his writings during his *New Republic* years (some of the best have been collected by Henry Dan Piper in *Think Back on Us . . . A Contemporary Chronicle of the 1930's*), and by the second edition (or second version) of *Exile's Return. Think Back on Us* records a struggle between Cowley's hope (during what he later called the pentecostal years) for the writer's identification with the cause of a socialist transformation of society and his later disillusionment with this possibility; the second edition of *Exile's Return* (especially in the prologue and epilogue) expresses on the whole a pragmatic attitude toward the relationship between the American writer and American society:

> As I read over these chapters written almost twenty years ago [Cowley states in the epilogue], the story they tell seems to follow the old pattern of alienation and reintegration, or departure and return, that is repeated in scores of European myths and continually reembodied in life. A generation of American writers went out into the world like the children in Grimm's fairy tales who ran away from a cruel stepmother. They wandered for years in search of treasure and then came back like the grown children to dig for it at home. But the story in life was not so simple and lacked the happy ending of fairy tales. Perhaps there was really a treasure and perhaps it had been buried all the time in their father's garden, but the exiles did not find it there. They found only what others were finding: work to do as best they could and families to support and educate. The adventure had ended and once more they were part of the common life.

By the time of the republication of *Exile's Return*, Cowley's interpretation of the writer in America had become governed by a kind of dialectic between a pragmatic concept of the writer's being that asserted his essential existence in society and an ideal concept of the writer's being that asserted his identity in the essential self. Cowley, to be sure, had taken a pragmatic attitude toward the literary life all along. At the beginning of "A Natural History of the American Writer," he refers to his long dedication to the customs of "my own tribe" and to "random notes" made over the years on "Where Writers Come From," "How They Get Started," "How They Earn Their Livings," "Their Domestic Habits," "Their Public Status," and "The Writer's Psychology." In "A Natural History" (which appears among the essays in *The Literary Situation*, 1954) these topics are treated with sagacity and wit, and Cowley (partly inspired by his desire to refute Dr. Edmund Bergler's interpretation of the writer as a neurotic) offers what is unquestionably one of the sanest inquiries ever written into the literary profession in America. But for all the emphasis on this profession as a functional group in American society, images of the writer as a man apart emerge in "A Natural History." A sense of the life of the writer as uniquely the life of the spirit echoes in the disquietude that Cowley says he felt when he shifted from bohemianism to responsible family living: "What I feared most and sometimes detected was a dryness of the heart." And it is plainly declared in the following comment in "A Natural History":

> For the writer properly speaking, language is not only the medium in which he works but also the medium in which he lives and breathes. His private universe consists of words, and no experience seems quite real for him until the revealing and magical words have been found for it. Sometimes he regards himself as a soldier fighting against the unknown and unexpressed; he is like a Roman legionary always serving on the frontier. Sometimes he is an explorer trying to broaden that civilized homeland which is the area of consciousness, by finding the proper words for new experiences.

In "A Natural History of the American Writer," Cowley wants to demonstrate that the writer is a normal right guy and in so doing seems to modify his attraction to the symbolist image of the writer as the isolated self, but the modification is more apparent than real. As a matter of fact, in the decade following his resignation from the

New Republic and preceding the republication of *Exile's Return* and the writing of "A Natural History," Cowley had firmly established the symbolist image of the writer as the archetypal image of the writer in American literary history.

In a well-known essay on Robert Frost (1944), Cowley objects to Frost because, although Frost talks about doing so, he does not, like other New England writers past and present, "strike far inward into the wilderness of human nature." Hawthorne does so, and in an essay of very considerable power written a few years after the Frost piece, Cowley shows how seminal Hawthorne's "cursed habits of solitude" became for American literature. For one thing, they created in him the "inner monologue." Hawthorne made this into a basic instrumentality of his art; himself both storyteller and listener, he repeated each story until the listener was satisfied with it. "This doubleness in Hawthorne, this division of himself into two persons conversing in solitude, explains one of the paradoxes in his literary character: that he was one of the loneliest authors who ever wrote, even in this country of lost souls, while at the same time his style was that of a social man eager to make himself clear and intensely conscious of his audience. For him the audience was always present, because it was part of his own mind." Still another paradox detected by Cowley in Hawthorne as a result of his "solitude and self-absorption" is his honesty about himself. "Under a veil of allegory and symbol," he followed Dimmesdale's passionate admonition in *The Scarlet Letter*: "Be true! Be true! Show freely to the world, if not your worst, yet some trait whereby the worst may be inferred."

The difference between the total achievement of Whitman and Hawthorne is, Cowley thinks, the result of Whitman's violation of his loneliness during the second part of his life. Earlier, in the time when he wrote his one great work, "Song of Myself," he had written as one "wounded and alone"—a tormented visionary, like Dostoevski descending into the underworld of the crippled and diseased, finding his identity with them, then coming into the sunlight again to see that the humanity above ground is in its inner being like that underground. But he put on the mask of the poet and prophet of the expansive national democracy of the average, and in trying to conform to a "preconception of what he should write"—in trying to conceive society as the reality of the spirit—became a lesser poet than he had been, attempting to envision an abstract world instead of dealing with the miraculous, infinitely concrete world that embodies spirit. "Hawthorne in his solitude wrote what he had to write." He obeyed his genius or his demon and in doing so became a founding figure in American literature, which speaking in general terms is a literature

> not broad and sweeping, but narrow and deep; not epical, but lyrical; not optimistic, but somber and self-questioning in its mood; not young, but middle-aged—one might almost say from the beginning; not realistic as a whole, but marvelously realistic in its grasp of details; not careless and uncouth, but often formalized and troubled by the search for perfection; not prevailingly social, but psychological, and interested from the first in what afterwards came to be known as depth psychology. On the whole it has been a literature of loneliness and one in which persons, however real in themselves, tend to dissolve into symbols and myths. Hawthorne's work continues to stand as one of archetypes, at the beginning of a double line that runs through James to Eliot, with all his imitators, and through Stephen Crane to Faulkner and Hemingway.

His sense of the American literary derivation from Hawthorne seems to be especially crucial to Cowley's appreciation of Faulkner's remarkable imaginative construct, Yoknapatawpha County, Mississippi. Although that harbinger of Faulkner's world-wide fame, Cowley's *Portable Faulkner* (1945), brings much more to the understanding of the Mississippi writer than his relationship to Hawthorne, nothing Cowley says is more fundamentally illuminating than the affinity he establishes between the New Englander and the Southerner:

> They stand to each as July to December, as heat to cold, as swamp to mountain, as the luxuriant to the meager but perfect, as planter to Puritan; and yet Hawthorne had much the same attitude toward New England that Faulkner has toward the South. The Civil War made Hawthorne feel that "the North and the South were two distinct nations in opinions and habits, and had better not try to live under the same institutions." In the spring of 1861, he wrote to his Bowdoin classmate Horatio Bridge, "We were never one people and never really had a country."— "New England," he said a little later, "is quite as large a lump of earth as my heart can really take in." But it was more than a lump of earth for him; it was a lump of history and a permanent state of consciousness.

Like Faulkner in the South, he applied himself to creating its moral fables and elaborating its legends, which existed, as it were, in his solitary heart.[3]

Cowley's empathy for Faulkner and the southern literary expression, it would seem, bears a fundamental relation to his feeling for the sense of alienation he discovered in the New Englander Hawthorne, and indeed perhaps developed out of this. Faulkner, like Hawthorne, Cowley implies, shared an estrangement from the nation imposed on American writers by their inability to participate in an authentic spiritual experience of its existence. Although the ideal of the nation as an existential autonomy has had a constant appeal to the American literary imagination, it has met an inherent opposition in the circumstances of American history and has remained, as Cowley discerns in his analysis of Whitman, an abstraction, impossible to embody in concrete story situations and genuinely realized characters. In the American writer's sensibility, the nation is paradoxically a symbol of exile and loneliness.

Cowley's own creative contribution to the American literature of loneliness is notable. Even though it consists in a single volume of poems, it is central to his career as a man of letters and to his interpretation of American literature.

Blue Juniata: Collected Poems ("This record of a life," as Cowley succinctly describes his book on the flyleaf of a copy he once gave me) is the lyrical center of Cowley's poetics of exile. The poems begin with his boyhood in the Juniata River country of Pennsylvania and "continue to the present." They were written over a period of many years, and some were reworked numerous times. Arranged in sections and provided with brief provocative introductions in poetic prose, they tell much of the story that is in *Exile's Return* (although there are no war poems). But how much more personally, intensely, and deeply they tell it is forecast in the first poem, the meditative, haunting depiction of "A Boy in Sunlight," "dozing awake like a snake on the stone," profoundly at home in a place in the world.

3 *The Portable Faulkner*, ed. Malcolm Cowley (New York: Viking Press, 1946), 22–23,

The land absorbs him into itself,
as he absorbs the land, the ravaged woods, the pale sky,
not to be seen, but as a way of seeing;
not to be judged, but as a way of judgment;
not even to remember, but stamped in the bone.

But if the boy is "half-animal," he is also "half-grown" and involved in the drama of dispossession still being enacted in the Juniata River homeland. It was a drama that had been going on since the first white men had come into the world of the Indians and, in their dispossession of the Indians and ravaging of the woods, had dispossessed themselves, sentimentalizing the pathos of the disaster in a banal but haunting frontier ballad:

Wild roved an Indian girl,
Bright Alfarata,
Where sweep the waters
Of the blue Juniata.

A young poet leaves the Juniata country—is exiled from the place of his boyhood and can never come back. The drama of his dispossession continues in New York; in the disorder of inflationary post-World War I Europe (young "pilgrims of art" bent on "following the dollar, ah, following the dollar"); back in New York, "The City of Anger" (the "city without landmarks, the home of lasting impermanence, of dynamic immobility"); and through the excitement and disillusionment of the revolutionary movement in the 1930s. Finally in *Blue Juniata* the poet, growing older, moves across the shadowy frontiers of "Another Country." This last section ends with "The Urn," the poem that concludes the first chapter of *Exile's Return*:

Wanderers outside the gates, in hollow
landscapes without memory, we carry
each of us an urn of native soil,
of not impalpable dust a double handful,

why kept, how gathered? was it garden mould
or wood soil fresh with hemlock needles, pine,
and princess pine, this little earth we bore
in secret, blindly, over the frontier?

—a parcel of the soil not wide enough
or firm enough to build a dwelling on

> or deep enough to dig a grave, but cool
> and sweet enough to sink the nostrils in
> and find the smell of home, or in the ears
> rumors of home like oceans in a shell.

In its context in *Exile's Return*, "The Urn" describes the survival of an image of nativity in the consciousness of the 1920s exile. In the story in this book, the exile returns from the "landscapes without memory" to seek his destiny in the destiny of his homeland. Thirty-five years later, placed at the end of the story in the collected poems, Cowley's larger record of his life and age, the reference of "The Urn" is greatly extended. This poem and several preceding ones in the final section of *Blue Juniata* ("Stone Horse Shoals," "Leander," "William Wilson," "The Living Water," "The Flower and the Leaf"), together with one graphic poem in the "Unsaved World" section ("Here with the Long Grass Rippling"), constitute a culminating enlargement of Cowley's fable of the Lost Generation. For they suggest that the origin of the theme of exile in Cowley does not simply relate to the exile of the writer's self from an American childhood and/or from American society. It derives more fundamentally from the sense of the self as irrevocably cast off from any social reference for its peremptory need to be.

Just when this divorcement of self and society began to be grasped by the literary imagination is difficult to document with exactness, but the loss of the old incorporation of the self in society and the consequences of this to the self are a major theme in *Hamlet*. The theme comes fully into view in the famous dictate of Polonius:

> This above all; to thine own self be true,
> And it must follow, as the night the day,
> Thous canst not then be false to any man.

In his inquiry into the moral life of the past four centuries, *Sincerity and Authenticity*, Lionel Trilling comments upon how much Polonius' advice demands our favorable response, in spite of the fact that we may attempt to interpret it as but another crafty pragmatic mouthing. Long before Emerson said that society is in conspiracy against the manhood of every one of its members, Shakespeare conceived Polonius as both the instrumentality and the manipulator of a new sense of society—a man who, as a self-serving opportunist, embodies society's degradation of the individual yet speaks for the ideal of the self's autonomy. By the time in history represented in Shakespeare's sensibility, society had already become the falsification of the self. Polonius's advice is based on that curious modern feeling that the self has of being dissociated from an integral self, of having lost, or of having been exiled from, some place where the self is whole. To thine own self be true: but where is the self—the original perdurable whole self—to be true to? The pathos of the counsel given by Polonius is patent in Hamlet's exclamation "To be, or not to be." The question is asked not merely in fear of what happens when one departs for the country from which no traveler returns; it is asked to bring up the problematical nature of being. It is posed as a reaction to the consciousness of the self and of the immense ambiguity of its dimensions. It is a question arising from the relationship of the conscience and the consciousness, conscience deriving from society and threatening to invade the consciousness with nightmares about the self, the self one was not true to and yet could not be, not knowing where to find it. The question is asked, furthermore, by one who shows a decided tendency toward assuming the doubleness of consciousness so characteristic of modernity. Hamlet is an observer of his own mind. Passionate though he is, he is the detached spectator: "I have that within which passes show."

The growth of the modern anxiety about the self, in the light of which we see the character of Hamlet, does not reach the moment of real urgency until the nineteenth century, when it begins to assume its twentieth-century proportions as the major subject of western literature. Cowley evidently first came upon the subject in his studies of the French symbolists during the 1920s, when he was not only reading them at first hand but seeing them and the whole symbolist mode through Paul Valéry's "high researches into the metaphysics of the self." To some extent, Cowley became a disciple of the prophet of pure and detached consciousness, and he published a translation of Valéry's essays in 1928, pointing out in the introduction that Valéry regarded literature as "a form of mental exercise, to be valued because it is difficult," and that his primary intention as a writer was "a defense of the conscious mind." When he began to study and write about the nineteenth-century American authors,

Cowley inevitably comprehended the parallels between writers like Baudelaire, Flaubert, and Rimbaud and their American contemporaries. He was particularly attracted to the New England writers, who had the symbolist mind and its capacity for detachment but had been tempered by a disciplined religious and moral sensibility. (Cowley had come to admire the cast of the New England literary mind in his Harvard years. When he reviewed Van Wyck Brooks's *Flowering of New England*, in the very midst of his Popular Front days, he made a point of stating his esteem for contemporary New England writers, both native and spiritual, praising "their scrupulousness and Harvard diffidence and half-concealed moral fervor, . . . the thin, stubborn integrity that has carried them through the years when so many other writers were being flashily successful.") In the instance of Hawthorne, the New England symbolism of consciousness emphasizes an alienation of the self from the community of mankind because the self has become estranged from the nature of being human; and it promises a discovery of the wholeness of the self if only the original sin, pride of intellect, which assumes such an intractability in modernity, can be overcome by an arduous journey "inward into the wilderness of human nature." In this journey there is to be overcome a hostility of the self—of the self in the image of the original sin, pride of intellect—to the society of man. But in the case of Emerson the New England consciousness stresses the cosmic character of the self. The self is God. In a universe in which the moral law radiates from the center to the circumference, there is no evil save in the incapacity of self-realization, a condition imposed on the self by the exigencies of society. For this reason, the self must utterly reject society and, in a state of ineffable, if ecstatic, loneliness, must seek its identity with the Over-Soul.

Cowley has recognized both sides of the New England symbolism of consciousness, the Hawthornean and the Emersonian. Thinking that he had found the remedy for the isolation of the self in a return to society through social revolution, he eventually realized that he had fallen into the sin of pride of intellect, and in this realization he found his way into Hawthorne, who saw in the reformer a fallibility of pride destructive to community. But Cowley was not led to share Hawthorne's opinion that the transcendentalism of his Concord neighbor was, far more than the pride of the social reformer, the epitome of folly. The journey of the soul in "The Over-Soul" is to Cowley a more essential element in the paradigm of the American poetics of exile than is the fearful journey of the soul into the depths of the forest in, say, "Young Goodman Brown."

> In common speech [Emerson says] we refer all things to time, as we habitually refer the immensely sundered stars to one concave sphere. And so we say that the Judgment is distant or near, that the Millennium approaches, that a day of certain political, moral, social reforms is at hand, and the like, when we mean that in the nature of things one of the facts we contemplate is external and fugitive, and the other is permanent and connate with the soul. The things we now esteem fixed shall, one by one, detach themselves like ripe fruit from our experience, and fall. The wind shall blow them none knows whither. The landscape, the figures, Boston, London, are facts as fugitive as any institution past, or any whiff of mist or smoke, and so is society, and so is the world. The soul looketh steadily forwards, creating a world before her, leaving worlds behind her. She has no dates, nor rites, nor persons, nor specialities nor men. The soul knows only the soul; the web of events is the flowing robe in which she is clothed.[4]

The Emersonian vision of the soul's neoplatonic odyssey across endless frontiers of consciousness registers the typical modern capacity for doubleness of consciousness; and in "The Over-Soul" Emerson is as much detached spectator of as participant in consciousness. His vision is a symbol of the "mind . . . aware of itself" and an affirmation of his austere faith: "A believer, a mind whose faith is consciousness, is never disturbed because other persons do not yet see the fact which he sees."

It is his own intimate involvement in the translation of this faith by the twentieth-century literary mind that has led Cowley to study Emerson, reading relatively obscure essays like "The Method of Nature" and the journals, as well as famous pieces like "The American Scholar." Henry Dan Piper has observed that during the 1930s Valéry's example of the man of detached consciousness shielded Cowley "from the temptations of orthodox Marxism—Stalinist or Trotskyite." Was not the example of Emerson also hovering over the literary editor of the *New Republic*? Writing *Exile's Return* in the

4 *Selections from Ralph Waldo Emerson*, ed. Stephen E. Whicher (Boston: Houghton Mifflin Company, 1957), 93.

1930s, Cowley sought to reject the literary quest for pure consciousness because it seemed to be the chief barrier between the American
writer and his acceptance of society as the norm of his existence. Responsibility for consciousness incorporated in the religion of art had
usurped the writer's proper moral responsibility for social values. A
rejection of consciousness proved to be impossible, one suspects,
not primarily because of Cowley's commitment to the amoral vision of Valéry, but because he made an association—of which Emerson is the exemplary American instance—between the quest for
consciousness and the intrinsic moral identity of the writer. The
quest for consciousness is the fundamental symbol of the modern
writer's being. It is only in and through his estrangement from society that he has a possible moral relation to society. He is an exemplification of the truth of being—namely, that the individual is the
world. The theory of the writer is intrinsically a poetics of exile.

Cowley has presented a further comment on the relation of the
Emersonian journey of the soul to the twentieth-century concept
of the self of the writer, in an important essay in which he traces
Conrad Aiken's crucial passage from "Savannah to Emerson."[5] This
is Cowley's most complete discussion, not only of Aiken, but of
Emerson and transcendentalism, and in it (although this is incidental to his intention) he explicates at greater length than in his essays on Wilder and Cummings the connection between the literature we associate primarily with the 1920s and the transcendental
ethos. (Born a little too soon, Aiken was not a fully accredited member of the lost and lucky generation, but he does possess the certification of appearing in Harold Stearns's *Civilization in America*.)
Cowley's analysis of Aiken in effect locates his advocacy of faith in
consciousness—which he called "the religion of consciousness"—at
the heart of the literature formed in the twenties, with its dedication to the redemption of the self's alienation from the sentiment of
being. Cowley stresses Aiken's insistence that the writer divide himself into two persons, observer and subject. The duty of the observer
is to make out of the observed self a construct of words representing

5 "Conrad Aiken: From Savannah to Emerson" first appeared in the *Southern Review*, n.s. 11 (Spring, 1975), 245–59. It is reprinted as Chapter 15 in Cowley's
—*And I Worked at the Writer's Trade* (New York: Viking Press, 1978), 231–48.

both an honest and an artistic use of language and serving to create an "artifact" (a poem, a novel) that will extend the human consciousness. Cowley makes a special analysis of Aiken's final artifact, a poem entitled "THEE." Comparing this to a fragmentary poem in Emerson's journals for 1831, which holds that "the soul of things is in thee," he comments: "Aiken gives a twist to Transcendental doctrine by stressing, first, the indifferent power of THEE [Nature], and then the dependence of THEE on the individual consciousness—with which it must 'meet and mate,' from which it learns to become more truly itself, and with which, perhaps, it must die." The twisting, or inversion, of the transcendental ethos results from the difference between the quest for consciousness viewed as an imperative of the moral law of the universe and as an imperative of the accidental nature of the human consciousness. But in either case, Emerson's or Aiken's, the imperative of the quest is the fulfillment of the self's lost wholeness, whether this be finally in the resolution of the self in the Over-Soul or in the integral mortality of nature and self. Either way, the journey of the self is finished, its exile ended, and the poetics of exile brought to a final statement.

Although Cowley in his interpretation of certain writers implies that an American poetics of literary exile is established in the transcendental paradigm of the soul's journey, he has discerned the lineaments of another and more awesome journey, one unrelated to the transcendental through either affirmation or inversion. I refer to his interpretation of Hart Crane. In distinct contrast to the attempts by some critics to link Crane with transcendentalism and to discover his motive in Emerson's recognition (as in *Nature*) of man's disunity with himself, Cowley links Crane with forces removed from the context of the Emersonian vision. Crane, like Rimbaud, pursued the paradoxical discipline of a deliberate derangement of the senses. Through "drunkenness, dancing, frenzied conversation, and sexual orgies," he entered into states of "heightened consciousness"—not for the sake of the experience itself, but for the sake of attaining the state in which poems could be created. Consciousness did not mean to Crane the abolition—either in the Over-Soul or in the extinction of the soul—of the temporal. To Crane, the poem was neither a paean to the correspondence of natural facts and spiritual facts nor an artifact of consciousness. He desired to unleash the primal energy of the magic in words, and to make the poem a work of magic. He was "like the sorcerer of a primitive tribe," employing the hallucinatory consciousness "to produce not poems only, but incantations and mantras that would have a magical power, evoking in the reader the same hallucinated visions that the poet had seen." As an authentic hallucinatory vision, a poem is not a countervention of time, but an intervention in time; a poem is a magical "structure" erected in time itself.

I am drawing on, and I hope not exaggerating, Cowley's careful analysis of Crane in *A Second Flowering*. But if I veer toward emotionality, it may be because I am more compelled by Cowley's poem "Leander" than by his essay.

> Regal and tired, O corpse that mapped the countries
> of ocean, saw pelagic meadows where
> the sea cow grazes, traveler who skirts
> the unicellular gardens of the foam:
> southward you drift, where archipelagoes
> of stars deflect the current, and waters boil
> with lava, through indefinite Marquesas,
> whirling in the typhoon, and off Cape Stiff
> in westerly gales your eyes commemorate,
> still tropical, the wax and wane of moons.
> Time is a secret frozen in your smile.

By the time he plunged off a ship into the ocean, Hart Crane had already destroyed himself by his inducements of extraordinary psychic states. There was no longer any way for him to write poems; and even though he had found alleviation from his homosexual compulsion for the first time in the love of a woman, the need for death had become absolute. In Cowley's remarkable poem (of which I have quoted the concluding stanza), the violent psychic quest that Crane made into the sources of poetry is imaged in the marvelous irony of the magical, hallucinatory, oceanic odyssey of the poet's "cold body / whittled by the sea." To be placed, not in contrast to, but in apposition with, the soul's journey in Emerson or in Aiken—this is one of the conclusive images in the writings of the Lost Generation of the exile of the self.

No one understands more than I my tendency to misrepresent

Cowley. If space permitted atonement here, I would attempt to rectify my remarks—with respect both to Cowley's relation to the poetics of exile and to a pragmatics of the writer's life—by observing in detail the extent to which his approach to the literary profession is, like that of William Dean Howells or Van Wyck Brooks, often infused with a poetry of literary community. Through the cultivation of a large personal literary acquaintance, through a gift for friendship, through generosity and compassion—I would not fail to say through love—and through his adherence to eclectic but substantial values of criticism, Cowley has urged upon American writers the image of a community based on both goodwill and discipline. He has urged too the extension of the community of American writers into the past (the "usable past"), finding his generation to be contemporaries of the mid-nineteenth-century generation. In *A Second Flowering* he calls our attention to how much the second flowering of American literature in the midsummer garden of the 1920s was a growth from the seeds of the first, which was so much a New England planting. The writings of the Lost Generation, he says, afford a brilliant retrospection on the work of the American romantics of the 1840s and 1850s. But in Cowley's central vision of his age, which is recorded in *Exile's Return* and the collected poems, the seeds of the first flowering fell into soil far from the pastoral world of pre-Civil War America. The landscape of the second flowering lay in another time and another country. We glimpse it in certain scenes in *Exile's Return*:

An artillery park near the western front on a rainy afternoon. Young American volunteer drivers under bombardment dash out from cover to gather up warm pieces of shrapnel, "collecting souvenirs of death, like guests bringing back a piece of wedding cake or a crushed flower from the bride's bouquet."

A "courtyard of a half-ruined chateau" on a July day in 1917 toward dusk. Artillery shells rumble overhead.

The German and the French heavy batteries, three miles behind their respective lines, were shelling each other like the Brushton gang throwing rocks at the Car Barn gang; here, in the empty courtyard between them, it was as if we were underneath a freight yard where heavy trains were being shunted back and forth. We looked indifferently at the lake, now empty of swans, and the formal statues chipped by machine-gun fire, and talked in quiet voices—about Mallarmé, the Russian ballet, the respective virtues of two college magazines. On the steps of the chateau, in the last dim sunlight, a red-faced boy from Harvard was studying Russian out of a French textbook. Four other gentlemen volunteers were rolling dice on an outspread blanket. A French artillery brigade . . . was laying down a barrage; the guns flashed like fireflies among the trees. We talked about the Lafayette Escadrille with admiration, and about our own service bitterly.

Removed from the world in which they occurred by sixty years and three more wars, we think of such scenes as belonging to an antique age when people sang about roses blooming in Picardy. But they are, to Cowley, the essence of the poetry of exile. These moments in the wasted garden that was the western front symbolize the crucial time in the germination of the second, the midsummer, garden of American literature—the exciting magical moment opening upon unlimited possibility, when the detached spectator began to look on the other spectators as well as on the spectacle and, further, to become aware of the power of being not only the observer of the observers but the observer of the observer himself. In the description of the charmed moments in the artillery park and the blasted courtyard, Cowley represents a singular transcendent conjunction of self, war, modern history, literature, and art in the consciousness, and the conscience, of a highly talented group of young American writers. This conjunction resulted in a unique enhancement of the modern spectatorial sensibility, even in the case of young American writers who for one reason or another did not get to the western front, and thus never had the exquisite and fabulous experience of the dissociation of self from childhood and from society that the ambulance drivers underwent as they watched themselves watching the destruction of remnants of the old community that had incorporated the self. They all became exiles in some degree: writers as different as Hemingway and Faulkner, Fitzgerald and Dos Passos, Thomas Wolfe and Robert Penn Warren, Hart Crane and Allen Tate, Conrad Aiken and John Crowe Ransom. All became makers of an American poetics of exile strangely placed at the heart of the second flowering.

This poetics is expressed in qualities of feeling and seeing that marked an age and entered into the style, the manner, of being a writer. Its primary symbol, the psychic and/or spiritual exile of the young writer from a homeland to an uncertain country from which there is no return, expresses the pervasive theme of modernity: the fragmentation and isolation of the self. This theme, developing as far back as Hamlet, is a secular reversal of the Christian theme of the assured destiny of the individual soul—symbolized as the individual's pilgrimage through life into death, the destination being either heaven or hell but in either event a certain country. Yet the writer who is cast off from his homeland, detached as he is from all that is familiar, has been liberated to witness the unfamiliar and, it may be, to cross as yet uncrossed frontiers of existence. There is the tremendous possibility that the wanderer outside the gates, haunted by rumors from home, may discover something of great import and send back a redeeming message from another country. It may be a message like that in "Leander," which is a vision of Hart Crane's own vision of the resolution of the secret of self and time in the hallucinatory experience of words. It may be a more essentially hopeful message. It may be some prophecy of a new flowering of the literary imagination. In Cowley's memorable poem "Stone Horse Shoals," a resurrectionary figure of the poet (the "tall man") says he has lived "a life that moved in spirals / turned inward like the shell of a seasnail"; but he speaks of shedding "my carapace" and after this death of witnessing "in another season" a transfiguration:

> a naked body climbing
> a naked seacoast, naked of the dead,
>
> naked of language. There are signs inscribed
> on stones and trees, familiar vocables;
> I hope to rise out of the sea as white,
> as empty and chalk-smooth as cockleshells.
> And children digging naked in the sand
> will find my shell and on it scratch new words
> that soon will blossom out . . . and bear
> new fruit, strange to the tongue of men and birds.

CODA / The Decorum of
the Writer

Nearly all of Malcolm Cowley's books, including his collected poems, are devoted to telling the story of the twentieth-century man of letters, particularly in his French and American guises. But except for the volume of poems (1968) and one other book, —And I Worked at the Writer's Trade (1978), Cowley's accounts are chronologically and thematically limited.[1] In fact, The Writer's Trade is the only book by Cowley that suggests a comprehensive vision of the literary profession. This is not to claim that the book is more than what it actually is, a collection of essays devoted to literary reminiscences and critical and historical interpretations and speculations, but anyone should grasp that the essays, which the author calls chapters of literary history, individually and collectively move beyond random recollection and incidental opinion.

I would suggest (and I do so here at the expense of ignoring its other interesting aspects) that The Writer's Trade is a compelling meditative exploration of the moral character—more broadly speaking, the ethical situation—of the twentieth-century writer. In the end, the book resolves the meaning of the story Cowley has been so much occupied with, that of his own generation—the "lost" but, as he puts it in a A Second Flowering, "lucky" writers who came into their own in the 1920s. The resolution lies quite simply in an association of the Lost Generation with "the notion that writing is a priestly vocation with its own strict ethical code." Cowley not only con-

---

1 This comment on Malcolm Cowley's —And I Worked at the Writer's Trade was written for the "Arts and Letters" section of the Sewanee Review at the invitation of the editor, George Core. In a sense, it is a sequel to the foregoing commentary on Cowley's career, which also appeared in the Sewanee Review.

ceives the generation of Hemingway and Fitzgerald to have been of the literary priesthood, but holds in effect that this generation possessed the transcendent truth of the literary vocation. He believes, furthermore, that in the 1970s the "religion of art," as "enforced by famous examples," may be held to be the permanent moral and metaphysical basis of the valid literary career. Indeed, he confidently states the binding commandments on the writer. Five in number, a "pentalogue" (but unlike the Decalogue no "guide to one's daily conduct as a spouse, parent, or neighbor" and no guard against the seven deadly sins, except perhaps for sloth), these declare to the artist (1) that he must "believe in the importance of art" and the "all-importance in his own life of the particular art to which he is devoted"; (2) that he must believe not only in his own talent, but also in its "universal validity," and so by any means necessary must strive to bring his talent to fruition; (3) that he "must honestly express his own vision of the world and his own personality, including his derelictions"; (4) that he "must produce grandly, to the limit of his powers," knowing a sense of guilt in the failure to produce; (5) that he must recognize that the work of art has "an organic shape and a life of its own . . . apart from the life of its maker and capable of outlasting it."

At first glance, his formulation of the code imposed on the literary artist may strike one as a recovery of a set of commandments that Cowley discovered in his youth. I refer to the "collection of beliefs" about the meaning of the literary vocation that he summarizes in *Exile's Return* (1934) from the letters and notebook entries written not long before he ended his European exile in the summer of 1923. Some of them conceived by Cowley himself, others taken over from his French acquaintances, these may be arranged without undue forcing in another pentalogue: (1) to be a man of letters one must be a man of *letters*, adopting not one role (such as essayist or novelist) but the "whole of literature as his province," and, moreover, devoting himself to it "as one might devote himself to God or to the Poor"; (2) the "man of letters, while retaining his own point of view, . . . primarily that of the poet, should concern himself with every department of human activity, including science, sociology, and revolution"; (3) since writers are ruined by early success, the young writer must be willing to make a fool of himself "in order to avoid being successful"; (4) recognizing that the "work of expanding the human mind to its extremest limit of thought and feeling" is the "aim of literature," the writer must avoid the "fallacy of contraction," allowing public life and social questions a full measure of his attention; (5) although the writer may "steal, murder, drink or be sober, lie to his friends or with their wives," he must in his writing give full allegiance to "high courage, absolute integrity and a sort of intelligence" that is "in itself a moral quality."

In the pentalogue of 1923, Cowley allows for the dedication of the contemporary writer to both society and art. On the one hand, he is a citizen of the Republic of Letters. In his allegiance to this realm, he is a descendant of the men of letters of the Renaissance and Enlightenment, who fostered the all-embracing critique of man, nature, society, and not less of God, which distinguishes modernity from all other ages. On the other hand, the writer is a literary artist, the figure of the man of letters who appears in the romantic movement and is more acutely defined in the symbolist intensification of romanticism. Although, in contrast with the medieval sense of the sociality of mind and art, both figures of the man of letters in Cowley's literary code idealize him as an autonomous entity, the first representation portrays him as an expression of the struggle for rationality. He is a figure of the Great Critique, combining detachment and a desire to understand and thus to control the moral meaning of man and the world. The second figure in Cowley's 1923 code, the man of letters as literary artist, presents an ideal of the artist as the perdurable self, opposed to society, striving to become integral in his own being. Yet the artist, Cowley insists, is not a development apart from the Third Realm. Amid the tensions of the nineteenth-century—the rise of the choate national state, the rise in the literary realm itself of an antihumanistic realm of science and technology—the image of the integral literary artist was thrown up by the literary realm as a major symbol of its continuing quest for moral autonomy. But the older image of the man of letters as detached moralist did not disappear in the newer symbol. A special aspect of the older image rather than a separate representation, the image of the literary artist expressed the motive underlying the movement of secular literature as this developed in the nineteenth century—namely the achievement of an ecumenical domain of the secular word with its own priesthood. Romanticism, symbolism, and, for that matter, the evolution of literary realism, Cowley implies, are essentially phases of the process (emphasized in the present studies as basic to the modern literary consciousness) that may be described as the divinization of the secular.

An analysis of Cowley's declaration of literary faith in 1923 raises the possibility that *Exile's Return* distorts the complex sense of vocation known to the writers of the 1920s, for the book reaches its climax in a deprecatory view of their devotion to art. Too much inclined to believe that art is "wholly individual and forever opposed to a stupid world," they were, Cowley says, moral failures as men of letters. Stressing the imperative emergence of the writer as revolutionist, Cowley sees him renouncing his false dedication to the religion of art and taking up a new faith in a radical politics that will forever alter the sterile society that encourages a purposeless commitment to art. Since the new literary faith in the America of the thirties meant a connection in some manner and degree with the proletarian movement in literature and with the Russian politics of world revolution, *Exile's Return* finally implies that the literary vocation must find its meaning in a consecration to Marxist principles. Yet the point may be made that the writer of the 1920s who took up the radical politics of the 1930s was not necessarily repudiating his inherited feeling for the literary life as a mixed realm of ideas and art. To eschew the man of letters as artist and to deny the religion of art in favor of a social vision of letters could be a way of recovering the humanistic amplitude of literature, of reasserting it as a far-ranging activity of mind and spirit that issues in a comprehensive moral criticism of man and his history. As a matter of fact, the recovery of the moral dominion of letters (as Cowley's 1923 code tends to demonstrate) was a more fundamental motive of the writer in the decade following the catastrophe of World War I than was the worship of art. As the 1929 crash and the subsequent depression deepened into economic crisis and threatened to become a civilizational debacle, it was entirely logical, if not quite inevitable, that the writer should seek to identify himself with his origin and continuity in the Great Critique—with the man of letters as philosophe. Nor did the writer have to be inclined toward political liberalism to do so. Allen Tate once likened the southern Agrarians to the French

Encyclopedists, which seems an unlikely comparison but is appropriate enough if one thinks in terms of the symbolism of the man of letters and the Third Realm. One might say that it was almost instinctive for literary intellectuals like Edmund Wilson and Cowley to fall under the spell of Karl Marx. Marx seemed to have brought politics and literature into a new relationship, greatly enhancing literature as a moral force in history. He seemed to have anticipated that the Third Realm—idealized by eighteenth-century publicists like Pierre Bayle, editor of *Nouvelles de la république des lettres*, as a classless cosmopolitan society of men of letters—would find its ultimate victory in history in a classless and stateless world. But by the later thirties the hopeful American literary liberals had begun to realize that Marxism as a political reality meant, not the connecting of politics to literature, but the direct assimilation of letters to the iron-fisted power embodied in the Stalinist state.

Cowley devotes only three chapters of his new book to the association between writers in the thirties and radical politics. In the fuller re-creation of that grey decade which he is now engaged in writing, he will no doubt deal at greater length with his perplexed reasons for adhering to the Stalinist line after Edmund Wilson and others had abandoned their dream of the Russian Revolution as the inauguration of a better state of man. In *The Writer's Trade*, he emphasizes how the complex politics of the later thirties appeared to present to him, as a liberal writer and editor (Cowley was literary editor of the *New Republic*), a pragmatic choice between Hitler and Stalin. Of course, the choice of Stalin was soon to be made by the United States as a whole, the politics of survival demanding that the enormity of the crimes against humanity committed by the Stalinist regime be ignored. But the man of letters in Cowley's position had another reason, I would think, for resisting the implication of Stalinism, one of a literary nature. This lay in the idealistic assumption, indeterminate yet vitalizing, that as "a free culture concerned with everything human" Marxism incarnated the moral polity of letters. To admit the degradation of Marxism in Stalinism implied the assimilation of letters by the state as the historical doom of the Great Critique and the Third Realm. And this was hardly all. The admission of such a fate for the literary realm carried a more intimate implication for the literary idealist: the suggestion of the inherent moral incapacity of men of letters to maintain among themselves a community of goodwill. In 1940, when Wilson charged Cowley with "giving hostages to the Stalinists in some terrible incomprehensible way," Cowley referred in one part of his reply to the hopelessness of a situation in which intellectuals, including Wilson, became "character assassins" and committed "symbolic murders." These, he said, "would be real murders if the intellectuals controlled the state apparatus," adding that maybe this "is part of the trouble in Russia."

Without intending to do so, Cowley conveys in *The Writer's Trade* the idea of a diminution of the man of letters and a depletion of the Third Realm in America since the 1930s. Emerging from the tone and temper of his history, the notion becomes most evident in the last chapter, "Rebels, Artists, and Scoundrels." This chapter moves curiously from a puzzled discussion of the "Love Generation" of the 1960s to a defense of the writer as artist. Observing that such writers as Joseph Heller and Thomas Pynchon belong to the 1950s and are not legitimate members of the Love Generation, Cowley concludes that the "actual leaders and spokesmen" in the sixties "were not men and women of letters." How are we to interpret the meaning of a generation that dreamed of "remaking the world and their own lives" but did not shape their dreams to any appreciable extent in any of the literary modes? Cowley does not make much of the Love Generation in definite evaluative terms; but in vaguely associating the 1960s with his vivid discussion of the "correlation between character and art" in the age of the Lost Generation, he apprehends, if only impressionistically, the novelty of the 1960s. For the first time in American history, a generational struggle to affect the moral course of the nation took place mostly outside the sensibility of literary order. Does the Love Generation—in its indifference to literary forms and its lack of feeling for literary ethics—testify to the complete assimilation of literature to politics?

It is misleading to suggest that Cowley's juxtaposition of the Love Generation and the Lost Generation is portentously pessimistic, when his inclination is forever to affirm a faith in the basic coherence and permanence of the literary mind and its works. But one cannot keep from observing that, in affirming the man of letters as artist at the end of his meditations on the literary life as he has known it for sixty years, Cowley has discarded the admonition in his early literary code against the fallacy of contraction. In his literary penta-logue of the 1970s, which centers in the fifth commandment of the old code, the man of letters as artist becomes the emblematic figure, not simply of the religion of art, but of the whole realm of modern letters. It is a dominion defined by a series of literary saints and martyrs: Flaubert, James, Mallarmé, Joyce, Thomas Mann, Proust, Hemingway, and Fitzgerald. "Art has its own hagiography and its Book of Martyrs," Cowley states. Positing a foil for the literary artist in the literary scoundrel, he declares that the two may be the same in their disregard of conventional morality, yet they show a narrow but profound difference in one respect. Unlike the scoundrel, an art-ist will never falsify himself in his art. The artist, like Hemingway, is obedient to the discipline of his vocation, to "decorum in the broad-est sense." Cowley speaks of Hemingway as living always with the feeling for life and death in taut tension. This was for Hemingway the condition and the imperative of decorum. His characters are symbols of decorum, or of the lack of it. But his style, striving ever to be in exact "harmony with the subject matter," is its pervasive symbol. The strict imposition of style on emotion—the palpable evocation of a landscape "remembered with a sense of precarious joy"—is in Hemingway a fulfillment of his own dictum: "A writer should be of as great probity and honesty as a priest of God." The dy-ing Proust, Cowley recalls, said this in another way. Dictating to his aged housekeeper at 3 A.M., he became unable to continue and broke off to pronounce a benediction on his own life and work: "I think what I've made you take down is very good. I shall stop now." Though Cowley once disdained the limits on the man of letters implied in the priestly image, he would in the 1970s seem to envision the sur-vival of the decorum of the Third Realm—of the discipline of good letters—as vested in the continuing power of the religion of art to shape the character of the writer. He sums up the precarious joy of his vision in an eloquently conclusive definition of the relation be-tween character and art: "No complete son-of-a-bitch ever wrote a good sentence." It is instructive to reflect how much the moral life of our culture may have depended on the symbolic distinction be-tween the literary saint and the literary scoundrel—on the fine difference between the near son-of-a-bitch and the perfect son-of-a-bitch—and on whether or not this ironic and essentially desperate symbol of our unstable propriety of mind and spirit now means anything at all.

9 / The Bard and
the Clerk

The literary connection between Donald Davidson and Allen Tate was remarkable not only for its duration, but also for its consistency and intensity, and for the depth of thought it provoked about literature and society. As revealed in their correspondence, theirs was a deeply experienced and indeed a covenanted relationship.[1] Now and again it suffered from marked disagreements and even lapsed into times of silence—and in fact did not endure in full mutuality of interests and aspirations for more than a third of its lengthy course—but it persisted until Davidson's death. Although the motive was no doubt an indestructible personal affection, it was more compellingly a sense of community that subsisted in a common all-absorbing vocation to literature.

In its underlying aspect, to be sure, the literary correspondence of Davidson and Tate constitutes a dialogue about the nature of the literary vocation in the past two centuries. It represents in this respect a significant contribution to the discussion of the crisis of the humanistic realm of letters. This crisis has been evident since it became clear in the last century that another realm, that of science, had erupted into history out of the realm of letters—and, moreover, that with its attendant technology this realm was the culminating expression of the long process of secularization that had begun in late medieval times and would, when the power it possessed was linked with that of the State, control history. It was at this point that a vivid sense of spiritual loss entailed in the decline of Chris-

---

1 *The Literary Correspondence of Donald Davidson and Allen Tate*, ed. John Tyree Fain and Thomas Daniel Young (Athens: University of Georgia Press, 1974).

tianity began distinctly to shape the modern literary vocation as a divinization of the secular word, with an accompanying elevation of the man of letters as secular priest. Recognized by every nineteenth-century writer of any depth who sought the motive of his career, the phenomenon of literary divinization was expressed symbolically and seldom became fully overt. One of the most direct attempts to set it forth may be seen in Thomas Carlyle's *On Heroes, Hero-Worship, and the Heroic in History*—in which, along with the hero as divinity, as prophet, and as king, we have the hero as poet and the hero as man of letters. It is possibly not so significant that Carlyle presents the grand geniuses of the creative imagination, Dante and Shakespeare, as "Saints of Poetry"—"really, if we will think it, *canonised*"—as that he finds an "unexpected" shape of the spiritual hero in the man of letters. The specific shapes that he appeals to are Johnson, Rousseau, and Burns, whom he considers to be "not heroic bringers of the light, but heroic seekers of it." Waiving the eccentricities and singularities of Carlyle's argument, we can see in his depiction of the "Man-of-Letters Hero" as "our most important modern person," the "soul of all" and teacher of the world, the burden of spiritual mission that the man of letters had begun self-consciously to assume by the middle of the nineteenth century or earlier. He does not necessarily assume the burden willingly or, for that matter, with a clear comprehension of what he is doing, but because men of letters, whether they know it fully or not, have become "the real working effective church of a modern country." Yet the organization of this church—the "Priesthood of the Writers of Books"—is not yet realized. Men of letters have an anomalous, a "disorganic," position in society; they may wander through it like an Ishmael, the literary life in modern society being at times "a wild welter of chaos." In this disorder, they seek to establish the rationale for the "organisation of the Literary Guild" that is yet to come: the teaching of belief to men who have become spiritual paralytics under his influence of the modern view that the world is a machine.

> But this I do say, and would wish all men to know and lay to heart, that he who discerns nothing but Mechanism in the Universe has in the fatalest way missed the secret of the Universe altogether. That all Godhood should vanish out of men's conception of this Universe seems to me precisely the most brutal error,—I will not disparage Heathenism by calling

it a Heathen error,—that men could fall into. It is not true; it is false at the very heart of it . . . One might call it the most lamentable of Delusions,—not forgetting Witchcraft itself! Witchcraft worshipped at least a living Devil; but this worships a dead iron Devil; no God, not even a Devil! —Whatsoever is noble, divine, inspired, drops thereby out of life. There remains everywhere in life a despicable *caput-mortuum*; the mechanical hull, all soul fled out of it. How can a man act heroically? [2]

He can act heroically by becoming a man of letters committed to changing the world view of modernity. "This must alter. Till this alter, nothing can beneficially alter." The view of the world as "instinct with Godhood, beautiful and awful, even as in the beginning of days" must be restored.

The relationship of Davidson and Tate hardly began in a conscious awareness of Carlyle's grand vision of men of letters as the priests of a restoration of an age of faith in the face of an age of science. Yet such a vision, it becomes clear as we read their letters, can be taken as the context of the inception of their literary correspondence and of its long continuance.

They originally discovered their personal literary community within the small provincial circle of the Fugitive acquaintance— within, that is, the group of young poets who read and criticized each other's poems for several years before 1922 and who, in that year, began publication of *The Fugitive*, a magazine of verse. A special communion between Davidson and Tate was established when Tate left Nashville in 1922. The two apprentices to poetry made an agreement to send their poems and accompanying criticism to one another. After the exchange had continued for something less than two years, Davidson's *An Outland Piper* was published by Houghton Mifflin. Tate looked upon this event both as tangible ratification of the value of their literary compact and as a revelation of its true significance: its implication of a spiritual community set against an alien world.

In the end it did not come to quite the same thing—this idealized community of alienation. It never came to quite the same thing. It is difficult to make a precise analysis of the root of it, but there was always a difference—a difference of temperament and personality,

---

2 *On Heroes, Hero-Worship, and the Heroic in History*, in *Works of Thomas Carlyle* (30 vols.; London: Chapman and Hall, 1897–99), V, 173.

subsisting in part in a difference in family history and in personal experience, and resulting in a difference of outlook upon and approach to the meaning of the literary vocation. We see the hint of the difference in a letter by Tate of March 14, 1924. Tate refers to Davidson's conception of their mutual devotion to poetry as "the life of adventure" and glosses this with the remark that it is the life of adventure because "it is the life of the soul"—"the life of the soul despite the incidental frustrations we meet and the merely human foibles we display and the temporary misunderstandings of the flesh we may suffer." Tate exclaims to his friend, "to your bow of burning gold I bring, in my meager way, what arrows of desire I can make for us in the momentary cessations of clamor in the physical world." This is of course the self-consciously literary, the heady stuff of a youthful literary idealist, but it is not to be dismissed. In his response to the publication of *An Outland Piper* as "a kind of event of the spirit, a culmination of an adventure beyond the accidents of everyday life," Tate recognized, if not altogether explicitly, an impulse in his own vision of the life in poetry that his friend did not entirely share: the poem conceived both as a symbolic expression of the dualism of the material and the spiritual and as an emblem of a transcendent alienation from the material world. Davidson, conceiving literature as the life of adventure, always tended to identify literary expression as the engagement of perception with the temporal and the mundane; he did not basically think of writing a poem as an act symbolic of the mind's capacity for transcendence. Tate tended always to do so. Although Tate might feel that he and Davidson were "approaching a common ground of principles, of which the fundamental one is that poetry must be the expression of a whole mind, not . . . a report of sensation, . . . a resolution of sensation through all the faculties of the mind," his emphasis on the subjectivity of the experience of wholeness opposes the essentially objective nature of the experience Davidson sought.

> I believe [Tate contends] that every person has a thought rhythm peculiar to himself, and this thought rhythm is identical with his special attitude to the world; hence a good poet is one who contrives an accurate symbolism for this special attitude. Nobody ever says anything about an external world; there are as many external worlds as there are persons (one is

tempted to add that therefore there is no external world at all that we can know); all that we are trying to do is to articulate the movement of thought, as if it were some vast snake which we must put together synthetically before we can look at the marvellous beauty and rhythm of the whole. The phrase, "poets are masters of life," only means that poets approach complete self-consciousness as a mathematical limit; they aren't mastering life, they are mastering themselves in the sense of understanding themselves.[3]

Needless to say, such an attitude represents no more than an aspect of the struggle on Tate's part to establish a theory or rationale of the task of the poet. Seeking to find the reason for being a poet, Tate moved toward an acceptance of the "dissociation of sensibility" as a dominant, controlling, and irredeemable fact of modern culture. Or at least this seems to have been his direction as Davidson saw it in 1927, when he tells Tate that he admires his recent poetic performance but does so without passion. Davidson explains:

> I think the reason is this. Your poetry, like your criticism, is so astringent that it bites and dissolves what it touches. You have decided that the opposite sort of poetry (say, an *expansive* poetry) can no longer be written in an age where everything is in a terrible condition. But this attitude does not merely lie behind your poetry; it gets *into* it, not in the form of poetry but of aesthetics, so that poem after poem of yours becomes aesthetic dissertations as much as poetry. Wherever your poetry is out-and-out argumentative . . . I follow you all the way and am nearly ready to say you are at your best; when you deal with *things themselves*, the things become a ruin and crackle like broken shards under your feet.[4]

Davidson applies this observation in particular to Tate's newly composed "Ode to the Confederate Dead," a poem which, he says, in effect argues that no poem can be written on a subject such as the commemoration of the valiant dead. Davidson admires the beautiful execution of the "Ode" and its "cold beauty." But, he asks, "where, O Allen Tate, are the dead? You have buried them completely out of sight—with them yourself and me. God help us, I must say. You keep on whittling your art to a finer point, but are you also not whittling yourself. What is going to happen if the only poetry you can al-

3 *Correspondence of Davidson and Tate*, 143.
4 *Ibid.*, 186.

low your conscience to approve is a poetry of argument and despair. Fine such poetry may be, but is it not a Pyrrhic victory?" In Davidson's view, Tate had defected from the great cause of poetry in modern times. Tate had violated their covenant: "I do not see how you think the battle between poetry and science can be won in such ways as you use, for do you not strive for and attain a rigidity as inflexible as the rigidity of science?"

Tate's reply to Davidson's cogent challenge to the "Ode to the Confederate Dead" is equally noteworthy. On the question of the possibility in modern times of an "expansive poetry" (a reference to poetry in the heroic or epic mode), Tate observes that Keats did not bring off either of his attempts at "Hyperion." In abandoning the second one, he showed the "whole fallacy of injecting 18th century philosophy into poetry, to take the place of myth." Tate adds significantly: "As for your [Davidson's] poems, I don't mean that the material is irrecoverable in the spatio-temporal sense; but that it is epistemologically—if this gets across." In other words, Davidson's endeavor in his own poetry to use the matter of the South as a means of conveying what Tate refers to in the "Ode" as "knowledge carried to the heart" cannot be considered wholly efficacious. The apprehension of this knowledge must be indirect. "Ode to the Confederate Dead"—ironically an ode about the impossibility of writing such an ode, but at the same time "an attack on those [*i.e.*, the Victorian poets] who, some years ago, removed the theme from the sphere of actuality"—dramatizes, Tate points out, a quarrel within his own mind, or by extension, within the modern consciousness. But in this quarrel no issue is joined. It is dialectical. Tate does not see his "Ode" as failing to project the battle between science and poetry. "There is no battle. . . . Art is just as rigid as science."

Nonetheless, Tate shared with Davidson a vision of reestablishing in modern fragmented scientific and industrial society a sense of the value of cultural wholeness. As he affirmed the loss of the heroic in poetry, he was on the verge of joining Davidson (together with John Crowe Ransom, Andrew Lytle, and Robert Penn Warren) in an active engagement with modernity. This would take the form of a heroic attempt at an inquiry into the epistemological meaning of the South and of an attempted recovery of the limits and validity of the historical and mythic South as the ground of, the source of, a unified sensibility—of "a knowledge carried to the heart." Tate had gone through a period in which he had paradoxically been sustained by a faith in art as a futile but necessary opposition to modernity, necessary if only as a personal redemption. He had more or less lost faith in the ideal of a community of alienation, but he had not, as Davidson feared, succumbed to solipsism. Instead, he had been seeking a way to make an effective critique of the subjectivity of modernism. In "Ode to the Confederate Dead," he had found the way. The South understood as a traditional society afforded a symbolic reference of a world in which intellect and emotion are harmonized.

In spite of his very active involvement in the publication of *I'll Take My Stand* and in the Agrarian movement, Tate's approach to the meaning of the South remained symbolic in nature and relatively detached. Much influenced by T. S. Eliot, whom he considered to be the greatest contemporary literary intelligence, Tate, as Eliot does in "Tradition and the Individual Talent" and "The Function of Criticism," saw the meaning of tradition from a broad civilizational perspective. Tate's commitment to the South was that of the cosmopolitan poet and critic. It was his cosmopolitan intellectualism that urged him toward the formation of an "academy of Southern positive reactionaries"—an academy that would embrace the discipline and organization of a total movement and "create an intellectual situation interior to the South." This situation would be based philosophically less on "the actual old South than upon its prototype— the historical and religious scheme of Europe." Tate declares, "We must be the last Europeans—there being no Europeans in Europe at present." If Tate's assimilation of the history of the South to European history is mingled with an apparent southern literalism, this should not be misinterpreted. He compares the Agrarian movement to "another and greater Southern movement," the Confederacy, which "foundered on the indiscipline of ideas." And he states flatly, "The Montgomery convention lost us the war." If this is a declaration of a neo-Confederate nationalism, it is as much or more an ironic metaphorical statement about the failure of the Old South to achieve a detached perspective on the logic of its position.

Tate's inclination to direct his engagement with modernity with a cosmopolitan intellectual austerity is to be seen in another instance, this in his reservations about Davidson's censure of Hemingway's writings as examples of "scientific ministration." Hemingway, Tate observes, "has that sense of a stable world, of a total sufficiency of character, which we miss in modern life"; and he possesses this "even though he has no historical scene to fall back on." If he "were a Southerner he would be just the novelist we are looking for—he would present us without any thesis at all. In other words, the ideal Southern novelist is the ideal novelist anywhere—I don't mean that Hemingway is the ideal novelist, only that he is nigh perfect in his own job—and ultimately there is no difference, for literature, between one thesis and another, in the sociological sense." Tate asserts that the Agrarian critics must be disinterested in literary judgments. In dealing adversely with any novelists, "we must attack them first as artists, and then show that their social attitude, because it is muddled, distracts the creative mind into mere propaganda and ruins the work of art." Tate concludes: "This could almost be made into a principle—that all great, or really good writers, must have a simple homogeneous sense of values, which incidentally are the kind of values we wish to restore." But Tate's dialectical imagination is not truly committed to seeking a restoration of a world established on a "simple homogeneous sense of values," save as the restored image of such a world (as presumably Hemingway's depiction of an ancient Spanish village like Burguete) would serve as an emblem of an integration of mind and heart, rebuking the dissociation of sensibility.

Up to a point, Davidson was willing to accept Tate's cosmopolitan perspective on literature and society. He allowed Tate to correct his disposition to assume a narrower view, taking to heart Tate's admonitions about Hemingway and "what you say about literary judgments in general, as not to be made from a sectional basis, but on the higher level." Davidson confesses, "I've felt for quite a while that I was in danger of losing balance and becoming merely a cantankerous localist, and your admonishment warms my conscience to its task." But Davidson drove toward a more absolute base of order than Tate envisioned—and this despite the fact that Tate turned at length to the authority of the Roman Catholic faith. The turning was a logical culmination of a quest for order conducted on the premise that the preservation of the ecumenical classical-Christian Western civilization is the proper goal of the man of letters. The mission to redeem Western ecumenicalism was not a premise of Davidson's thought. His cultural vision was precosmopolitan; his mind harked back, we might say, to the time before the Stoics set forth the idea of a transcendent polity of mind. Davidson, Louise Cowan points out in her brilliant essay on his career, "conceives that the tradition exists among members of a society, who have a real, though spiritual, bond and a cumulative and undying history which they—and their ancestors—have created."[5] Sharing in this continuity is made possible "by communion and pietas," not by "retrospection" or by "a mere program of wide reading." In "Why the Modern South Has a Great Literature," Davidson terms a traditional society one "that is stable, religious, more rural than urban, and politically conservative." But it must be more than the sum of these elements: it must be rooted in "family, blood-kinship, clanship, folk-ways, custom, community." The South, Davidson believed unrelentingly, represented such a society not only in historical actuality, but also in a present actuality that was integrally a part of the past reality. He believed, too, that the actuality could be preserved.

In a famous passage (in "The Profession of Letters in the South") explaining the literary achievement of the modern South, Tate says it was made possible by "a curious burst of intelligence" that occurs when a traditional culture and a modern culture come into conflict. But the burst of intelligence does not last and cannot be extended beyond the inevitable passing of the old ways. Commenting on "Why the Modern South Has a Great Literature," Davidson recognizes the same motive in the South's twentieth-century literary demonstration, but he is unresigned to the loss of the traditional society. He implies, on the contrary, that the process need not remain "unchecked" if the southern writer will follow what he knows in his bones as much as in his brain. The literary defense of tradition, Davidson always held, has been inadequate or misguided. Poets and critics—men of letters—have allowed the epic and ballad, the drama,

5 "Donald Davidson: 'The Long Street'," in *Reality and Myth: Essays in American Literature*, ed. William E. Walker and Robert S. Welker (Nashville: Vanderbilt University Press, 1964), 101.

and the lyric poem allied to music to disappear. From Baudelaire t
Tate, they have compromised with or yielded to the enticing but de
ceptive subtleties of modernism, allowing the dictates of the literar
intellect to corrupt or abolish the basis of expression in the modes c
oral narration and song. Davidson had a certain empathy for a kin
of bedrock paganism. He had a conception of the sensibility unifie
in a preprint, even a preliterate, prehistorical age—in a culture exist
ing in and through an organic traditional consciousness, as oppose
to an articulated historical consciousness; in a community forme
long before the differentiation of the realms of State, Church, an
Letters. This vision, if never fully developed, and forever in conflic
with his wide learning and his role as a member of the academic pol
ity of letters, constantly underlay the activity of Davidson's mind
It accounts, among other things, for his obduracy in promoting Agrar
ianism as a highly tangible cause. The passion of Davidson's advocac
puzzled Tate, who sensed it before *I'll Take My Stand* was publishe

> There is one feature of our movement that calls for comment. We are no
> in the least divided, but we exhibit two sorts of minds. You and Andrev
> seem to constitute one sort—the belief in the eventual success, in th
> practical sense, of the movement. The other mind is that of Ransom an
> myself. I gather that Ransom agrees with me that the issue on the plan
> of action is uncertain. At least I am wholly skeptical on that point; bu
> the skepticism is one of hoping to be convinced, not by standing aside t
> watch the spectacle, but by exerting myself. In other words, I believ
> there is enough value to satisfy me in the affirmation, in all its conse
> quences, including action, of value. If other goods proceed from that, al
> the better. My position is that since I see the value, I am morally obli
> gated to affirm it.[6]

After the active Agrarian days were over, Tate was vexed by Da
vidson's conviction that the Agrarian group had failed to accomplis
anything.

6 *Correspondence of Davidson and Tate*, 241. Judged by the dispute over the title of
the Agrarian symposium, which developed at the last moment before its publica
tion, the division appears to have been Tate, Lytle, and Warren as opposed to
Davidson and Ransom. The problem that Tate saw was the failure to "appeal
through the title to ideas." The title *I'll Take My Stand* left the authors of the sym
posium open to the charge of advocating a literal agrarianism, Tate says, and af
forded critics an opportunity to ridicule poets and intellectuals for pretending to
be farmers.

You evidently believe [he wrote to Davidson in 1942] that agrarianism was a failure; I think it was and *is* a very great success; but then I never expected it to have any political influence. It is a reaffirmation of the humane tradition, and to reaffirm that is an end in itself. Never fear: we shall be remembered when our snipers are forgotten. I have had a certain disagreement with you from the beginning; you have always seemed to hold to a kind of mystical secularism, which has made you impatient and angry at the lack of results. We live in a bad age in which we cannot do our best; but no age is good.[7]

Tate's assertion of a distinction in the Agrarian impulse between reaffirming the humane tradition and a "mystical secularism" directed toward specific political results suggests that he had comprehended in his friend's motive as an Agrarian something approaching a will to control history. Davidson would, he felt, ironically effect a reversal of the secularization of history by virtue of a special and absolute knowledge of the truth of the South. This knowledge, as much as the knowledge claimed by the advocates of Progress, brooked no doubt of its efficacy. Tate did not draw implications so drastic as these perhaps; but the term "mystical secularism" may well bear the import of an almost Manichaean version of history, and there is surely some justification for glimpsing in Davidson's mind the drama of a struggle between the forces of light (an organic Agrarian society of the South) and the forces of darkness (a dehumanized industrial society of the North). The drama took a poignant personal turn in 1945 when Ransom published in the *Kenyon Review* a renunciation or his Agrarian commitment, deeming it to have been an act of nostalgia.[8] Davidson took Ransom's commentary on Agrarianism as an act of surrender to the enemy, if not of downright defection. "Anybody can now observe that Ransom of the North talks differently, if not oppositely from Ransom of the South; and can also see that Ransom of the North has put himself on the side of the strongest battalions. What next?"[9]

The correspondence does not show what came immediately afterward. But a few years later Tate expressed his agreement with an-

7 *Correspondence of Davidson and Tate*, 328–29.
8 See "Art and the Human Economy," *Kenyon Review*, VII (Autumn, 1945), 683–88.
9 *Correspondence of Davidson and Tate*, 345.

other criticism of Agrarianism by Ransom. He "alluded to our old views of the late twenties," Tate explains to Davidson, "when we were rebelling against modernism, and pointed out that we never got much further than Nostalgia because no historic faith came into consideration. I think there's a great deal in that. We were trying to find a religion in the secular, historical experience as such, particularly in the Old South. I would now go further than John and say we were idolaters. But it is better to be an idolater than to worship nothing, and as far as our old religion went I still believe in it."[10] Tate's identification of Agrarianism as a divinization of secular history may be understood as a clarification of what Tate had meant two years earlier when he had referred to Davidson's "mystical secularism." Tate was able to make it, we can surmise, because he had himself now embraced Catholicism and could see more clearly the phenomenon of the divinization of the literary mind and the attendant desperate alienation that men of letters undergo when they engage in the futile struggle to alter temporal history so that the Godhead may be restored. A differentiation between temporal history and supratemporal history became the basis of Tate's vision of the man of letters in "The Man of Letters in the Modern World" (1952). Men of letters have, he says, constituted a cult, an idolatry, "like the *parvenu* gods" of "decaying Rome." But their function has not been entirely impaired. Culture is dependent on the "use of the letter . . . [,] in the long run our one indispensable test of the actuality of our experience." The man of letters has the "power of discrimination"— the power to choose between language that expresses reality and language that dooms men to a mechanical version of reality. The man of letters is primary in keeping open the possibility of man's apprehension of the truth of his destiny beyond time.

If Davidson replied to Tate's letter about the Agrarian idolatry, the reply is not recorded in the published correspondence. The implication in Tate's letter is more drastic than in Ransom's statements about Agrarian nostalgia, for Tate suggests that the Agrarian perception was blocked off from actuality by its confusion of profane and sacred history. But, it may be assumed, Davidson did not

10 *Ibid.*, 370.

grasp this suggestion with certainty. He saw no confusion in Agrarianism, his conception of actuality not truly including its dual nature in the temporal and metaphysical dimensions of existence. Davidson's conception of the mission of the literary vocation remained nontranscendent. In fact, by the time he wrote "A Mirror for Artists," his contribution to the Agrarian symposium, Davidson had taken his stand on the function of the poet as critic. In order to survive in an industrial age, the poet may retire "more deeply within the body of tradition to some point where he can utter himself with the greatest consciousness of his dignity as an artist. He is like a weaponless warrior who plucks a sword from the tomb of an ancient hero." But Davidson does not see the plucking of the sword as a secret, merely aesthetic gesture. He indicates that, as a critic of society, the poet may come forth into "the common arena, assuming the guise of a 'citizen.'" He may become a farmer or he may run for Congress, but he must take a stand "against the industrial devourer—a stand that might prove to be a turning point." A warrior-bard concealed in a Congressman—the image is not preposterous if we accept Davidson's view of reality. He wanted to join literature and politics, to create a viable southern resistance movement against industrialism, and to take action. History can be changed, if the true source of the South's history in the ancient heroic society is understood.

In the first part of "The Man of Letters in the Modern World," Tate says: "While the politician, in his cynical innocence uses society, the man of letters disdainfully, or perhaps absentmindedly withdraws from it: a withdrawal that few persons any longer observe, since withdrawal has become the social convention of the literary man, in which society insofar as it is aware of him, expects him to conduct himself." He is suggesting, Tate says, "the melancholy portrait" of himself. He concludes his analysis of the man of letters, as has been indicated, by describing the capacity of the man of letters to keep open the knowledge of redeeming transcendence inherent in the discriminating use of the letter. This is his ultimate and only true function.

In his literary correspondence with Donald Davidson, and in his writings generally, Allen Tate's vision of the modern Priesthood of the Writers of Books derives from his major literary inheritance: the spiritual cosmopolitanism—the high culture—of Western Civilization. Tate aspired to emulate the moral and aesthetic heroism of the great poets and clerks, from Dante to Eliot. This is the tradition of the literary vocation that we respond to most readily, for it is the one we are most familiar with. Still, the sense of the vocation of the heroic bard is not entirely lost to us. Davidson's struggle to recover it and to define for America a conception of the man of letters as bard demands our attention. Carlyle had intimated the importance of such a conception in his assessment of the various types of the man of letters by acknowledging the significance of Robert Burns. He was, Carlyle says, "a piece of the right Saxon stuff: strong as the Harz-rock, rooted in the depths of the world;—rock, yet with wells of living softness in it."

10 / The Legend of the Artist

> Who shall unriddle the puzzle of
> the artist's nature?
>
> —Thomas Mann

aulkner is not only the major writer of the South; he is an embodiment of the legend of the modern literary artist. My concern is with the inception and early development of this representation—with, as I shall call it, Faulkner's literary novitiate.
Marked by his search into the mystery of the identity of the writer,
this period of his career can be traced in certain figurations of the literary artist that appear in his work from *The Marble Faun* through
The Sound and the Fury. At first, Faulkner sought the identity of the
artist—to be sure, of himself—as though this belonged to the mythic
consciousness of existence. Eventually he discovered the identity of
the writer to be implicit in his consciousness of the modern self-
consciousness of history.

No doubt a systematic, comprehensive treatment of the subject
that I suggest is much to be desired. I offer a few reflections on it, beginning with some remarks on the evolution of the literary priesthood.

In his essay on *Don Quixote,* Thomas Mann draws a contrast between the healthy ego of Cervantes, an artist whose creativity in-
hered in the feudal corporateness, and the melancholy ego of the
modern writer, whose creativity flaps wanly about like an ailing
eagle in the abstract freedom of bourgeois culture.[1] But ironically, in
his admonition to us about the diseased and rootless ego of the literary artist, Mann is talking about himself as much as about anyone
else. Still more ironically, in establishing Cervantes as a model of

1 "Voyage with Don Quixote," in *Essays by Thomas Mann* (New York: Vintage
Books, 1957), 325–69.

the artist rooted in a traditionalist Christian society, he is wish-
fully misinterpreting the actual situation. Cervantes, like Shakespeare, is an anticipation of the artist as "ailing eagle." He creates in
Don Quixote, as Shakespeare did in Hamlet, the figure of a displaced
poet trying to find his way in a time that has become disjointed. He
lived in the age when, under the dispensation of modern history and
science, the Christian polity began to fall into irremediable disrepair; when a culture of icon, ritual, and hierarchy became subject to
the literalism of the Reformation (and to the even more destructive
literalism of the Counter-Reformation); when the powerful tendency
of Christianity to become a secular movement—to assume the secular design of a gnostic Puritanism—began to overcome a static,
cosmopolitan Christendom.

In the ensuing fragmentation of the cosmopolitan tradition, which
had been rooted in the Christian assimilation of the pagan cultures,
the poet's nostalgia for the world in which art was part of a unified
community urged the preservation of the supranationalism of the
old time. In the struggle to do so, the poet (I use the term in its wid-
est application) of great talent or genius began to lose his association
with cosmopolitan mind and to become identified with mind as
world-historical. The poet became a creature of history and yet assumed a responsibility for history. It was a lonely state to be in, and
one in which he must constantly define and redefine his vocation or,
as it came to be ever so curiously put, his function.

In his essay on *Don Quixote*, we see Thomas Mann adding another
small bit to the story he was, either overtly or by implication, engaged in writing—and not less in living—throughout his career: his
version of the legend of the literary artist. In such an engagement—
marked by confusions, contradictions, ambiguities—he was doing
nothing singular. He obeyed an imperative of the writer for perhaps
the last four hundred years, one greatly intensified in the last two
hundred: namely, the writer's personal responsibility for determining the meaning of the literary vocation. Typically a modern literary
career begins and ends in a quest for its meaning. It is as if the writer
is always trying to give birth to himself. This situation—foreshadowed in Dante and Petrarch, made plain in Shakespeare and Cervantes, and stated in Donne, Pope, and Johnson—is written large in

writers from Rousseau and Goethe to Hemingway and Faulkner. If the burden of self-creation falls on the painter and the sculptor, it bears more heavily on the literary artist; for the Western literary artist inescapably feels that he is involved in the essence of the civilization of which he is a part. This is a civilization founded historically on verbalization—on the spoken and written word: on rhetoric and grammar, on the use of the word and the discipline of the letter. The literary artist is inextricably attached to the expression and meaning of the word in the whole culture, even when the wholeness has been fragmented. If the art of the word fails, the poet fails; if the poet fails, the art of the word fails. In either case, the poet believes, the civilization fails. Believing that the relation between poetry and civilization is indivisible, the writer feels a solemnity in his vocation. That in his quest to fulfill it he sometimes yields to neurosis is not surprising.

And yet, for all the solemn sense of singularity he may experience, the writer knows that creativity only seems to be ingenerate in the self and that no artist, whatever his innate talent, truly begets himself. In his lonely search for meaning, he eventually discovers his affiliation with the modern community of those who are alienated in the word. In my remarks on Donald Davidson and Allen Tate, I have pointed out that Carlyle calls this the modern Church, or the Priesthood of the Writers of Books; Blake, and later Joyce, refer to it as the "priesthood of the eternal imagination." Embodying what Thomas Mann called the "unalienable cultural Christianity of the Western world," this realm functioned in the Renaissance as the world center of the Christian and classical (or pagan) dialectic concerning the nature and order of being. In the century of the Enlightenment, Peter Gay says, the philosophes transformed this dialectic into a "struggle for autonomy." Attempting "to assimilate the two pasts they had inherited—Christian and pagan"—they thought that in pitting "them against one another," they would "secure their independence" and attain to "criticism and power." Gay sees the "philosophes' rebellion succeeding in both of its aims: theirs was a paganism directed against their Christian inheritance and dependent upon the paganism of classical antiquity, but it was also a *modern* paganism, emancipated from classical thought as much as from

Christian dogma. The ancients taught the philosophes the use of criticism, but it was modern philosophers who taught them the possibilities of power."[2]

The emancipation of a modern paganism resulted in a world in which all the gods of myth and tradition, classical and Christian, are, as Hume says, silent; and the silence is filled with the voices of Hegel and Marx proclaiming a counterrevelation: man's self-interpreted vision of world history. A condition of mind occurred in which man, employing a never-ceasing critical investigation of his physical and societal environment, postulated himself as the master of existence. But the result of man's control of history—the assumed fruition of the great rationalist assimilation of knowledge—was a specialization of mental function and a mechanization of thought and morals. Romanticism and symbolism renewed the pagan and Christian dialectic, directed by the inspiriting motive, in an increasingly anomalous struggle to penetrate the mystery of being, of discovering a new mode of revelation—at the least of asserting the mystery of consciousness against, as Peter Gay defines it, the modern paganism of rationality.

In its resurgence, the pagan-Christian dialectic—involving the pre-Enlightenment paganism, the modern paganism, and Christianity—assumed at once a more varied, a more complex, and a more subjective character. Nothing in the manifestation is more apparent or more striking than the fulfillment of a tendency evident as far back as Petrarch: the conferring on secular literature of the status of the Holy Word. This phenomenon was accompanied by the opening of the priesthood of the imagination, not only to those writers who were prophets and revealers, like Blake, but to those who were, like the symbolist poets in France, radical experimenters with words and fabricators of a new literary language. Literary seers and craftsmen together made an irregular spiritual government, a polity of the literary mind, dedicated, we may say, to creating out of the diverse contents of the cultural dialectic an irregular myth of creativity, a myth of the artist's self-interpretation and self-fulfillment. This myth has many aspects, but everywhere we turn in modern writings, from

2 *The Enlightenment: An Interpretation. The Rise of Modern Paganism* (New York: Vintage Books, 1968), xi.

Wordsworth's "Intimations of Immortality" to Eliot's *The Waste Land*, we find it implied in its multiple complexities. Founded in subjectivity and emotionality, it is perhaps best described in broad terms as an imperative mode of the artist's imagination of self. If the community of literary artists had a supranational character, it was conferred by a supranational underground of the literary mind that bore the aspect of a precarious order of world-historical neurotics. I do not speak disparagingly; the literary priesthood was no place for spiritual sissies. Admission to this order was not by vote of an academy and assuredly not by acknowledgment of the public, but by self-admission, following a self-imposed novitiate in which the writer strained to satisfy himself as to the authenticity of his calling by a self-interpretation of, as Hemingway would have said, how "good" he is. If the priesthood of the imagination has fallen away with the last of its great exemplars—Mann, Yeats, Eliot, Joyce—its primary authority was everywhere still obvious before modernity came to an end with World War II.

The modern literary priesthood undoubtedly exercised its power most intimately over aspirants to literary careers when they were tangibly in touch with it, nowhere more so than in Paris. But in the age of printing, the omnipresence of the Book and the Periodical has been determinative. When a young mind of potential literary genius encounters enough books and magazines, he may, without experiencing its tangible embodiment, recognize his true homeland in the Republic of Letters. William Faulkner appears quite early to have done so. By the time he returned from Canada following his service in the Royal Air Force during World War I (he was twenty years of age), he had, like the young Hemingway, conferred upon himself the status of a novice in the priesthood of the imagination and indeed had envisioned a place for himself in the inner circle of the modern literary order. This can be said despite Faulkner's contention in 1925, when he had entered upon the advanced stage of his novitiate, that his first verse was only to aid in "various philanderings" and to make the "youthful gesture . . . of being 'different' in a small town."[3] His difference from the townspeople, as he knew, was real.

3 Joseph Blotner, *Faulkner: A Biography* (2 vols.; New York: Random House, 1974), I, 422.

186 The Brazen Face of History

I say all this advisedly, of course. I do not wish to distinguish unduly between the somewhat mystical concept of "novitiate" and the rather more mundane one of "apprenticeship." As Richard P. Adams, James B. Meriwether, Joseph Blotner, and others have so well demonstrated, Faulkner served a very deliberate and professional apprenticeship. Assessing his capacities in the light of his earliest writing experience, and regretfully abandoning verse for prose fiction, he determined upon not just being, but learning how to be, a storyteller. Yet serving his apprenticeship (self-imposed, although emulative of the craftsmen available to him through reading and, in a limited degree, in person) he served a novitiate in the essentially spiritual order of minds formed by the divinization of secular literature in the nineteenth century. Young Faulkner deliberately set out to discover and to articulate the legend of the modern literary artist—to make his own version of the myth of self-creativity. He intended to create a legend of himself as a priest of the imagination.

If we had an orderly record of Faulkner's disorderly, yet purposeful, wide-ranging reading, his exploration of the cultural dialectic might be traced systematically. The fact is that we hardly need to have the list of books he read, since the drama of his imagination may be deduced with considerable certainty from his writings. It was shaped by his involvement in one prominent aspect of the myth of creativity, the myth of the Great God Pan.

In her meticulous study entitled *Pan: The Goat God*, Patricia Merivale offers an illuminating inquiry into the main facets of the myth of Pan in modern times, especially in the English and American literatures of the past two centuries (in which, for reasons that are not very clear, Pan has been most active.)[4] Although Professor Merivale includes no more than two or three passing references to Faulkner, her elucidation of Pan's appearance in the romantic and Victorian periods and on into the twentieth century provides us with a sizable context for the development of Faulkner's imagination. Of the greatest importance, I would think, is the description in *Pan: The Goat God* of a special phase within what I have referred to as the

4 *Pan the Goat-God: His Myth in Modern Times* (Cambridge, Mass.: Harvard University Press, 1969).

modern cultural dialectic. This is a Pan-Christ dialectic.

The ultimate source of the Pan-Christ argument may be an incident recorded in Plutarch's *Moralia*. During the reign of Tiberius Caesar, legend holds, a voice was heard announcing the death of the Great Pan. This mysterious incident was given such intriguing interpretations—including that by the fourth-century Christian scholar Eusebius, who linked Pan's death with Christ's purgation of demons from human existence—that nearly two centuries later it is still known. Identified with Christ, Pan was blended with the Christian God in the concept of a universal lordship. Of the various versions of Pan's fate upon the coming of Christ—whether he was transformed into a demon or made coequal with Christ—nineteenth-century literature stressed the first. One of Elizabeth Barrett Browning's worst but most popular poems, "Pan Is Dead," celebrates the victory of Christianity over the pagan gods. Employing Pan as a summary symbol, Mrs. Browning condemns all pagan myths in the light of Christianity. Despite its popularity, this condemnation of pagan mythology, bearing comparison with the defense of Christian supernaturalism by Chauteaubriand, represents a minority attitude. The dominant poetic attitude in Mrs. Browning's day stressed an equation between Christianity and the repressions of the industrial age. Heine spoke for many nineteenth-century poets when he said "that the gloomy workaday mood of the modern Puritans spreads itself over all Europe like a gray twilight," making a connection between the Reformation culture and the rise of the industrial-technological age. This theme is the connection implicit in Theophile Gautier's vision in 1852 of the yielding of "Jupiter to the Nazarean":

> A voice says: Pan is dead!—The shadow
> Stretches out.—As if on a black sheet
> Upon immense and gloomy sadness
> The white skeleton becomes visible.

A more complex, and on the whole more important, representation in the nineteenth-century poetic mind of a Pan-Christ confrontation is found in Robert Browning's "The Bishop Orders His Tomb at St. Praxed's Church" (1845). The Bishop exclaims:

> Those Pans and Nymphs ye wot of, and perchance
> Some tripod, thyrsus, with a vase or so,

> The Saviour at his sermon on the mount,
> St. Praxed in a glory, and one Pan
> Ready to twitch the Nymph's last garment off,
> And Moses with the tables.

Underlying Browning's ironic assimilation of the sacred and profane in this poem, Patricia Merivale says, is the remarkable feeling of the poet for the psychological equilibrium of Pan as both goat and god.[5] The Bishop's mind as he specifies the details of his tomb is poised on this equilibrium. This observation can be extended. Browning's sense of poetic values is significantly focused on the basic meaning of the Pan-Christ argument: the restoration of the sexuality of art. The satyrs, nymphs, and fauns ranging through the nineteenth-century imagination—often being affronts to Christian values, as Mrs. Browning saw—belong to the impulse to rediscover through artistic vision the mythical basis of culture in the biology of male and female, and the variations thereof. The same crisis of meaning in the Christian conception of history that called for the elevation of Christ over Pan in the legend of Pan and Christ, we may reflect, provoked the appearance of historical minds like Nietzsche and Freud.

Once the sexuality of art began to be comprehended in a wider perspective, that of a sexuality of history, the Pan-Christ dialectic receded in poetry. But it found continuing expression in the more broadly social medium of modern times, prose fiction, its most vivid expositor being D. H. Lawrence. In his later career, Lawrence became associated with a startlingly literal identification between the Pan-Christ pairing and the nature of the artist. In fact, a painting by Dorothy Brett portrays Lawrence as both Pan and Christ on the Cross. Seated on a rock, Pan's usual resting place, the bearded Lawrence as Pan, his hoofed hands upraised, is looking at the bearded Lawrence as Christ hanging on the Cross. What is even more intriguing is that Lawrence himself painted a similar picture.[6] At this stage, the Pan-Christ situation reaches an absurd yet profound impasse. The literary artist as both the pagan goat god and the crucified virgin God

---

5 See *ibid.*, 1–16, for a discussion of the origins of the Pan myth; 77–133 for a discussion of Pan in mid-nineteenth-century writings. The translation of Gautier's poem is on p. 107; Browning's poem is quoted on p. 86.
6 See *ibid.*, Illustration No. 15, following p. 144. Also, see 195–219.

represents the ultimate mystery of the literary artist; yet within the representation there is an unresolved, and unresolvable, tension. The rebellion in art against a rationalistic modernity cannot reconcile its divided sources: a vision of man's destiny rooted in a cosmic mythology and yet attached to the Christian historical revelation.

The modern fractured myth of creativity is implicit in the early stage of Faulkner's literary novitiate, notably in *The Marble Faun*, *The Marionettes* (a one-act play), and various sketches and short stories. A pastoral poem in structure, *The Marble Faun* is more ambitious than has ordinarily been recognized. A parallel to, possibly an anticipation of Eliot's *The Waste Land* (some of the individual poems in Faulkner's first book were written before 1920, although the book was not published until 1924), *The Marble Faun* is based on nothing less than an intention to express the modern cultural dialectic. It attains a considerable complexity of meaning. The faun, a creature of Pan and a figure of the modern poet, speaks out of his imprisonment in a work of art, a statue of a faun set in a formal garden. Of indeterminate location, the garden represents the lapsarian garden of modernity, in which, significantly, "that quick keen snake / Is free to come and go," but the faun is forever "marble-bound." His bondage is subtly related to the freedom of the snake, inasmuch as the faun imagines himself gliding "like a snake" to peer into a glade where Pan sits on a rock brooding beside a hushed pool. The faun's consciousness of the snake—the biblical snake who destroyed the cosmological innocence of the first garden—is associated with his desire "for things I know, yet cannot know." These would include the whole cyclical sequence of the seasons, the joys and the sadnesses of the natural progression from birth to death—spring, summer, autumn, winter. The introverted longing for the world that responded to the piping of Pan is associated, not only with the frustration symbolized by the snake in the garden, but by the intrusion into the garden of the arty people who pause to admire the statue of the faun and by the dancers who at night beneath paper lanterns move ungracefully "to brass horns horrible and loud."[7] These intruders, we

---

7 *The Marble Faun and a Green Bough* (New York: Random House, n.d.). This is a photographic reproduction of the two volumes, originally published in 1924 and 1933, respectively. Quotations from *The Marble Faun*, 12, 16, 46.

might say, are "modern pagans." Eliot would call them the "hollow men." The corruption of the natural world by a Christianity that is in alliance with the philosophy of the modern machine society—to a quite discernible extent Faulkner succeeds in embodying something like this vision in his first work. Significantly, he does so through a complex perspective: the faun's tormented consciousness of being conscious. The faun's sense of the dispossession of Pan is an emblem of the suffering induced by the depletion of the sexual basis of culture and the turning in on the self.

In his next work, *The Marionettes*, Faulkner engages the sexual theme more boldly. (Actually, according to Noel Polk in his careful study of the manuscript of the play, a more decided engagement is forecast in a contemplated but discarded version of *The Marble Faun*.) Faulkner again presents the displacement of the pagan garden of fecundity and the imprisonment of the natural or instinctual in a formal garden. The image of Pan appears in a statue of a faun like the one in *The Marble Faun*, but in *The Marionettes* the contrast between the mythic world of the goat god and the sterile world of modernity is drawn far more graphically than is the contrast between Arcadia and modernity in *The Marble Faun*. What occurs in the garden of the faun—the frustration of the truth of art and the integrity of the artist—is symbolized in Pierrot's impotent lust and Marietta's delight in meretricious adornment. The rape of Marietta—Pierrot's dream of raping her—depreciates the sexuality of the human spirit as this is represented in the legend of Pan the ravisher of nymphs. As a figure of the poet, Pierrot suggests an image of the terror and violence inherent in psychic repression. This image is enhanced by the suggestion that Pierrot's psychic aggression against Marietta is really against himself, that, as a matter of fact, the two characters are aspects of the same condition of spirit.[8] The Pierrot-Marietta relationship foreshadows the obsessive concern that Faulkner was to develop with the ambiguities of the masculine and feminine duality in life and in art.

How thoroughly the young Faulkner's imagination of the poet was being caught up in the question of the sexuality of art becomes

8 See Noel Polk, "William Faulkner's *Marionettes*," *Mississippi Quarterly*, 26 (Summer, 1973), 247–80.

clear in "Nympholepsy." Unpublished until recently, this sketch is an expansion, done in early 1925, of one entitled "The Hill," published in 1922 in *The Mississippian*. In both the first and second versions of this strange little piece, Faulkner finds his protagonist in a youthful wanderer and dreamer. He resembles the author himself, although it would appear that he is a midwestern youth, an itinerant farm laborer, who is following thresher crews northward with the wheat harvest. After a day's harvesting, facing the usual prospect of "cloddish eating, and dull sleep in a casual rooming house," the youth is hoping that "a girl like defunctive music, moist with heat, in blue gingham, would cross his path." But when he dimly glimpses a feminine figure and begins to pursue her, she turns out to be no blue-gingham country girl. In an increasingly furious chase after this elusive creature, he slips into a dark stream. As he struggles to keep from drowning, he feels the touch of a "swift leg" and the "point of a breast." Then he sees "her swing herself, dripping, upon the bank." But his further pursuit of the creature—"her body, ghostly in the moonless dusk, mounting the hill"—is futile. He is left to wonder in despair: "But I touched her." And to return to labor another day surrounded by "all the old despairs of time and breath." In depicting the experience of possession by a nymph (common enough in ancient times), Faulkner explicitly identified the theme of the psychic repression of the poet, or artist, with the Calvinistic work-ethic society. This is made more explicit by certain symbols employed in the sketch, especially the church spire and the courthouse. Both in the protagonist and in the setting of "Nympholepsy," Faulkner for the first time locates the pagan-Christian dialect on the American scene and more or less definitely associates it with his own quest for vocation.[9]

Presumably at about the same time he revised "The Hill" as "Nympholepsy," Faulkner wrote a sketch of greater import in his literary novitiate than anything he had set down before. Entitled "Out of Nazareth," this was published in the New Orleans *Picayune* on Easter Sunday, 1925. One of several sketches he contributed to the *Picayune* during the period he lived in the New Orleans French Quar-

9 "Nympholepsy," ed. James B. Meriwether, *Mississippi Quarterly*, 26 (Summer, 1973), 403–409.

ter (the first six months of 1925), "Out of Nazareth" clearly intends, as Carvel Collins has said, for the reader to infer a parallel between its protagonist, another wandering youth, and the figure of the young Christ. Seventeen years old, he has left his hometown in the Midwest; with no destination in mind, he lives indifferently by himself or among other wanderers, enjoying a sense of peace and at oneness with nature and man. Eventually he comes to New Orleans, where one morning in Jackson Square he is seen by Faulkner and his friend William Spratling, the painter, standing "beneath sparrows delirious in a mimosa," against the background of "a vague Diana in torturous escape from marble draperies." The youth's face is brooding upon the spire of St. Louis Cathedral, or perhaps "something in the sky." Spratling exclaims, "My God, look at that face." Faulkner continues: "And one could imagine young David looking like that. One could imagine Jonathan getting that look from David, and, serving that highest function of which sorry man is capable, being the two of them beautiful in similar peace and simplicity—beautiful as gods, as no woman can ever be. And to think of speaking to him, of entering that dream, was like a desecration." But when the marvelous youth—Faulkner calls him David, but the youth never gives his name himself—responds to their attention, they take him to lunch. They find out that he always carries a "battered 'Shropshire Lad'" (acquired by chance) and that he has written a story about his journeying. Faulkner presents David's own story verbatim. Save for attempts at literary style here and there, it is a very simple report of the youth's experiences on the road. "Some of the words mean nothing, as far as I know," Faulkner comments, adding parenthetically "and words are my meat and bread and drink." But, he says to change David's word "would be to destroy David himself." Faulkner's intention is obvious. The name given the youth ("I am the root and offspring of David, and the bright and morning star." Rev. 22.16), such details as his fondness for sleeping in hay with cattle, together with the emphasis on the idea that in a virginal purity and innocence he is "serving his appointed ends," confirm the relation of the youth to Jesus. The references to Houseman's poems and to the narrator's dedication to words make explicit Faulkner's association of the young Jesus in "Out of Nazareth" with his own search for the meaning of the vocation to which by this time he had come to feel a complete commitment. The quest, it will be noted, takes on an austere prophetic quality. David appears against the background of Diana, the goddess of chastity. His eyes look heavenward; he leaves a message of hope about the ordinary people he has met in his wandering. The message may have literary flaws and unknown words in it, but it is sacramental. It is the authentic expression of David. Faulkner distinctly symbolizes the implication of Christ in the mystery of the writer's vocation and, to be sure, relates the implication to the identity of a writer who had come out of Oxford, Mississippi, and who, as David says about himself in the story, might someday return to his hometown, the place of his nativity.[10]

So far as I am aware, no writer, and certainly not Faulkner, became so literally involved in an image of the writer drawn from the Pan-Christ dialectic as did D. H. Lawrence. But the Lawrentian extreme points up the importance of the visionary source of the modern literary vocation in a pagan-Christian opposition and reconciliation. And there are, interestingly enough, two related short stories by Faulkner, written probably in the mid-1920s, that suggest Lawrence. Both are about the same character, Wilfred Midgleston, a former draughtsman for a New York architectural firm. In "Black Music" the narrator encounters Midgleston in a Caribbean port named Rincon, where as an old man he lives a barfly existence, sleeping in an attic in a roll of tarred roofing paper. In the story that he recounts to the narrator, he tells how he was transformed by the god Pan into a faun. Existing in this transformed state for one day, he is used by Pan to frighten Mrs. Van Dyming, wealthy patroness of the arts, from her Virginia estate. The arty matron has planned to build a replica of a Roman theater on the site of a stand of native grapevines. Midgleston, whose purpose in going to Virginia had been to consult with Mrs. Van Dyming about plans for the theater, flees to the Caribbean island and remains there, a true believer in Pan. If "the Bible says them little men were myths," Midgleston knows differently.[11]

---

10 "Out of Nazareth," *New Orleans Sketches*, ed. Carvel Collins (New Brunswick, N.J.: Rutgers University Press, 1958), 102, 104, 110.
11 *Collected Stories of William Faulkner* (New York: Random House, 1950), 805. The entire story occupies 799–821.

The comic mode of "Black Music" is countered by the surrealistic poetry of "Carcassonne," the second story about Midgleston. Rolled up in his tar paper bed, the old man becomes pure poetic conscious- ness. He is "on a buckskin pony with eyes like blue electricity and a mane like tangled fire, galloping up the hill right off into the high heaven of the world." His ecstatic flight is mingled with images of the medieval crusades (knights "riding against the assembled foes of our meek Lord"); of the Crucifixion ("But somebody always killed the first rate riders"); of the Resurrection; and of the "dark and tragic figure of the Earth, his mother." The theme of Faulkner's surrealis- tic elaboration of an analogy between poetry and Christianity seems to be stated in the declaration, *"I want to perform something bold and tragical and austere."* [12] To be a first rate rider is to be crucified for it. Faulkner apparently seeks to depict in Midgleston both the pathos of a defeated poet and the ironic victory of his imagination.

The decisive stage of Faulkner's literary notiviate may be traced in the unfolding of the legend of the artist in the increasingly complex and subtle interplay of classical paganism, modern paganism, and Christianity in *Soldiers' Pay, Mosquitoes, Flags in the Dust,* and *The Sound and the Fury.* This evolution, I realize, cannot here be set forth in the detail required for satisfactory analysis, but I shall at- tempt a partial outline.

In *Soldiers' Pay,* Faulkner creates the dialectical interplay chiefly through the relationships among three characters: Donald Mahon, the World War I pilot who has been shot down over Flanders and, horribly scarred and in a comatose state, is returned to his small- town home in Georgia to die; Donald's father, the Reverend Mr. Ma- hon, rector of the Episcopal church in the community, an outwardly professing Christian who is no longer, if he ever was, an inwardly believing one; and Januarius Jones, described as "a late fellow of Latin in a small college," a brash, enigmatic person who just shows up one April day at the rector's garden gate. All three of these characters bear the mark of Pan. Before the war Donald had run naked in the moonlight and made love to Emmy, the servant girl, whom he trans-

12 *Ibid.,* 899. "Carcasonne" is to be found on 895–900.

formed, so to speak, into a nymph. Donald, a devotee of "A Shropshire Lad," is a figure of the poet as faun, and bearing his battle scar
he is a sacrificial victim, a type of the wounded and dying god. The
rector has one great passion, a beautiful rosebush in his garden. He
awaits its first bloom with the impatience of a young man expect-
ing his mistress, and the blooming rose brings him an ecstacy like
that known to "the old pagan who kept his Byzantine goblet at his
bedside and slowly wore away the rim kissing it." Jones is a satyr.
Grossly sensual, forever in a state of "nympholepsy," and would-be
seducer both of Emmy and of Cecily, Donald's intended, he is suggestive of the Pan who became satanic at the time of Christ's crucifixion and may be taken as the demonic inverse of Donald Mahon.
Jones finally accomplishes his seduction of Emmy while the service
for the burial of the dead being said over Donald echoes in her mind
("I am the Resurrection and the Life, saith the Lord") and taps sound
distantly from a local Boy Scout's bugle. *Soldiers' Pay* ends with the
rector standing outside a shabby Negro church, which has a "canting
travesty of a spire," listening to "the crooning submerged passion of
the dark race," who had made a "personal Father" out of the white
man's "remote God." Then he takes his way back "along the mooned
land inevitable with to-morrow and sweat, with sex and death and
damnation."[13] In *Soldiers' Pay* there is creative passion left neither
in classical paganism nor in Christianity. Only the alien dark race
has any harmony with existence. To a certain extent, Faulkner succeeds in dramatizing the waste land in terms of the life of a little
Georgia town. The central figure in this world is a humanitarian
deist or, it could be, a total skeptic, who yet wears the cloth, the Reverend Mr. Mahon. While not a writer, Mr. Mahon is obviously literary. As he strolls his formal garden, where he worships a beautiful
rose—to him, a perfected symbol of love—he not only seems to represent a type of the modern literary sensibility, but may even be taken
as a specific image of the priesthood of art. Like the marble faun, he
is a poet imprisoned in a formal garden; or, to use another image of
Mr. Mahon's situation, he is sealed in a Byzantine vase of surpassing
beauty. Save for certain intimations of their potential viability, both

13 *Soldiers' Pay* (New York: Liveright Publishing Corporation, 1954), 61, 297, 319.

Pan and Christ are inert forces in the moribund community of *Soldiers' Pay*.

But the conception of the artist's power to imagine does not reach an impasse in this novel. On the contrary, Faulkner's first novel marks a considerable expansion and complication in imaginative power, particularly in the way in which the dialectical interplay in the story establishes a relationship between the sexuality of art and the sexuality of the human community as represented in time and place by Charleston, Georgia.

In *Mosquitoes*, Faulkner might well seem to have contemplated something like a full-scale approach through classical myth to the meaning of the artist's nature in the modern age. The outstanding theme of the novel announces itself clearly in the beginning as the sexuality of art and the artist. It is never certain whether Gordon, the French Quarter sculptor who worships his own abstract statue of a virgin, or Mrs. Maurier, the wealthy patroness of art whose yacht, the *Nausikka*, is named for the virgin Nausicca in the Odyssey (and whose own condition, as it turns out, is that of a psychic, if not technical, virginity), is the chief character in the novel. The exploration of the sexual motivation of creativity, or the lack of it, is ruthlessly pursued by Faulkner in a talky comedy about a mixed bag of New Orleans artists and wealthy and petty bourgeoisie who embark on the *Nausikka* for a trivial and aborted little cosmological odyssey around Lake Pontchartrain. Faulkner weaves into his drama a whole complex of references and allusions to the classical myths dealing with the sexual nature of man. He even brings himself in briefly as a dark faunal little man who is a "liar by profession" and, it is implied, a bit of a goat. But the central insistence in *Mosquitoes* is Christian. Gordon, who is described as having a "faunlike face" and in various ways is associated with "pipes" and "centaurs' hooves," finds his basic meaning in his having suffered the somewhat obscure "auto-gethsemane" that his abstraction of the virginal girl—a torso only, headless, armless, legless—represents. Mrs. Maurier in part resembles the Nausicca of Joyce's *Ulysses* (Gertie McDowell, the devotee of pseudoart), in part the innocent Nausicca of the *Odyssey*, who has her first, and possibly only, awakening to love in her impossible longing for Ulysses. Gordon intuits the suffering behind the masked face of Mrs. Maurier and makes a clay molding of her face "that exposed her face for the mask it was, and still more, a mask unaware." A character called "the Semitic man" throughout the novel explains the history of Mrs. Maurier to the provincial Dawson Fairchild, a novelist who resembles Sherwood Anderson. Giving a specific account of Mrs. Maurier's marriage of convenience to a man twice her age—a former plantation overseer and a rank and crafty opportunist—the Semitic man establishes her character in the historical and social circumstances of the South. Although the introduction of this kind of historical specification into *Mosquitoes* is awkward and increases its disparate quality, it points to the major direction Faulkner's dialectical apprehension of the ground of art and the character of the artist was beginning to take—this is to say, toward the historicity of art. Further evidence of Faulkner's intention is provided in the best-known scene in *Mosquitoes*; usually compared to the Circe episode in *Ulysses*, this is the episode following the scene in Gordon's studio where the Semitic man relates the story about Mrs. Maurier—a surrealistic scene in which the Semitic man delivers a description of genius as "that Passion Week of the heart." He refers to Dante, who "invented Beatrice, creating himself a maid that life had not had time to create, and laid upon her frail and unbowed shoulders the whole burden of man's history of his impossible heart's desire." As the poet's creation of a figure to bear the weight of the burdened history of impossible desires of the human heart, Beatrice suggests the Christian sense of the primacy of history—the unredeemed history of the human heart in conflict with itself—the source, Faulkner would say twenty-five years later, of all storytelling.[14] In the Semitic man, Faulkner came into the understanding that art is a part of history—the understanding that is implied in Gordon's intuition of the meaning of Mrs. Maurier's face and that is explicated by the Semitic man. It is to be noted that both the Semitic man and his sister Eva Kauffman are significant figurations of the poet in *Mosquitoes*. Faulkner ascribes some of his own poems to the latter, including an important one called "Hermaphroditis." This poem is a comment on the legend of Hermaphroditis and Salmacis the nymph, who, after

14 William Faulkner, *Mosquitoes* (New York: Dell Publishing Company, 1962), 119–20, 40, 266–70, 277–81.

Hermaphroditis bathes in her pool, desires him but is rebuffed, and who, following her appeal to the gods, is forever joined to Hermaphroditis. Eva is either an active or latent lesbian; it is not clear which. But either way she descends from Sappho of Lesbos and is in her present guise a poet of the modern historical dispensation. Her brother is a younger version of the "Wealthy Jew" in the *New Orleans Sketches*, a poetic apostrophe to the type of the Jew of world history, who says to the gentiles, "No soil is foreign to my people, for have we not conquered all lands with the story of your Nativity?"[15]

In his attempt to explore the sexuality of art in *Mosquitoes*, Faulkner sighted a momentous subject. This is the modern concept of the historical nature of sexuality, which is the concept that the sexuality of individuals and families is inherent in the process of history. Assigning all the mysteries of the sexual nature of existence—biological and spiritual—to the given social structure, this concept holds that the modes of sexuality are subject to historical and sociological, and to legal and scientific, interpretation and prescription. It severely diminishes mythic and/or religious celebration of the mysteries of birth, life, and death.

Once he began to glimpse the significance of the assimilation of sexuality—of, that is, the fundamental nature of the familial community—into the modern concept of history, Faulkner, we can conjecture with assurance, was compelled to the subject of his own physical and spiritual inherence in history: to the substantive implication of his family in the history of Oxford, Lafayette County, the State of Mississippi, the South, the nation, and the world. He was seized by the modern "agenbite of inwit": the necessary experience of undefinable remorse that the consciousness of the artist undergoes when he realizes that an arrangement of human relations that had seemed to his childhood vision to embody both a natural and mystical permanence in truth embodies a process of historical alteration. Faulkner's experience of isolation came to him in its typical attenuated American guise (the American settlement having been from the beginning an attenuation of the traditional community): a small-town youth's sense of the evanescence of time and a nostalgia for the lost

<hr>

15   *Ibid.*, 202–209; *New Orleans Sketches*, ed. Collins, 38.

scene of boyhood; for, as Faulkner put it in the period when he first began to devote his writing to the world of his nativity, the "simple bread-and-salt of the world." But having become a writer, he required more than a "touchstone" of the past. He must "recreate between the covers of a book the world I was already preparing to lose and regret." And the dimensions of this world—his own little postage stamp of the world—expanded prodigiously under the pressure of his genius as a literary artist once he commenced the sacramental act of preserving "my belief in the savor of the bread-and-salt." The act of memorial re-creation became an act of historical creation. Faulkner's story of his world became, as the Bible is, an improvement on God, who, Faulkner observed in the exalted moment of his new-found vision, "dramatic though He be, has no sense, no feeling for theatre."[16] Faulkner—like Balzac and Flaubert, Hawthorne and Melville, and not least Dickens—experienced the counterrevelation, which is to say, a vision of the drama of modern man's comic, pathetic, and in moments, tragic inherence in his own untranscending history.

But Faulkner's mind was too complex to subscribe easily to an imagination of historical process as man's fate. His identification with Pan, the cosmological poet, was never to yield entirely to an identification with the role of the purely historical poet. The morphology of myth remains vivid in Faulkner's vision; it merely becomes recessive. While the process can be detected only approximately, it is fascinating to observe the ever-growing complexity and sublety that the cultural dialectic assumes in Faulkner's mind as it began to be embodied in the history of Yoknapatawpha County. When Faulkner began to conceive his vision of Yoknapatawpha County, he appears to have made his first effort to get into focus in the story of Flem Snopes and the Frenchman's Bend people a novelistic plan largely conforming to what Polonius would have called a "comical-pastoral-historical" story. "Father Abraham," as he called his uncompleted work, resembles George Washington Harris' Sut Lovingood tales and Mark Twain's *Adventures of Huckleberry Finn*; both Harris and Mark Twain combine a pastoral sensibility (drawn

16 Blotner, *Faulkner*, 531–32.

ultimately, as all Western pastorals, from classical paganism) with a strong feeling for historical realism. In Faulkner's case, he was so conscious of his connection with Pan that, according to Blotner, he drew on the back of one page of the manuscript of "Father Abraham" (evidently at the time he was writing the arresting fragment) a picture of himself as a faun, his back against a tree, piping the music for the dance of two fantastic creatures, half lamb and half rocking-horse.[17] He could have had in mind nothing more than the entertainment of a child, but the sketch may also be taken as a symbol of Faulkner's ironic concept of himself. Perhaps the amusing portrait of himself as a faun piping a dance for half-real and half-man-made creatures was a farewell to the role of the poet as a faun; or perhaps it anticipates the subtle role Pan would play in the governing perception of the literary artist in *The Hamlet* some fifteen years later, the novelist as pastoral parodist.

Abandoning "Father Abraham" and turning his attention to the composition of *Flags in the Dust*, a story much closer to being a "touchstone of the past," Faulkner for the first time entered intimately into the historical perspective. In fact, the subordination of a mythic to a historical frame of reference in *Flags in the Dust* is a notable feature of the first Yoknapatawpha novel. The historical perspective takes command; myth and tradition undergo the depredations of history. The Sartorises exist in an aura of regret for the past; as though transplanted directly from medieval France into Mississippi, they live their lives in nostalgia. Caught up in the intangible sense of having been deprived of the past, they have longings known to persons in historical societies but unknown to people in mythic and traditional ones. The young Sartorises are destroyed trying to incorporate the airplane and the automobile, symbols of modern history, into their reaction to it. Byron Snopes prowls the community, writing his obscene love letters to Narcissa. But in the telling, *Flags in the Dust* is objectively representational. For all the emphasis on history in the novel, Faulkner embodies this in no character in the story. His increasing sensitivity to the isolation of the individual in history—to the assertion of history against the individual

17 *Ibid.*, 529–31.

and the attempted assertion of the individual against history—waited its fuller expression in his discovery of a character who was a world-historical poet. He was looking in the depths of his imagination for his Hamlet or Don Quixote, his Roderick Usher, his Ishmael.

He found Quentin Compson.

Of course, he had probably known Quentin for some time before he found out his identity in *The Sound and the Fury*—if he ever truly found it out. Quentin may have been too close to him for his detached comprehension. I believe Louis D. Rubin, Jr., is surely right when he says that Joseph Blotner's biography of Faulkner offers convincing evidence of the affinity between Faulkner as a boy and youth and Quentin.[18] But so far as the fictional employment of Quentin is concerned, we know that Quentin's role as the prophet and—shall we say?—the historian of the conscience and the consciousness of the Compsons was likely to have been the center of "Twilight," a projected story from which *The Sound and the Fury* most immediately developed. Joseph Blotner is inclined, moreover, to attribute the writing of the short story entitled "A Justice" to a period before the composition of *The Sound and the Fury*. In this story, Quentin's role as narrator is definitely established. He is the twelve-year-old boy who recalls the story Sam Fathers tells him about the circumstances of his birth. In the conclusion of this story, the scene is set for Quentin's future role as moral historian. Grandfather and the children get in the buggy to go back to town from the farm, and Quentin remarks that Caddy had "one fish, about the size of a chip, and she was wet to the waist." Then Quentin says: "We went on, in that strange, faintly sinister suspension of twilight in which I believed that I could still see Sam Fathers back there, sitting on his wooden-block, definite, immobile, and complete, like something looked upon after a long time in a preservation bath in a museum. That was it. I was just twelve then, and I would have to wait until I had passed on and through and beyond the suspension of twilight. Then I knew that I would know. But then Sam Fathers would be dead."[19]

Twenty-five years after he wrote *The Sound and the Fury*, Faulk-

---

18 See Rubin's review of Blotner's *Faulkner* in *Chronicle of Higher Education*, 8, No. 25 (March 25, 1974), 11–12.
19 "A Justice," *Collected Stories*, 360.

ner told Jean Stein, "Ishmael is the witness in *Moby Dick*, as I am Quentin in *The Sound and the Fury*."[20] It is quite possible to think that Faulkner was confused in his remark. Did he actually mean to say, "as I am Quentin in *Absalom, Absalom!*" This would seem to be more logical, for in this novel the central storytelling role of Quentin is patent. More than this, the overt presence of Quentin as a character is far more extensive; so it might seem that Faulkner's full interest in Quentin did not develop until the writing of the story about Sutpen. But the evidence indicates that the presentation of Quentin in *Absalom, Absalom!* is secondary to that in *The Sound and the Fury*. Quentin as he is at Harvard during the month before his suicide gains his authenticity from his large presence in *The Sound and the Fury*.

On the face of it, such an emphasis on Quentin appears to contradict the well-known four-fold perspective of *The Sound and the Fury*. The first three sections are told by Benjy, Quentin, and Jason, respectively, the last by an omniscient narrator. But where is the informing consciousness pervading *The Sound and the Fury*? And where does it derive from? Who is the truly responsive witness to the scene when Caddy in her muddy drawers climbed the tree to look in on the mourning for Damuddy? It is not the mindless Benjy nor the rationalist Jason, but Quentin, who had told Caddy to take off her dress and had splashed water on her so that she slipped and fell down in the stream and got mud on her drawers. It is the virginal Quentin who conceives an incestuous love for Caddy, not because he would ever actually commit incest, but because, through "some presbyterian concept of its eternal punishment," he could "cast himself and his sister both into hell . . . where he could guard her forever and keep her forevermore intact amid the eternal fires," and so escape forever from the burden of history.[21] In Quentin's relationship with Caddy, the response of sexuality to the forces of history is symbolized more powerfully than it is in "The Fall of the House of Usher," *Pierre*, or *The Turn of the Screw*, as powerfully as in *Madame Bovary*. But what is still more powerful, I think, is the implication the theme de-

20 Blotner, *Faulkner*, II, 1522.
21 See *The Sound and the Fury* (New York: Vintage Books, 1954), 365–71, for the scene in Dilsey's church.

velops in Quentin's agonized interior monologue. I mean the historicism of consciousness—the implication in *The Sound and the Fury* of how, in the modern world, bereft of mythic and traditional order save as this appears in the trappings of nostalgia, the "dark, harsh flowing of time" is channeled directly into the sensitive self instead of into the family and the community. In these cold waters, Quentin strives for a purchase on the symbols of order; carrying on his crazed struggle to save the "frail doomed vessel" of his "family's honor," he transforms honor into doom—willfully yielding the vain myth of himself as a savior to implacable historical imperatives. I mean, too, the way Caddy (according to that prose poem, the Compson genealogy, which Faulkner wrote fifteen years after *The Sound and the Fury*) in her inextricable attachment to Quentin lives out his love of death—his impotence, his incapacity to love, his isolation. She names her half-anonymous bastard child after him because the child is truly Quentin's heir—the girl Quentin who disappears out of a window with the money she stole from Jason (though it was rightfully hers) and is never seen or reported upon again. But Caddy, whom Faulkner says he loved passionately, had to be reported upon again. And she is. She is a creased and recreased photograph from a glossy picture magazine folded in the hand of the shocked, mousy librarian Melissa Meek. In the photograph, sitting beside a middle-aged Nazi staff general in "a chromium-trimmed sports car," is Caddy, still beautiful, serene in her damnation, a figure in the obscene Nazi historical perversion of a pagan societal mythos. Disappearing in an unspeakable *Götterdämmerung*, Caddy knows her doom and accepts it, understanding somehow her role in Quentin's struggle with history. Understanding that if to Benjy she was partly a mother, partly a nymph of water and trees, and to Jason a worthless bitch, she was to Quentin a symbol of his resistance to history and so was caught up in the remorseful, murky historicism of her brother's consciousness of time, sex, death, and damnation. Caught up, we might say, in the power of the God of John Knox, a power that Quentin in his puritan desperation had ruthlessly arrogated to himself. If it is true, poetically speaking, that Faulkner wrote the first three sections of *The Sound and the Fury* under the impress of a witness like Quentin Compson, no dying god but a world-historical neurotic and self-defeated historian, it helps to explain why, in writing the Benjy section, he had felt, as he was to say later, an "ecstasy and also a bafflement." He had known the ineffable joy of the self-certification of his creativity; he had experienced the transcendent fulfillment of his long novitiate in the literary priesthood. But when he had finished the section, had he not also—for all his talk about failure with his novel —experienced the feeling of being enclosed in a perfected work of art, as though he had sealed himself in that same Byzantine vase the Reverend Mr. Mahon refers to in *Soldiers' Pay*? Faulkner says that he wrote Quentin's and Jason's sections trying to clarify Benjy's. But he knew that he had not written three discrete interior monologues. In the tortured account of the familial relationships of the Compsons as told by each of the three narrators, he had dramatized the imprisonment of sexuality in history. Still, he had made the inner truth of the modern writer's consciousness of existence—that is to say, his self-conscious awareness of the subjection of his consciousness to history (symbolized most prominently in the novel by Quentin's vision of his incestuous relation with Caddy)—the theme of Benjy's and Jason's sections no less than of Quentin's. He had identified the consciousness of each narrator with the historicity of the literary artist as he had found this in Quentin.

This is an insight that Faulkner glimpses, I think, in a curious depiction of the southern literary artist in a preface to *The Sound and the Fury* that he set down in 1933, five years after the writing of the novel, but never published. Faulkner states—although in what he evidently thought of as a kind of prose poem and thus in condensed, somewhat enigmatic language—that the person who elects to be an artist in the South does so on his own because the South, having been dead since the Civil War, has no art. The choice involves the southern writer in violence. Once it might have been physical; southern writers were given to horsewhipping or shooting editors who maltreated their manuscripts. But now the violence is psychic. Since the southern writer is isolated from his environment, leaving him with only himself to write about, he has to make the necessary connection with his world, although it is dead and lacks even the sense of artistic tradition available in Chicago. He must join his self-created will to art with what history has made of the South: "Because it is himself that the Southerner is writing about, not about his environment: who has, figuratively speaking, taken the artist in him in one hand and his milieu in the other and thrust the one into the other like a clawing and spitting cat into a croker sack. And he writes."

> We seem to try in the simple furious breathing (or writing) span of the individual to draw a savage indictment of the contemporary scene or to escape from it into a make believe region of swords and magnolias and mockingbirds which perhaps never existed anywhere. . . . Each course is a matter of violent partizanship, in which the writer unconsciously writes into every line and phrase his violent despairs and rages and frustrations or his violent prophesies and still more violent hopes. That cold intellect which can write with complete detachment and gusto of its contemporary scene is not among us.[22]

But in *The Sound and the Fury*, Faulkner says, he can see after five years that he tried both to indict and to escape the South at one time. What he means is that he had put art and artist integrally into the story, without the awareness of thrusting the first into the second by main force. He had entered into the depths of meaning that he articulated fully only once—this later on (and with the climactic simplicity of a truth revealed)—in *Absalom, Absalom!*, when in the "iron New England dark," Quentin says of the South, "I don't hate it."

Once he looked through Quentin's eyes at Sam Fathers distanced in the mythic twilight and moved with Quentin's mind toward the day when he would pass from the ahistorical childhood vision of the old people into the knowledge of modernity, Faulkner discovered in Quentin the first profound portrayal of his own imagination—a fiction, yet a symbol of a deep inner reality, a powerful apprehension of modern existence. (And besides that, it may be that Faulkner discovered a symbolic brother who assumed one of Faulkner's deepest longings, the desire for a sister). Through Quentin, Faulkner could pass beyond the attachment to myth, tradition, or revelation; beyond the vision of the cyclical pattern of existence, or of the pattern in the climactic events of Christian history: the Nativity, Crucifixion, and Resurrection. He could experience how, these possible faiths failing, the consciousness knows only a relentless and an entire inherence of body and spirit in the historical process.

Faulkner was never truly to transcend his identification of the

---

22 "An Introduction to *The Sound and the Fury*," ed. James B. Meriwether, *Mississippi Quarterly*, 26 (Summer, 1973), 412.

imagination of the literary artist with the compelling historicism of
the modern consciousness of existence. He obviously rebelled against
it in his later works—in the Nobel Prize speech and at great length
in the much-abused non-Yoknapatawpha novel, *A Fable*. His first
and most powerful rebellion occurred early—in *The Sound and the
Fury* itself, specifically in the last section in which, he says, he attempted "to get completely out of the book" by employing an omniscient narrator. Yet essentially this narrator presents the testimony
of three interrelated witnesses to the enclosure of modern existence
in history. One of these is Dilsey. A more basic witness is the Negro
preacher, the Reverend Shegog, who delivers the Easter sermon in
the little church Dilsey attends on the day after Caddy's daughter
has run away and while Jason is pursuing her. A visitor to Jefferson
from St. Louis, Reverend Shegog is a highly educated man, although
he is little and looks like a monkey. The outstanding feature of this
St. Louis preacher, however, is his dual nature. He is actually two
men. In one guise, the Reverend Shegog sounds "like a white man"
as (controlled and poised like a man on a tightrope) he delivers a
carefully phrased message in a cold, level, educated, rational voice.
But then he pauses and in a different tone announces, "Brethren and
sisteren, I got the recollection in the blood of the Lamb!" In the moments that follow, his diction becomes "negroid." "Bredden en sis-
tuhn," he exclaims as he is transformed into a folk preacher, "I got
de rickliskshun en de blood of de Lamb!" Telling the story of the
moment in history when history is transcended in the Crucifixion
and Resurrection, his words become incarnate in his body and he becomes an icon of the slain God, "a serene and tortured crucifix."
Christ is present in the little Negro church in Jefferson, Mississippi,
on April 8, 1928. Yet strangely, although Dilsey and the congrega-
tion witness and, if unknowingly, participate in a movement beyond knowledge into faith, the omniscient narrator—the Faulkner
who is trying to get out of the story—does not discern in the movement into faith an assured movement beyond history into the eternal. "There is only one relation to revealed truth," Kierkegaard says,
"believing it." The realization of the Kingdom of God in a movement beyond history is a matter of profound faith on the part of Dilsey, yet her experience of this truth is associated with Shegog's vision

of the "power and the glory." And the St. Louis preacher is a self-conscious actor. Regardless of the depth of his impulsion to change roles in the midst of the service, he is quite aware of the transformation. His act suggests an ambivalent relation between revealed truth and history, between the eternal and the temporal. Dilsey's sorrowing vision of the Compsons as she departs from the service—"I've seed de first en de last"—bears no imputation of the histrionic. But ironically it tends to resolve the equivocal drama of the Easter service in a vision of the unredeemed, and unredeemable, imprisonment of the human condition in history.[23]

At the end of the fourth section of *The Sound and the Fury*, Quentin's witness returns. In the ironic moment when Luster swings the buggy to the left instead of to the accustomed right of the Confederate memorial on the square and all the order of Benjy's world is suddenly destroyed, Quentin—though he has been dead for eighteen years and though he was already a ghost when he drowned himself in the Charles River, Cambridge, Massachusetts, June 2, 1910—is once again fully present in the story, the dark consciousness of a South still living its death in history.

It has been kept in mind, I trust, that in remarking upon Faulkner and the legend of the artist I have been speaking about the artist in the modern age. The term *modern age* is still a convenient one to use, but, as we all know, the modern age is ceasing to be. In this age the society of myth and tradition was displaced by a society of history and science. What kind of society will displace the modern society? We of course do not know. We cannot imagine an existence that is not historical.

Life is a tale "told by an idiot, full of sound and fury, / Signifying nothing." This statement of futility by Macbeth—together with Hamlet's soliloquy, "To be or not to be"—is the first formulation of what I have awkwardly termed the historicism of consciousness. Shakespeare experienced in his imagination of Hamlet and Macbeth the imposition of the burden of history that the consciousness had to assume with the depletion of the life of the consciousness incorporated in myth and in traditionalism. By its very nature, this is not

23 *The Sound and the Fury*, 336–38.

a theme that can be inherited by one generation after another. In one way or another, it has been discovered in each generation of literary artists since Shakespeare, the discoveries growing more poignant as the sense of the mythic and the traditional have become more and more marginal in the consciousness. One of the most compelling experiences of the impingement of history upon the fading margins of myth and tradition occurred in the literary imagination of the post-World War I American South. Quentin Compson is the preeminent legend of this imagination. He knew what Hamlet and Macbeth knew, and Caddy, out of her love for her loveless brother, shared what he knew with him. And Faulkner—who created the brother and sister and who ruthlessly imagined their terrible images of the world—shared with both of them what they knew.

11 / A Fable of Civilization

How the world of truth became a fable.
—Nietzsche, *Twilight of the Idols*

L et me treat in a somewhat more comprehensive way a complex and subtle topic I have approached before in remarking on Faulkner: his sense of his ory in relation to civilization.[1] My discussion will regard three aspects of his outlook. I shall comment on the subject of the modern novel. Defining this as the myth of the past in the present, or the literary myth of modern history, I will point out the relation of this myth to the literary consciousness in America. In this connection I shall also observe that Faulkner's version, or vision, of the novelistic subject includes not only the myth of the past in the present but the loss of this myth, together with the threatened loss of the very capacity of the imagination to make mythic constructs of existence. Finally I shall observe that as, under pressure of his vision of the myth of the past in the present, Faulkner invents a highly particularized myth of history, the story of Yoknapatawpha County, he implies a larger myth of man. In remarking on the larger myth—which struggles to emerge out of the Yoknapatawpha myth but is never clearly articulated—I will attempt to consider the meaning of Faulkner's largest non-Yoknapatawpha work, *A Fable*, in what I conceive as its crucial, pivotal relation to the Yoknapatawpha stories.

The source of my concept of the literary myth of modern history and its bearing on the southern novel has been referred to before in this

1 Besides the preceding chapter, see Lewis P. Simpson, "Sex and History: Origins of Faulkner's Apocrypha," in Evans Harrington and Ann J. Abadie (eds.), *The Maker and the Myth: Faulkner and Yoknapatawpha* (Jackson: University Press of Mississippi, 1978), 43–70.

volume. It is a critical and historical revelation I share in common
with every student of southern letters: Allen Tate's recognition of
the significance of twentieth-century southern fiction in "The Profession of Letters in the South" (1935). Let me reproduce in full the
familiar passage in this essay:

> The Southern novelist has left his mark upon the age; but it is of the
> age. From the peculiarly historical consciousness of the Southern writer
> has come good work of a special order; but the focus of this consciousness
> is quite temporary. It has made possible the curious burst of intelligence
> that we get at a crossing of the ways, not unlike, on an infinitesimal scale,
> the outburst of poetic genius at the end of the sixteenth century when
> commercial England had already begun to crush feudal England. The His-
> tories and Tragedies of Shakespeare record the death of the old régime,
> and Doctor Faustus gives up feudal power for world power.[2]

As the poetic drama was the form inherent in the Elizabethan literary subject, the novel, Tate recognizes, is the form demanded by
the subject of twentieth-century literature. The literary subject in
both Elizabethan England and the modern American South is the
same: the intense historical consciousness peculiar to an age that is
at "a crossing of the ways." In such a period of endings and beginnings, the sense of time is heightened and a writer's consciousness
struggles not only with the number of changes that are occurring,
but, and more profoundly, with their implications for his vision of
human existence. The writer is acutely aware of life as it has been
known, and will no longer be known. In the Elizabethan age, the response of the literary imagination to the crisis in the vision of existence was made in the plays of Marlowe and Shakespeare; in the
South of the 1920s and 1930s, the response, as Tate sees it, is being
made by such novelists as Elizabeth Madox Roberts, Caroline Gordon, Thomas Wolfe, Andrew Lytle, and William Faulkner. Yet in his
analogy between the Elizabethan literary situation and that in his
own world, Tate fails to make a clear discrimination between the
modern novel and the Elizabethan poetic drama. The Elizabethan
tragedies respond to the declining vision of a world in which human
events, obedient to a transcending myth of fate or destiny, move to-

2 Allen Tate, "The Profession of Letters in the South," in *Essays of Four Decades*
(Chicago: Swallow Press, 1968), 533–34.

ward a climactic resolution. The novel answers to the need for a
form to express the vision of a new and strange world in which the
epic and/or tragic vision of time is being displaced by the assumption of time in the image of the mechanical clock—by the strange
feeling that history is not a series of actions but a time process, in
Quentin Compson's image, "a minute clicking of little wheels."[3]

The need for the novel that was first answered by Cervantes' *Don
Quixote* not only anticipates the shift in the modern consciousness
from the mythic and traditionalist to the historical rationale of existence, but also diagnoses the psychic consequence of this alteration: the comic and pathetic individualism that occurs when, dis-
lodged from the society of myth and tradition—from the cosmic
sacramentalism of Christendom—the person begins to acquire, as
we say, a personality. The Knight of the Sad Countenance becomes
a self and goes in search of an identity in history. The individual, as
creature of historical time, as a historical self—this is a theme in all
modern literature in whatever form it is cast. But in the novel, it appears with a singular concentration and comprehensiveness. The
juxtaposition of the society of myth and tradition and the scientific-
historical society in the acute consciousness of the novelist assumes,
as in, say, *Pamela, Tom Jones, Tristram Shandy,* and *Madame Bovary,* the proportions of a literary myth of modern history. The novelistic vision translates the continuous dialectical tension established by the pressure of the past upon the present into a story in
which the old society asserts its spectral but undeniable presence in
the modern society.

In American literature the myth of the past in the present waited
for its expression upon the expanding historical signification of the
American Revolution. Receiving its first tentative formulation in
the hastily written but discerning novels of Charles Brockden Brown,
it came into distinct American versions in James Fenimore Cooper's
stories about Leatherstocking, Edgar Allan Poe's tales about Roderick Usher and Ligeia, Nathaniel Hawthorne's depictions of Hester
Prynne and the Reverend Mr. Dimmesdale, and preeminently in
Herman Melville's story of Ishmael, Ahab, and Moby-Dick. But, it

3 *The Sound and the Fury* (New York: Vintage Books, 1954), 94.

may be noted, the stories of Poe, Hawthorne, and Melville were not written primarily in the light of the Revolution; they appeared in the foreboding light of an approaching civil war in the new nation. In the great and terrible illumination of this conflict, when it came, the true past of the American existence—its deep substance in the ancient terrors of European history—found out the present. The nation that, flouting all the historical evidence certifying man's irresistible disposition to folly and evil, had based itself on the premise that man is a rational and beneficent being, had within seventy years of the establishment of the Great Experiment in human nature engaged in one of the bloodiest internecine conflicts in history.

Yet the post-Civil War American novelistic vision by no means focused in a pessimistic view of history. Henry James, believing the truth of American history still to lie in the dynamics of the great moral experiment, opposed the essential innocence of the self liberated from the past to the evil intrinsic in the self implicated in European experience. The other most substantial American novelist of post-Civil War America, William Dean Howells, also supported the moral superiority of the American present. Both James and Howells, to be sure, felt that asserting the triumph of American innocence was their historical responsibility as American authors.

Among the determinate motives of American novelists, none is more ironic, nor so fundamental and so rich in meaning, as the compulsion to regard the individual as being responsible for history. The logic of this imperative is inescapable; it is the American idea in essence. Operating with an intense historical consciousness of what they were doing, a band of British subjects, centered in a few such cosmopolitan men of letters as Benjamin Franklin, Thomas Jefferson, and John Adams, became the first people in the annals of man deliberately to subvert the assumption that the past is necessary to the present. Having successfully culminated this treason against Church and State and against all the mythic, traditionalist, and ceremonial structures of the mother country, they invented a republic purged of these structures; and, whether they fully intended to or not, dedicated the new nation to the historical fulfillment of the self. The American became the first person in history fully to experience an internalization of history—to identify his sense of being as a person with the sense of being in history. This meant that the American became the first person to be haunted, not by a mythic and traditionalist past, but by the historical past—a past that may be as immediate in its presence as today's newspaper.

The more complex American storytellers have been ironically aware that our equation of self and history threatens the imaginative response to the literary subject of the West, the myth of the past in the present, that if the writer accepts the equation between self and history, he moves beyond the dialectical drama of the crossing of the ways. Such an intimation of the meaning of American historicism has been harbored in the American literary mind as a kind of secret knowledge. Its unspoken presence is evident in literary nationalists like Emerson and Whitman as well in cosmopolitan conservatives like James and Eliot. One of its overt, or almost overt, manifestations occurs in Mark Twain, who, in spite of some argument about the matter, is basically to be understood as southern. I refer to his ironic inversion of the drama of the past in the present in *A Connecticut Yankee in King Arthur's Court*. As a prophetic work, this novel transcends the mythic connection between past and present and assumes the quality of a large historical vision. Hank Morgan —the morally ignorant but inventive Yankee who takes on the responsibility for the history of the Middle Ages in the name of the American doctrine of progress and in doing so destroys a world—is significant enough to stand beside Don Quixote. While the Knight of the Sad Countenance graphically represents the crossing of the ways, Hank suggests its appalling resolution.

Twentieth-century southern writers, however close to James in sensibility, resemble Mark Twain in their apprehension of the power of history to resolve the modern literary dialectic. Their perception is not altogether owing to the South's heritage of defeat. The catastrophe of the Civil War confirmed intimations of historical displacement that had preyed upon southerners from the early days of the Virginia settlement. Like the adventitious rise of tobacco smoking in Europe, to which it was inextricably linked, chattel slavery was no part of Anglo-Saxon myth and tradition. On the contrary, the drastic effect of its casual introduction into the American South represents the radical power of modern history once it began to center in a world marketplace. Southerners understood that slavery was a historical accident and called it their "peculiar institution"; but, history demanding that they justify it as part of their civilizational heritage, they came to look upon it as providential.

In the encompassing sense of the terms *letters* and *literature* still obtaining in the nineteenth century, both the defense of slavery and the abolitionist attack on it were literary. Defending the peculiar institution, southern men of letters attempted to adapt the slavery system to the general literary subject in Western culture, the myth of the past in the present. They envisioned a slave society conducted by a free and egalitarian order of masters, who were at once committed to operating in a world marketplace economy and recovering and maintaining a viable patriarchal social structure. In seeking to project their vision, southern writers followed the ultimate imperative of the modern historicist ethos: they rewrote history to make it conform to historical necessity. They placed the southern literary mind, as Henry James perceived, under the interdiction of a "new criticism"—a southern critique of history.[4] This in effect meant a drastic assimilation of both the southern writer and his subject matter to the present emergency of the state. The southern literary imagination was thus strangely bereft by the desperate means through which it sought to fulfill itself. In the southern literary consciousness of the 1840s and 1850s, the dialectical tension of the past in the present was increasingly resolved in an immitigable historicism. Until the southern literary imagination should be opened to the subject of the past in the present, the southern novelist had no subject, even though it was implicit in a commitment to history that obsessed the southern self in its blood and bone.

A larger vision of southern history was slowly beginning to open to the novelist in the South when World War I erupted. But this cataclysmic event forcibly directed his attention outward toward the meaning of world history and, in doing so, toward the meaning of the South in this context. The Civil War and the South's defeat took on the character of events symbolizing the southern participation in the whole civilizational drama of the past in the present. The south-

4 Henry James, *The American Scene* (New York: Charles Scribner's Sons, 1946), 374. *Cf.* the remarks on James in chapter 4.

ern situation became emblematic of the crossing of the ways in Western civilization, and the southern literary artist could view himself
both as observer of and participant in the crisis. Mark Twain had
glimpses of the possibilities open to the novelist who would grasp
southern history both sympathetically and ironically, bringing into
focus the fate of a slave society that had been both historical novelty
and anachronism. Faulkner was to see the southern situation in full
and to capture the entire drama of the South's representation of the
past in the present.

In accomplishing this great task, Faulkner made an imaginary southern world of which he was, as he said, sole proprietor—a county in
northern Mississippi modeled on his home county of Lafayette, with
its county seat of Oxford. He called his creation Yoknapatawpha
County and named its seat Jefferson. But in spite of the fact that his
invention and peopling of Yoknapatawpha is a major achievement
in twentieth-century literature, Faulkner did not uniformly maintain the proprietorship of his mythical county during the forty years
he wrote about it. At about midpoint in his authorial career, his
imaginative grasp of it weakened. His lapsing hold on Yoknapatawpha may be partially attributed to burdensome personal circumstances. It may be traced more surely, I think, to two literary circumstances.

The more obvious of these was the falling off from the conviction
that there is an equation between integral selfhood and art. In the
preceding chapter in this book, I remarked upon certain aspects of
the origin of this sense in Faulkner. To this discussion it is eminently
worthwhile to refer again to Lionel Trilling's insistence on how
personal modern literature is—how much it derives from the desire
to authenticate the existence of the writer, to invest it with what
Rousseau isolated amid the modern anxieties as the "sentiment of
being." This sentiment, as exemplified in Rousseau, Schiller, and
Wordsworth, calls for the writer to be strong but not powerful. It is
"not concerned with energy directed outward upon the world in aggression and dominance, but, rather, with such energy as contrives
that the centre shall hold, that the circumference of the self keep
unbroken, that the person be an integer, impenetrable, perdurable,

and autonomous in being if not in action."[5] Trilling points out that
the vaunted doctrine of the impersonality of the artist—the seemingly paradoxical insistence in modern literature that "the poet is
not a person at all, only a *persona*"—is a strategy of the sentiment of
being. That the progress of an artist is, in Eliot's words, "a continual
extinction of personality" or that it is, in Joyce's view, a refinement
of the personality "out of existence" are ways either of relieving the
fatigues of the self in the struggle for being or of attributing to it "sha-
manistic power." In Faulkner's case, the strategy of impersonality
appears to have been invoked as the author in midcareer sensed a
lapsing of his selfhood in art and sought to protect it by, in effect,
stationing a persona to guard its circumference. In 1949 he declared
in a letter to Malcolm Cowley: "It is my ambition to be, as a private
individual, abolished and voided from history, leaving it markless,
no refuse save the printed books: I wish I had had enough sense to
see ahead thirty years ago and, like some of the Elizabethans, not
signed them. It is my aim, and every effort bent, that the sum and
history of my life, which in the same sentence is my obit and epitaph too, shall be them both: He made the books and he died."[6]
Faulkner's most moving appeal to the doctrine of the impersonality
of the artist—and the saddest one—occurs in a letter in the spring of
1953 to Joan Williams, the youthful would-be writer of whom he
was enamored. He mentions his progress on *A Fable*:

> I know now—believe now—that this may be the last major, ambitious
> work; there will be short things, of course. I know now that I am getting
> toward the end, the bottom of the barrel. The stuff is still good, but I know
> now there is not very much more of it, a little trash comes up constantly
> now, which must be sifted out. And now, at last, I have some perspective
> on all I have done. I mean, the work apart from me, the work which I did,
> apart from what I am. . . . And now I realize for the first time what an
> amazing gift I had: uneducated in every formal sense, without even very
> literate, let alone literary, companions, yet to have made the things I made.
> I dont know where it came from. I dont know why God or gods or who-
> ever it was, selected me to be the vessel. Believe me, this is not humility,
> false modesty; it is simply amazement. I wonder if you have ever had that

5 *Sincerity and Authenticity* (Cambridge: Harvard University Press, 1972), 99.
6 *Selected Letters of William Faulkner*, ed. Joseph Blotner (New York: Random
House, 1977), 285.

thought about the work and the country man whom you know as Bill Faulkner—what little connection there seems to be between them.[7]

In thus virtually disclaiming an awareness of any connection between person and persona, between his life and his art, Faulkner (depicting himself as a Mississippi primitive somehow chosen to be a vessel of God) was far away from the moment of the fulfilled self-interpretation of the modern literary artist—the moment when self, art, and subject had fused in the vision of *The Sound and the Fury*. In the writing of this book in the late 1920s, Faulkner had realized the power of the sentiment of being. Indeed, this realization is the fundamental theme of the remarkable commentary on *The Sound and the Fury* mentioned previously,[8] in which he says that the southern writer must, "figuratively speaking," take "the artist in him in one hand and his milieu in the other and thrust the one into the other like a clawing and spitting cat into a croker sack." The southern writer, Faulkner implies, seizes upon the unarticulated power of art in the South in a manner comparable to that through which Allen Tate says (in "Religion and the Old South") the modern southerner must appropriate the unarticulated religious power of the South, through violence, meaning a psychic ferocity. No doubt both Faulkner and Tate were, forty-five or fifty years ago, in the grip of the same imperative: the need of the modern southern writer to grasp his essential identity, his being, through the act of writing. Out of this necessity, Tate wrote his "Ode to the Confederate Dead," grabbing the poet, the living cat, and thrusting him into the inert sack, which thereupon became alive with the cat. But Tate's inclination in his most famous poem is towards adherence to the decorum of the persona, as can be seen in "Narcissus as Narcissus," a description of his labor on the poem several years after its composition (during which he kept returning to the poem and revising it), whereas Faulkner's comment on the writing of *The Sound and the Fury* affirms a personal intimacy with the act of art and represents a complete violation of the decorous regard for the masking of the person of the creator. To

---

7 *Ibid.*, 348.
8 "An Introduction to *The Sound and the Fury*," ed. James B. Meriwether, *Mississippi Quarterly*, 26 (Summer, 1973), 410–15.

be sure, it describes the writing of the first part of the novel, the Benjy section, as a sacramental certification of Faulkner's personal being as an artist.

> The story is all there, in the first section as Benjy told it. I did not try deliberately to make it obscure; when I realized that the story might be printed, I took three more sections, all longer than Benjy's to try to clarify it. But when I wrote Benjy's section, I was not writing it to be printed. If I were to do it over now I would do it differently, because the writing of it as it now stands taught me both how to write and how to read, and even more: It taught me what I had already read, because on completing it I discovered, in a series of repercussions like summer thunder, the Flauberts and Conrads and Turgenievs which as much as ten years before I had consumed whole and without assimilating at all, as a moth or a goat might. I have read nothing since; I have not had to. And I have learned but one thing since about writing. That is, that the emotion definite and physical and yet nebulous to describe which the writing of Benjy's section of *The Sound and the Fury* gave me—that ecstacy, that eager and joyous faith and anticipation of surprise which the yet unmarred sheets beneath my hand held inviolate and unfailing—will not return. The unreluctance to begin, the cold satisfaction in work well and arduously done, is there and will continue to be there as long as I can do it well. But that other will not return. I shall never know it again.[9]

Like Tate's vision of the South, the Yoknapatawpha vision grew out of Faulkner's evolving consciousness of the tensions of self and art, as these were integral in the subject of the literary myth of modern history—the story of the crossing of the ways embodied in the South. Joseph Blotner quotes from a fragmentary self-review of his writing set down by Faulkner in the mid 1920s: "So I began to write, without much purpose, until I realized that to make it truly evocative it must be personal, in order not only to preserve my own interest in the writing, but to preserve my belief in the savor of the bread-and-salt" (of, as he puts it in the same discussion, "the simple bread-and-salt of the world").[10] In other words, Faulkner was compelled to write by the need to experience the intimacy of his own being in the historical moment. The experience corroborated what he had already learned, less directly, in his prior writings: the self has its being in

9 *Ibid.*, 414–15.
10 *Faulkner: A Biography* (2 vols.; New York: Random House, 1974), I, 532.

history in proportion to its resistance to history, or to its own historicity. The effective image of the self is the obdurate image of the artist, who, deeply scrutinizing the self's hostility to the historical society, controls and shapes an ideal of autonomous being. The implied center of the Yoknapatawpha saga—and notably of its four greatest novels: *The Sound and the Fury, As I Lay Dying, Light in August,* and *Absalom, Absalom!*—is Faulkner's version of the exemplary self of the artist.

But this self achieves its presence in a work of art not only through craft, but also through its implication in the subject. The day never came when Faulkner did not possess something worth saying and the ability to say it well; the day did come when the unreluctance as well as the ecstacy were gone. The ecstasy had come in experiencing the momentary revelation of the self's wholeness triumphant against the consciousness of the self's historical fallibility; the unreluctance, from the conviction of the recurring historical reality of the experience. By the time Faulkner published *Go Down, Moses* in 1942, the modern sense of selfhood in art was beginning to be undercut by the awareness of a diminishment of the novelistic subject. Like his contemporary Hemingway, Faulkner sensed by the time he came to middle age that, although World War I had heightened the dialectical play of the crossing of the ways in the modern literary imagination, it had also forecast the complete eclipse of the literary myth of modern history.

Such an awareness on Faulkner's part—his implied recognition of the disappearance of the past in the present as cultural theme and substance in the final historicizing of the mythic, ceremonial, sacramental world of Christendom—is a basic inhibitory influence on his largest non-Yoknapatawpha vision. This is the vision of Western civilization he struggled to set forth in *A Fable*. Begun in 1944, this novel occupied its author for ten years. A novel that may seem less compatible with Yoknapatawpha than any other of the non-Yoknapatawpha works—a piece that may seem to have intervened in and been detrimental to the development of Yoknapatawpha—*A Fable* bears an important relation to Faulkner's fictional dominion. Indeed, it essentially affords a significant demarcation of first and second cycles of the Yoknapatawpha tales. In the first cycle, published between 1929 and 1942—*Sartoris, The Sound and the Fury, As I Lay Dying, Sanctuary, Light in August, Absalom, Absalom!, The Hamlet*, and *Go Down Moses*—Faulkner achieved a major representation of the dialectical drama of the crossing of the ways. He performed the task, he said, in the sweat and agony of the spirit, yet, as he also said, in joy and, in a few moments, in ecstasy. The novels of the second cycle, published between 1948 and 1962—*Intruder in the Dust, Requiem for a Nun, The Town, The Mansion*, and *The Reivers*—written with labor but evidently with less joy and never in ecstasy, are a record of the decline of the civilizational or cultural rationale of the Yoknapatawphian subject.

A Fable, it may be said, is nothing less than an attempt to confront this decline and to arrest it. It is an effort to assert the fundamental rationale of Faulkner's vision of Yoknapatawpha, that is, its service as a microcosmic image of the literary myth of modern history.

This is not to say that in the first cycle of Yoknapatawpha stories Faulkner comprehends the dialectical play of past and present in balanced tension. His attitude toward his subject is conditioned from the beginning by his sensitivity to its impermanence. In the pre-Yoknapatawpha publications—the poetic sequence called *The Marble Faun* and the novels *Soldiers' Pay* and *Mosquitoes*—Faulkner implies his awareness of the depletion of the Western mythic constructs and of the threatened loss of the myth-making capacity of the imagination. He invigorates, complicates, and expands the implication of poetic dispossession in the initial cycle of Yoknapatawpha works, transforming the life of the little patch of world that he staked out as his own into a drama of the subversion, or betrayal, of the older order of myth and tradition by the southern commitment to modern history. Exploring the character of Quentin Compson III —a character with whom he was fully empathetic and who is closer to being a fictive representation of the author than any other character in his stories—Faulkner developed a powerful symbol of the traumatic interiorization of modern history in the self. Quentin's strivings to transcend his feeling of guilt for the lapse of his family into disorder and decay lead him to imagine a myth of supreme damnation: he commits incest with his sister Caddy and the two are consigned forever to hell. But Quentin's desire for a supratemporal reference for his agony avails nothing against his ruthless historical consciousness. In *Sanctuary*, Faulkner's disposition to a historicist outlook would seem virtually to prevail. Temple Drake sitting at the last with her father in the Luxembourg Gardens—sullen, discontented, spiritually dead, while the music of Massenet dies in the descending twilight—is a symbol of the historical triumph of the waste land. Still, as the music and the whole scene in the garden of the dead queens suggests, the tension between the mythic and historical forces underlying the novel is vividly present. In *Light in August*, Faulkner creates a more explicit tension between myth and history by presenting a tangled situation in which he contrasts the Protestant anguish over history and sexuality and (as Faulkner described it in an interview) "a luminosity older than our Christian civilization." Coming "from back in the old classic times" of "fauns, satyrs, and the gods," this illumination, a light from Olympus suggested by the quality of light in a Mississippi August, is, Faulkner said, what the title of the novel refers to. In *Light in August*, the story of Lena Grove is set against that of Joe Christmas and Joanna Burden. Modernity can never betray Lena. She walks, Faulkner states, in the light of "that pagan quality of being able to assume everything." Unashamed of the desire for her child, Lena follows convention and tries to find the child's father. "But as far as she was concerned, she didn't especially need any father for it, any more than the women that—on whom Jupiter begot children were anxious for a home and a father." Lena lives in the "luminous lambent quality of an older light than ours."[11] On the other hand, while Lena has her identity in the survival of cosmic being in man's consciousness, Joe Christmas and Joanna Burden are creatures of history and are doomed by its imperious necessities. In their lives, and in the life of the Reverend Gail Hightower, Faulkner perceives the chief source of the modern historicist ethos as Protestant Christianity. Answerable for the meaning of their lives, Joe, Joanna, and Hightower remind us of how complex the American burden of history becomes when the Jef-

11 Frederick L. Gwynn and Joseph L. Blotner (eds.), *Faulkner in the University* (New York: Vintage Books, 1965), 199.

fersonian and Protestant convictions of the self's obligation to history are joined; and they further remind us that such a union has characterized the southern vision of the self.

The contention of the mythic-traditionalist and the historical modes of being is more expansively dramatized and investigated in *Go Down, Moses*. The sections in this novel called "The Bear" and "Delta Autumn" tell about Isaac McCaslin's rejection of his heritage because of the curse of slavery. In his act of renunciation Ike declares himself answerable for history, yet his subsequent attempt to imitate the life of Christ is equivocal and probably, though he does not realize it, a way of evading a responsible self-existence. Insofar as Ike illustrates the endeavor of an educated, sensitive person to return to the mythic-traditionalist mode of being, he demonstrates the impossibility of the attempt. There can be no return from the self-consciousness of history to the mythic existence, not even for one who as a boy has been privileged to enter at least into the margins of the mythic. To live in the Olympian light is possible only for an atavistic creature like Lena.

The character in the first cycle of Yoknapatawpha tales who appears to come closest to a convincing transcendence of the modern bondage to historical consciousness is Dilsey in *The Sound and the Fury*. According to Faulkner's metaphysic of endurance as exemplified in Dilsey, the survival of the mythic consciousness and the imperatives of the historical consciousness unite in the unending drama of the human heart in conflict with itself. In this drama Faulkner seeks a myth of modern man. This myth would center, not in the struggle of man to achieve historical selfhood, but in his universal capacity to endure his own nature as man, in enduring this to realize his goodness and his evil, and in this realization to prevail over his confinement in historical circumstance. Nonetheless, considered as a whole, the first Yoknapatawpha cycle does not pursue the quest for a compelling, transcending myth of man with assurance. Faulkner's vision of his subject, the past in the present as evinced in the American South, is oriented toward a deprivation of a mythic-traditionalist past by a materialistic present and always inclines toward history as the controlling center of existence.

Obedient to the dialectical shape of his subject, however, Faulkner refused to seal his image of Yoknapatawpha in historical determinism. When World War II broke out, his sense of resistance to history was accentuated. After the war was won, he wrote to his stepson Malcolm Franklin in 1943, "We must clean the world's house so that man can live in it in peace again." Meanwhile, Faulkner had begun work on a project that had originated in a Hollywood producer's idea for a movie script about World War I. The idea involved a dramatization making use of legendary questions about the identity of the anonymous soldier buried under the Arch of Triumph. Combining the story of a mutiny of French troops on the western front with the notion that the Unknown Soldier is Christ, Faulkner eventually began to write a long story or novella and finally a full-length novel about World War I. In late 1944, when he was still thinking about a story of around fifteen thousand words, he explained his conception to Robert Haas of Random House as follows: "The argument is (in the fable) in the middle of that war, Christ (some movement in mankind which wished to stop war forever) reappeared and was crucified again. We are repeating, we are in the midst of war again. Suppose Christ gives us one more chance, will we crucify him again, perhaps for the last time." Faulkner added that he did not intend "to preach at all." He summed up his argument: "We did this in 1918; in 1944 it not only MUST NOT happen again, it SHALL NOT HAPPEN again, i.e. ARE WE GOING TO LET IT HAPPEN AGAIN? now that we are in another war, where the third and final chance might be offered to save him." [12] He was putting his story "crudely," he told Haas, but it is clear that by this point Faulkner had discovered in his World War I story a challenge to explore his thought and emotion about the nature of man through a deep inquiry into the moral structure of Western civilization. As the inquiry became more elaborate and more intricate, it assumed the form of a massive, stylized, philosophical, and allegorical fable about the nature of modern existence. Moving beyond the boundaries of Yoknapatawpha, Faulkner committed himself to the broadest possible frame of novelistic reference in his search for a myth of man.

Faulkner's undertaking was bolder than, if not as successful as,

---

12 Blotner, *Faulkner*, II, 1154.

Milton's attempt to write the epic of the fall of man. Milton had a story to tell that held for him the truth of faith: he believed the poet could justify the ways of God to man. Faulkner, having no received truth of faith, sought to justify the ways of man to man by a mythic construction of his own devising. He envisioned the justification as being the intervention in history of the son of man, bringing the message that man has the capacity to spiritualize his own history. Utilizing a radical adaptation of the central part of the Christian myth, the events of the Passion Week, Faulkner intends in *A Fable* to transfer the Christian myth into the realm of a mystical humanism, which in his writings had developed as an uncertain foil to the grinding historicism of modernity. To this end *A Fable* presents two exemplary fables. One is the tall tale, drawn from the realm of southern comedy, about the horse thieves, the British sentry and the Reverend Tobe Sutterfield, and the marvelous three-legged racing horse. The other is the story, derived from religious myth, of the corporal and his father (the supreme general of the Allied forces), about the mutiny led by the corporal, and the subsequent events of the "Passion Week." Apposite to each other, the fabulous tales become mingled in the novel. By associating it with the story of the incredible horse, Faulkner obviously intends to transfer the Christian story into a fable illustrating man's imaginative power to transform his history into transcendent myth. In the story about the horse, a deputy pursuing the thieves thinks the fugitives are as good as captured when a large reward is put up for their apprehension and the return of the horse. The "sum, the amount of the reward—the black, succinct evocation of that golden dream" on the poster—insures their fate, since a "simple turn of a tongue" will bring someone "that shining and incredible heap of dollars." The thieves are "doomed not at all because passion is ephemeral (which was why they had never found any better name for it, which was why Eve and the Snake and Mary and the Lamb and Ahab and the Whale and Androcles and Balzac's African deserter, and all the celestial zoology of horse and goat and swan and bull, were the firmament of man's history instead of the mere rubble of his past), nor even because the rape was the theft and theft is wrong and wrong shall not prevail, but simply because, due to the sheer repetition of zeros behind a dollar-mark on a printed

placard, everyone within eyerange or tonguespread . . . would be almost frantically attuned to the merest whisper regarding the horse's
whereabouts." A story of unnamable desires and dreams is translated into folklore and myth; and the tale of the groom, the Negro
preacher, and the stolen horse, far from beginning the "mere rubble
of the past, the detritus of the historical record," has become a part
of the living "firmament of man's history." [13]

But *A Fable* strangely fails in its larger purpose: to place the story
of the corporal in the firmament of man's history. The fundamental
reason for this, I think, is revealed in Faulkner's exchange with a
student at the University of Virginia in 1957:

> Q. Can you make any comment on the part that the Old General plays in
> *A Fable*, who seemed to me to take two distinct, different parts if not
> more, in the theme of Passion Week, including the Three Tempta-
> tions? Would you care to elaborate at all on that character?
> A. Well, to me he was the dark, splendid, fallen angel. The good shining
> cherubim to me are not very interesting, it's the dark, gallant, fallen
> one that is moving to me. He was an implement, really. What I was
> writing about was the trilogy of man's conscience represented by the
> young British Pilot Officer, the Runner, and the Quartermaster Gen-
> eral. The one that said, This is dreadful, terrible, and I won't face it
> even at the cost of my life—that was the British aviator. The Old Gen-
> eral who said, This is terrible but we can bear it. The third one, the
> battalion Runner who said, This is dreadful, I won't stand it. I'll do
> something about it. The Old General was Satan, who had been cast
> out of heaven, and—because God himself feared him.
> Q. Well, what—the thing that puzzled me was that, going back, as far as
> I could gather, he also had been the father of the Corporal.
> A. Yes, that's right.
> Q. And that is what has somewhat puzzled me in the allegorical—
> A. That was part of Satan's fearsomeness, that he could usurp the legend
> of God. That was what made him so fearsome and so powerful, that
> he could usurp the legend of God and then discard God. That's why
> God feared him. [14]

The student's hesitant and fumbling little inquisition broke off,
but he had made a vital point. The Christ who is crucified in *A Fable* is conceived by Faulkner to be the son of man because he is the

13 *A Fable* (New York: Modern Library, 1966), 160–61.
14 Gwynn and Blotner (eds.), *Faulkner in the University*, 62–63.

son of Satan, the rebel against God. At the funeral of the old general before "the vast and serene and triumphal and enduring Arch," the protest against militarism by the corporal's disciple, the runner, hardly persuades us that the part of man's conscience that says "I'll do something about it" actually can do or wants to do anything about it.[15] In the "trinity of man's conscience" the voice of the runner is subordinate to that of the old general saying "This is terrible but we can bear it." It is the old general—Satan himself—and not the runner (in spite of Faulkner's attempt to make the disciple of the corporal the hero) who personifies the attributes of man most celebrated by Faulkner: the strength to endure his fate as the creature of his own history, and pride in his strength. The most eloquent and persuasive rhetoric in *A Fable* is the old general's. It is his (Satan's) apology for man that, in the temptation scene, strikes the truest note in the novel. Man, the old general asserts, will survive even the destruction to be wrought by "his enslavement to the demonic progeny of his own mechanical curiosity."

> O yes, he will survive it because he has that in him which will endure even beyond the ultimate worthless tideless rock freezing slowly in the last red and heatless sunset, because already the next star in the blue immensity of space will be already clamorous with the uproar of his debarkation, his puny and inexhaustible voice still talking, still planning; and there too after the last ding dong of doom has rung and died there will still be one sound more: his voice planning still to build something higher and faster and louder; more efficient and louder and faster than ever before, yet is inherent with the same old primordial fault since it too in the end will fail to eradicate him from the earth. I don't fear man. I do better. I respect and admire him. And pride: I am ten times prouder of that immortality which he does possess than ever he of that heavenly one of his delusion. Because man and his folly—"
>
> "Will endure," the corporal said.
>
> "They will do more," the old general said proudly. "They will prevail."[16]

The supreme general (whose declaration of man first appears in guise of Faulkner's Nobel Prize Address) knows what will happen in history. Moreover, he not only knows the futility of the myth of sacrifice that the corporal is once again bequeathing to man, he knows

15 For the funeral scene, see *A Fable*, 433–47.
16 *Ibid.*, 352–54.

that his son knows its futility. As the old general parts from his son, the corporal says, "Good-by, Father." The father replies, "not good-by. . . . I am durable too; I dont give up easily either. Remember whose blood it is that you defy me with."[17] The corporal does indeed know his own blood. Both he and the dark angel who fathered him know that another futile sacrifice of it is necessary as a symbolic reaffirmation of the continuity of history in its essential meaning, the drama of man and his folly. This drama endures the rejection of even the noblest sacrifice; it never transcends itself. Insofar as man prevails, he prevails *in* the endurance of his history and not *over* it. This, I would suggest, is the underlying sense of one of the most powerful yet enigmatic scenes in *A Fable*. I speak of the one when the French army chaplain comes to the corporal with his priestly "gear" —"urn ewer stole candles and crucifix"—to administer the Last Sacrament.[18] But first he must follow an order from the old general to make a final plea to the corporal to reconsider his commitment to martyrdom. In the course of his discussion with the corporal, the priest realizes that he has lost a Christ whose presence is invoked in the transcendent mystery of the Mass, the Christ of the institutional Church (the Lamb of God who takes away the sins of the world), and found in the illiterate corporal a Christ who appears as the human spirit in human history (as Faulkner said in his letter to Robert Haas, "some movement in mankind which wished to stop war forever"). To atone, it would seem, for his, or the Church's, delusion about the nature of the human spirit, for the failure to recognize the true meaning of the crucifixion as an act affirming man's nature, the priest runs a bayonet into his side. He repeats the ritualistic thrust of the spear by the Roman soldier into the body of Christ at Golgotha, in this gesture identifying himself with the Christ who is the creature of history and with the corporal, who is the son of the proud angel who fell into human history.

Although *A Fable* refers often to the ironic dualities that mark human existence, the novel culminates in no vision of mundane history differentiated from a transcending firmament of history. In fact, although the question of whether or not Satan has verily usurped

17 *Ibid.*, 356.
18 *Ibid.*, 367.

the legend of God is raised solely as poetic possibility in *A Fable*, the identification of the dramatic, story-telling, literary imagination with the "dark, splendid, fallen angel" is unmistakable. (Faulkner's depiction of the educated and matchless parable-maker, the Christ of the New Testament, as an illiterate is part of the strategy of the novel.) If there is any doubt about the identification of Satan as world-historical poet, it is removed when we compare the rhetoric of the old general with that of the famous Nobel Prize address. In *A Fable*, Faulkner not only accepts a fall of modern man from the mythic into the historical mode of existence, but also concludes that the modern literary imagination cannot reverse this fall. Man's immortality is the unending succession of mortal lives in human history. This is the idiom of being.

The stories of the second Yoknapatawpha cycle confirm the unstated conclusion of *A Fable*. In them the association of a myth of man with the crossing of the ways—with the dialectic involving a mythic-traditionalist past and a historical present—gives way to the conception that the myth of man consists in his fall into a historical condition that is unredeemable save in his struggle, ultimately futile, to redeem it.

We note how in *Intruder in the Dust* Chick Mallison finally refers his participation in the history of Jefferson to the stasis of the actor's role. The actor has some control in the interpretation of the part he plays, but in any event he plays the role to its assigned conclusion. What Chick learns—I do not mean to say overtly—is that the community of man is the drama of history. Each person plays his role in the drama, but the mythic firmament, the supporting ground of transcendent meaning, is no firmer than Gavin Stevens' rhetoric. It is just that—rhetoric. The opposition of historical actuality and mythic transcendence in *Intruder in the Dust* is a static, not an evolving, drama.

This is true too of *Requiem for a Nun*. Faulkner invents a redemptionary scheme not unlike that in *A Fable*; but it is more bizarre in its effect, for it is accommodated to a realistic rather than to a fabulous story. Condemned to hang for murdering Temple's baby, an act she has committed in order to save Temple from herself, Nancy can hardly be taken as a symbol of a secularized Christ legend. The story about Temple and Nancy describes Nancy as a nun and the bride of Christ, not as the daughter of man, and so projects the Christian story as, conceivably, historical reality. Brought into juxtaposition with Faulkner's assimilation of history and myth in the progressive unfolding of the story of Jefferson in the eloquent prologues to the three acts of the novel-play, Nancy's literalistic acceptance of the necessity of sin, suffering, faith, and redemption contrasts vividly yet subtly with the transference of history into the mythic imagination—so "vast, so limitless" in its power to "disperse and burn away the rubble-dross of fact and probability, leaving only truth and dream."[19] Nancy's violent act of murdering the baby and her own imminent death by execution recall the grim blood sacrifices recorded in the Bible, each an act performed in the name of a divinely decreed historical scheme. To escape her suffering, Temple tries to conceive of herself as existing only in the present. She is Mrs. Gowan Stevens; Temple Drake is dead with a dead past. Prompted by the moral tutelage of Gavin Stevens and Nancy, Temple responds to Gavin's dictum: "The past is never dead. It's not even past."[20] Accepting the truth of history, she comes to life as a living soul. But whether the soul can have a resting place without a full faith in a literal heaven transcending empirical history thereupon becomes Temple's anguished question. Resisting Nancy's simple admonition, "Believe," Temple reflects the Shakespearean mood Faulkner had drawn upon twenty years earlier in *The Sound and the Fury*. "What about me?" she asks. "Even if there is one [a heaven] and somebody waiting in it to forgive me, there's still tomorrow and tomorrow. And suppose tomorrow and tomorrow and then nobody there, nobody's waiting to forgive me—"[21]

The last two novels of the Snopes trilogy, *The Town* and *The Mansion*, make explicit a theme Faulkner implies in *A Fable, Intruder in the Dust*, and *Requiem for a Nun*—history is the pathetic deprivation of the mythic existence. Actually this theme is anticipated in the first Snopes novel, *The Hamlet*. In this story, Flem and Eula are up to their ears in conventional existence but bear always the signs of their

19 *Requiem for a Nun* (New York: Random House, 1951), 226.
20 *Ibid.*, 92.
21 *Ibid.*, 283.

beginnings in Faulkner's fascination with satyrs and fauns, demons and goddesses. Doomed by their presence in history but undoomed by the conflicts of the human heart, they exist in a curiously ambivalent connection to the historical motives that provide the context of their lives. Faulkner strives in *The Town* to make them vulnerable to the force of warring human passions. But he is uncertain of their strengths and fallibilities. He makes them convincing neither as displaced creatures of myth nor as creatures of a historical society. Eula kills herself in *The Town*. Ostensibly she is obedient to social convention, wanting to save her daughter, Linda, from the knowledge that Flem is not her father. But, as Ratliff discerns, she kills herself to escape the town's efforts to reduce her to human status. A goddess displaced in history has had enough of it. In *The Mansion*, the last volume of the Snopes trilogy, Flem also has had enough. He sits in his lonely mansion as though waiting for his brother Mink to come and kill him. When Mink shows up with a rusty pistol that misfires and has to be recocked, Flem makes no gesture to save himself.

Faulkner remarks in a prefatory note to *The Mansion* that between the initial conception of the Snopes story in 1925 and its completion in 1959 he had "learned . . . more about the human heart and its dilemmas."[22] What he had learned, generally speaking, was mostly a confirmation of what he knew to begin with—namely, that the myths that represent the human heart in its complex desires and conflicts belong, not to a realm that transcends human history, but to the heart's impossible longing for transcendence. The diminution of the dialectical drama of the past in the present in Faulkner's imagination eventuated in a tendency for Faulkner (like the later Mark Twain) to envision history as morally nihilistic yet eloquently pathetic. In *The Mansion*, the interwoven stories of Flem and Eula, Gavin Stevens, V. K. Ratliff, Linda Snopes, and the others arrive at the simple, bleak summation of all human motives pronounced by Stevens and Ratliff:

> "There aren't any morals," Stevens said.
> "The pore sons of bitches," Ratliff said.
> "The poor sons of bitches," Stevens said.[23]

22　*The Mansion* (New York: Vintage Books, 1959), ix.
23　*Ibid.*, 429.

This austere resolution of the literary myth of modern history—of the moral drama of the past in the present as the subject of the literary imagination—is mitigated by Mink's compelling perception of his ultimate fate, as this is interpreted by the omniscient narrator of the last chapter of *The Mansion*. Mink, lying down on the earth, feels himself "following all the little grass blades and tiny roots, the little holes the worms made, down and down into the ground already full of the folks that had the trouble but were free now . . . all mixed up and jumbled up comfortable . . . equal to any, good as any, brave as any, being inextricable from, anonymous with all of them: the beautiful, the splendid, the proud and the brave, right on up to the very top itself among the shining phantoms and dreams which are the milestones of the long human recording—Helen and the bishops, the kings and the unhomed angels, the scornful and graceless seraphim."[24]

The signs in the firmament of myth are assimilated into the long human recording; the mythic consciousness is identified with the pathos of human history. It is to be expected that Faulkner's last novel, *The Reivers: A Reminiscence*, displays merely the vestiges of the great drama of myth and history that runs through the Yoknapatawpha saga. Lucius Priest, the eleven-year-old boy who is the teller of the story, is to some extent an autobiographical persona. Although the story he relates has sharply realistic elements, Lucius concludes the monumental series of stories with an affectionate, nostalgic celebration of the events in his life in the year 1905. The civilizational tension of the crossing of the ways quietly vanishes in a past that has no present. *The Reivers* completes the story Faulkner had begun even in his earliest writings: the story of the fall of myth into history. If we consider fable to be less than myth—to be essentially an intervention of the skeptical, moralizing, and civilizing literary intelligence in the mythic sensibility, Greek, Roman, or Christian— we may say that Faulkner's work as a whole, Yoknapatawphian and non-Yoknapatawphian, in an ultimate sense constitutes a fable of history and civilization.

24 *Ibid.*, 435–36.

12 / What Survivors Do

What do survivors do?
—Lancelot Andrewes Lamar in Walker Percy,
Lancelot (1977)

My intention is to identify an aesthetic of memory as a formative element in southern fiction. Although my argument hardly extends from identification into analysis, I trust that a discursive, and rather personal and impressionistic, approach to the problem I propose will supplement the discussion in the two preceding chapters and will suggest directions for a more rigorous inquiry into the labyrinthine facets of memory and history, not only in the writers who are taken up here but in others who might well be considered.

In the small community of Texas where I grew up, there were several old people who had been citizens of the Confederate States of America, a nation that came into historical existence for four years and then was destroyed. But, as I recall, the emblems of this apocalypse who walked about in the town square—in one or two cases members of the family circle—were to me figures of a certain disappointment, or of a kind of disenchantment. They failed to fulfill my expectations of what survivors of the Confederacy should properly be like. The failure was owing no doubt to the fact that my requirements for historical heroes were derived chiefly from the same place Tom Sawyer got his—various popular sentimental fictions. But I tried to do the best I could with the materials at hand.

To cite a particular instance, I remember that for several years a pathetic old man appeared at our back door one morning each week, one hand firmly grasping the handle of a yellow lard can. My mother would take the lid off and fill the can about three-fourths full of milk. Then she would carefully and firmly push the lid down into place. The milk was always skimmed. It wasn't that the milk of human kindness ran thin in my mother's heart. Although four or five Jersey cows may have oversupplied us with milk, all the cream in it was needed for a large family. But I secretly thought we ought to do better by the old man, for he was, my mother said, a veteran of the Confederate Army. And having read Thomas Nelson Page's *Two Little Confederates* (a handsome Christmas present) until the book fell apart, and having gone on to more advanced stories of the sufferings and bravery of the Confederacy, I easily conceived of him as an authentic hero. One day I learned from my paternal grandmother, who knew everybody in the county and remembered the Civil War with disconcerting accuracy, that the recipient of my mother's benevolence was not a heroic survivor of the Lost Cause. He had been a forager for somebody's outfit, a mere boy at the time of the war, never in any battle, big or little. The discovery, I remember, left me feeling that, in some indistinct way, I had been betrayed. Of course, I did not realize as a kid in the 1920s that this surviving boy forager of the Confederacy was a far more complex and exciting embodiment of history than any character in the fictions of Thomas Nelson Page. I did not realize this any more than Tom Sawyer grasps that the Negro Jim represents something far more profound than an opportunity to effect a splendid romantic rescue of a captive according to Alexandre Dumas' imitation of a lost heroic age. I indulged myself in a conventional piety of memory but had no sense of the irony of such self-indulgence, which is not strange. It was hard for a boy of southern family to come by a sense of literary irony.

Save for Mark Twain and George Washington Cable, virtually no writers of the later nineteenth-century South ventured beyond pieties associated with remembrance. Indeed, southern literary culture was glutted with the piety of memory, as the fifteen volumes or so of the Library of Southern Literature, published in the first decade of the twentieth century, convincingly demonstrate. My father owned these books with pride, and I read them with devotion; and I have yet scarcely escaped their influence upon my literary education. When he was still in his teens, my father had aspired to at least a part-time literary career, combining his literary interests with his interest in the law. He published locally one book of verse of stultifying sentimentality. I recall to this day two lines from a poem about a boy who went bad and paid the consequences: "And there between the earth and sky / A wicked boy was hanged." My father also wrote stories. One was about a southern lad who became a martyr by being blown to smithereens in the Spanish-American War. It was called "The Sentinel Boy of the Maine." The other story was a noble tale about southern lovers who restore their lives following the Civil War. Called "Love Amid the Ruins," this work was in several chapters and pretty ambitious. An obscure forecast of the apocalyptic theme in Walker Percy's novels, one may even fancy for it a connection with literary history.

In some ways, it is worth remarking, my father had a better literary education than is common today. He knew Latin and read the standard pieces—Tacitus, Cicero, Virgil, and others. He read the New England writers, including Emerson to some extent, although Longfellow was his favorite. (I remember his copy of Longfellow's collected poems, with a declaration inscribed on the flyleaf "Commenced to commit this book to memory on April 15, 1893.") He read some of the better novelists, including Dickens and Thackeray. He read Tennyson and Browning (from whom he got the title "Love Amid the Ruins"). And it goes without saying that he was familiar with the two greatest literary resources in the English language, Shakespeare and the King James version of the Bible. He knew the latter intimately. But by and large—and this was true long after he ceased to think of literary composition save in terms of public address, for which he had a considerable renown—my father regarded literature as existing for the inculcation of religious and moral principles and the perpetuation of cultural pieties. Although he had a keen sense of irony, he saved this for the private realm of male storytelling. When a group of lawyers got together to talk shop, the pieties were handled roughly enough, or some of them. But never in public. The ironies were for the law office after the door was closed, for the fishing or hunting trip, for a little circle of men standing in front of the drugstore.

These personal recollections serve, I hope, to make a simple but highly significant point that I have more than once noted in discussing the South. In the literary sensibility of the South, there was for a long time an excess of piety and a deficiency of irony. This situation was by no means peculiar to the southern literary mind, but in southern literary expression the rhetoric of pious remembrance was general and obligatory; it was more difficult than elsewhere in the nation for even a talented writer to achieve independence from convention. Meanwhile, the writer in the South had around him waiting for realization—had closely around him in the very community he lived in, no matter how small—the richest literary subject matter in America, and among the richest to be found anywhere in the world. It consisted in nothing less than the whole intricate irony of the South living the long aftermath of its confused and disastrous attempt to establish itself in history as a nation. In the southern vision, this nation would have represented the truth of the American Republic as it had been founded in 1790, the rest of the original republic having by 1860 erred too far from the fundamental truth. Can history defeat truth, even the truth of the nation-state, which has been accepted by the modern world as the singular repository of truth and its carrier in history?

Southern writers faced this awesome question by evading it. They intended to assimilate all visions of the South—the never-never land of kindly masters and happy darkies called the Old South, the post-Civil War South of the Brahmin redeemers, and the rising, industrializing New South—in the grand metaphor of a transfigured South, a South that had become, as Robert Penn Warren has said, a City of the Soul.[1] The all-embracing piety of their response to the historical significance of the Civil War protected southern men of letters from its terrifying implication: the ironic historicity of the redemptive order assumed to have been permanently established by the American Revolution and, the inevitable corollary, the fallibility of any redemptive order.

The southern repression of historical irony is a tenuous subject. I am not at all sure that it can be rendered in tangible terms. But in the neglected work referred to previously in these pages, *The American Scene*, Henry James comes close to doing so:

1 *The Legacy of the Civil War: Meditations on the Centennial* (New York: Vintage Books, 1964), 14.

I can doubtless not sufficiently tell why, but there was something in my whole sense of the South that projected at moments a vivid and painful image—that of a figure somehow blighted or stricken, discomfortably, impossibly seated in an invalid-chair, and yet fixing one with strange eyes that were half a defiance and half a deprecation of one's noticing, and much more of one's referring to, any abnormal sign. The deprecation, in the Southern eyes, is much greater to-day, I think, then the old lurid challenge; but my haunting similitude was an image of the keeping-up of appearances, and above all of the maintenance of a tone, the "historic" high tone, in an excruciating posture.[2]

The pathetic figure of the defeated South, maintaining the historic high tone—that is to say, the memorial high tone—against historical fate, may be taken as the quintessential image of the restraint imposed by the piety of memory on the capacity of the southern literary and artistic psyche to comprehend historical reality. The consequence of this prohibition is made explicit in James's description of the Confederate Museum in Richmond. Here, amid what seemed to him the barren memorabilia of an abortive nation, James found it "impossible to imagine a community [the South] of equal size, more disinherited of arts or of letters." Culturally speaking, the South was one "great melancholy void." Memorial art introduced into this void, James thought, only enhanced the emptiness, as for example Richmond's monumental but "stranded, bereft" equestrian statue of Robert E. Lee by Mercié. Yet, contemplating the southern vacancy, James had the prescient intimation that it would be filled.

The moral . . . seemed to me . . . the touching inevitability, in such conditions, of what I have called the nursing attitude. "What on earth—nurse of a rich heroic past, nurse of a fierce avenging future, nurse of any connection that would make for *any* brood of visions about one's knee—wouldn't one have to become," I found myself inwardly exclaiming, "if one had this great melancholy void to furnish and to people!" It was not, under this reflection, the actual innocent flare of the altar of memory that was matter for surprise, but that such altars should strike one, rather, as few and faint. They would have been none too many for countenance and cheer had they blazed on every hilltop.[3]

2 *The American Scene* (New York: Scribner's, 1946), 377.
3 *Ibid.*, 387.

What would the southern piety of memory become if subjected to the pressure of a literary imagination comparable to James's? Although he could not articulate it with any precision, James foresaw the transformation of this piety into the subtle, complicated, and pervasive structure—or aesthetic—of memory that came into full flowering in Western literature after World War I. The communion with the southern subject matter in *The American Scene* announces the distinct possibility, in the very face of James's harsh strictures on southern culture, that a flowering of modern literature will occur in the South.[4]

I say a flowering of modern literature in the South. I think it is more accurate to say this than it is to refer to a modern flowering of southern literature. In contrast to those writers who belonged to the generation immediately following the Civil War, gifted southern writers born in the later 1890s and in the first decade of the twentieth century responded to the ironic mode of the modern literary mind. In so doing they discovered the omnipresent subject of modern letters: man's idea of himself as a creature of his own conception of history, and his resistance to this idea. To put this in another, and more specific, way, southern writers discovered the modern resistance to the disappearance of the community of kinship, custom, and tradition; they found, furthermore, that this resistance is complexly, tantalizingly present in the southern memory. They did not find this out all at once. However intuitive in character, the discovery resulted from hard work in apprehending the motives and methods of modern literary irony. Their teachers were varied, although Flaubert, Turgenev, Proust, Mann, Joyce, Yeats, and Eliot formed a common core of masters. In summary, the education that southern writers gained from such masters consisted in learning that modern culture is a historical phenomenon. Far from being bardic or epic, or in any sense col-

---

4 In the first part of this comment, I have drawn on certain materials that I have made some use of elsewhere, particularly in "The Southern Novelist and Southern Nationalism," in *The Man of Letters in New England and the South: Essays on the Literary Vocation in America* (Baton Rouge: Louisiana State University Press, 1973), 201–28; "Some Prefatory Notes on Garnishing and Peopling a Void," *Southern Review*, n.s. 8 (Autumn, 1972), xv–xix; "The Civil War: Written and Unwritten," *Southern Literary Journal*, 7 (Fall, 1974), 132–34.

lective in expression, it takes its character from an isolation—an interiorizing—of history in the individual consciousness (and particularly in the consciousness of the writer).

I have never encountered a more fitting symbolization of the self-conscious southern appropriation of the twentieth-century literary mind than the decorations that the Mississippi writer George Marion O'Donnell had on his office wall at Louisiana State University when he was teaching there in the later 1940s. O'Donnell (who died in 1962) was too young to have been a contributor to the Agrarian manifesto, *I'll Take My Stand* (1930), but he did witness his discipleship to the Vanderbilt group by taking part in the symposium called *Who Owns America?: A Declaration of Independence* (1936). The ornaments he had on his wall, however, reflected less a polemical than a memorial cast of spirit. There were three: a photograph of his grandfather in the uniform of a Confederate officer, his grandfather's sword, and a photograph of the death mask of Proust. O'Donnell also had, I think, a photograph of Joyce, but this hung apart from the trio of major symbols, which were arranged above his desk. The symbolic arrangement no doubt represented O'Donnell's chief ambition, to write a trilogy of novels about the life and death of the South.[5] He had become privy to the secret of Proust: an elaborate, compelling coalescence of memory and history in the trained and disciplined literary consciousness. But, for whatever reason, O'Donnell was never able to make Proust's secret work in his own writing; and he never got beyond a fragmentary composition of *No More, My Ladies*, the title he gave his projected trilogy. It could be that he attempted in too literal a way to seize on the Proustian vision of the search for lost time and so short-circuited his imagination, bypassing his own instinctive life for the sake of imitating Proust. It could be that he was intimidated by the example of an older writer of his own state, William Faulkner, who had powerfully realized the possibilities of the ironic quest for the meaning of memory in modernity in such works as *The Sound and the Fury, Light in August*, and *Absalom, Absalom!* In fact, O'Donnell grasped Faulkner's significance at a time when few had, and in his essay entitled "Faulkner's Mythol-

5 I have commented on O'Donnell's significance in "O'Donnell's Wall," in *The Man of Letters in New England and the South*, 192–200.

ogy" presented one of the first illuminating critical comments on his novels.[6] Today O'Donnell's interpretation of Faulkner's world seems to be narrowly conceived. But his thesis—"Faulkner is unable to sustain his traditionalism at all, and the forces of antitraditionalism become the protagonists"—remains fundamentally evocative. In his doomed struggle to assert the continuity of past and present, Faulkner, as O'Donnell sees his stories, creates a world populated by a variety of lonely, anxious survivors of the community of myth and tradition who are pitted in a losing fight against the morally destructive forces of history represented by the multitudinous Snopes clan. The conception of this conflict is based not simply on Faulkner's reverence and regret for the old community, but also on his deep apprehension of the passionate drama of the self's bewildering experience of the transformation of an assumed metaphysical and moral order into the dehumanized present-day society of history and science. O'Donnell's version of Faulkner suggests that he follows the Proustian or Joycean, the whole modern, expression of memory as a resistance to historicism. His work is an elaborate and central exemplification of the modern memorial motive in southern fiction.

The southern aesthetic of memory, as we would expect, has expressed itself more in novelistic practice than in critical formulation. But our insight into its structure has lately been illuminated in an essay by one of its most sensitive and accomplished practitioners, Eudora Welty. In this essay, called "Some Notes on Time in Fiction," Miss Welty envisages "time" as entirely synonymous with the modern historicism of consciousness. She comments, among other things, on the disturbance or disruption of chronology in modern fiction: "If a point is reached in fiction when chronology has to be torn down, it must be in order to admit and make room for what matters overwhelmingly more to the human beings who are its characters." She continues:

> Faulkner has crowded chronology out of the way many times to make way for memory and the life of the past, as we know, and we know for

6 O'Donnell's essay on Faulkner may be conveniently found in *Faulkner: A Collection of Critical Essays*, ed. Robert Penn Warren (Englewood Cliffs, N.J.: Prentice-Hall, 1966), 23–33.

what reason. "Memory believes before knowing remembers," he says (in *Light in August*). Remembering is so basic and vital a part of staying alive that it takes on the strength of an instinct of survival, and acquires the power of an art. Remembering is done through the blood, it is a bequeathment, it takes account of what happens before a man is born as if he were there taking part. It is a physical absorption through the living body, it is a spiritual heritage. It is also a life's work.[7]

The work of the southern storyteller has been shaped, in Miss Welty's retrospective vision, by the exigent force of the memory against history. It has been formed by the very drama engendered in the effort to translate an instinct into the order of art—to, we might put it, make the flesh into the word.

Such a struggle did not come into being until early modern times —the age of Shakespeare and Cervantes—and did not reach its definitive stage until the present century. This is not to say that the literary registration of memory as an instinct of survival against history is uniquely modern. The fear of history, and the origin of memory, are to be traced to the initial differentiation of the historical from the cosmic consciousness of existence. Memory, the ancients said, is the mother of the muses. But it would appear that remembering as an art of the psychic—the spiritual—survival of the individual did not come into being until the culture of kinship and custom, of tradition and myth, began to give way altogether to the culture of rationality. In the society of mythic and traditionalist order, memory is not a means of personal survival, as it is in Proust, Faulkner, and Miss Welty. It is not even a separate function of consciousness. In the traditionalist society, memory is yet in the flesh and in the blood. Miss Welty would have memory still function as instinct. But in her formation of the aesthetic of memory she comprehends modernity and the Cartesian severance of flesh and word together with the consequence. This is the looking upon everything—man, nature, place, time, and God—as subject to the dominion of history. Not of history as a story; on the contrary, of history as an ineluctable process or series of processes, which may be regarded either as teleological or blankly purposeless. In this situation, memory became, not a spiritual heritage, but a "life's work." If I interpret the poetry

7 "Some Notes on Time in Fiction," *Mississippi Quarterly*, 26 (Fall, 1973), 490.

of her remarks correctly, Miss Welty sees the modern novel as a trans-figuration of history: "Mann, attacking the subjectivity of man's knowledge of time, and Proust, discovering a way to make time give back all it has taken, through turning life by way of memory into art, left masterpieces that are like clocks themselves, giant clocks stationed for always out in the world, sounding for us the high hours of our literature."[8]

Resistance to the historicism of the modern consciousness has not impelled all twentieth-century American novelists to emulate the Proustian quest to transform history through the individual memory into art. It has often been observed that there is little recognition of family or community in Hemingway. Corporate existence is not real to him. What is real is the isolation of the self in history. The only countervailing reality is the refuge that the self finds in some tiny, fragile enclave of love: Jake Barnes and Lady Brett in *The Sun Also Rises*; Lieutenant Henry and Catherine in *A Farewell to Arms*; Robert Jordan and Maria in *For Whom the Bell Tolls*. The momentary resistance to history symbolized by such relationships is based on a strategic avoidance of memory. The rule of the Hemingway hero, his technique of survival, is don't think about it. With consummate irony, Hemingway uses the power of the word to say over and over, don't let the flesh become articulate in the word. This for the writer is the same thing as saying, don't let the memory believe. This astringent negativity toward memory moves us strongly, celebrating as it does a self-decreed resistance to the individual's envelopment in history through his perception of his own autonomy.

But the rejection of memory did not appeal to Hemingway's contemporary in the South. It was hardly a possibility for him. He knew a different kind of resistance to history. He had been born into a community that existed in a tension toward history, a culture of memory that history has paradoxically effected in the South. Contrary to the illusion it has fostered, the southern culture of memory is in no basic sense a perpetuation of the traditionalist world of kinship and tradition. Representing the southern society as a memorial image of this world, its motive is a cultural nostalgia directly opposing the histor-

8 *Ibid.*, 491.

ical reality of the South. The motive was present before the Civil War as well as after it. Subject to a divisive and fragmenting Protestantism, the Old South found no center in a unified religious authority and thus was without a prime requirement of a traditional society. Nor was the Old South (although its chief business was agriculture), in the usual signification of the term, a traditionalist agrarian order. It was an unprecedented political economy, a modern chattel slave society, which found its symbol in the pastoral and patriarchal plantation but could conceivably—in a fuller realization of its essential nature than was permitted by historical circumstances—have also found its representation in the industrial slave city. It might too have found its representation in empire. Southerners were visited by recurrent dreams of a vast slave dominion. Embracing Mexico, Central America, Brazil, the Caribbean islands, this progressive empire would foster a cotton economy that would redeem the world from poverty and war. There was not much difference between the Old South's dynamic of historical destiny and the New South movement in the generation after Appomattox. The New South, Henry W. Grady said in his famous speech before the New England Society in 1886, "understands that her emancipation came because through the inscrutable wisdom of God" the antebellum South's "honest purpose was crossed, and her brave armies were beaten." God has decreed, Grady said, that the South's destiny is to embrace the sacred trinity of education, science, and industrialism. Having been forced to give up slavery, the aspect of its existence incompatible with modernity, the South, in Grady's vision, would now fulfill its role in the culture of historical process. The novels of the New South continue a reaction to this culture that is present in the preceding antebellum novels, exuding the nostalgic yet at time stangely ironic atmosphere pervading such key Old South novels as John Pendleton Kennedy's *Swallow Barn* and William Gilmore Simms's *Woodcraft*.[9] But in the postbellum stories, there is a compounding of the atmospheric

9 "The New South," in *The Literature of the South*, ed. Richard Croom Beatty, Floyd C. Watkins, Thomas Daniel Young, and Randall Stewart (Atlanta: Scott Foresman, 1952), 492. See Lewis P. Simpson, *The Dispossessed Garden: Pastoral and History in Southern Literature* (Athens: University of Georgia Press, 1975), 43–64.

quality. In a plantation novel like Page's *Red Rock*, the antebellum
society appears as the memory of a society that is in itself the memory of some presumed, actual, archetypal society.

When the Proustian-Joycean literary mind began to take over in the
South (asserting its presence in Faulkner, O'Donnell, Miss Welty,
Robert Penn Warren, and the many other writers who belong to the
"Southern Renaissance"), it repudiated the simplicities of the southern culture of memory but not its deeper symbolic meaning. It affirmed what was emblazoned on O'Donnell's wall: its own underlying continuity with the southern novelistic imagination. It disclosed,
emotionally if not analytically, that the southern aesthetic of memory is imbedded in the European matrix of memory, and so greatly
complicated and enlarged the possibilities of the southern novelist.
The continuation of these possibilities, not only in writers from
whom we expect their lasting assertion, like Eudora Welty and Robert Penn Warren, but in writers of later vintage, must be recognized
as one of the important forces of twentieth-century southern letters.
The power of the continuation is especially to be noted in southern
writers who ardently desire to free themselves from the work of
memory.

I am thinking expressly of Flannery O'Connor and Walker Percy.
As committed Roman Catholic writers, they may be considered ec-
centrics in a still largely Protestant South; but not only are they the
most remarkable southern fictionists of the past twenty-five years,
they are pivotal figures in the resolution of the drama of history and
memory in southern fiction.

Talking about the future of fiction in 1960, Miss O'Connor said:

> There is no literary orthodoxy that can be prescribed as settled for the
> fiction writer, not even that of Henry James, who balanced the elements
> of traditional realism and romance so admirably within each of his nov-
> els. But this much can be said. The great novels we get in the future are
> not going to be those that the public thinks it wants, or those that critics
> demand. They are going to be the kind of novels that interest the novel-
> ist. And the novels that interest are those that have already been written.
> They are those that put the greatest demands on him, that require him to
> operate at the maximum of his intelligence and his talents, and to be true
> to the particularities of his own vocation. The direction of many of us

will be more toward poetry than toward the traditional novel.[10]

These remarks, which belong to Miss O'Connor's noted defense of the grotesque in southern fiction, suggest (although one assumes with no intention on her part) that the author of *Wise Blood* and *The Violent Bear It Away* is putting a period to the time when southern writers were engaged in "garnishing and peopling" the "melancholy void" that was the South of Jamesian vision. Even though Miss O'Connor speaks about the importance of a "shared past, a sense of alikeness and the possibility of reading a small history in a universal light" as literary attributes of the South, she says that the identity of a region is "not made from what passes, but from those qualities that endure, regardless of what passes, because they are related to truth."[11] In her sense of the South, its enduring quality is not remembrance; it is something "known only to God, but of those who look for it, none gets so close as the artist."

> Every serious writer will put his finger on it at a slightly different spot but in the same region of sensitivity. When Walker Percy won the National Book Award, newsmen asked him why there were so many good Southern writers and he said, "Because we lost the War." He didn't mean by that simply that a lost war makes good subject matter. What he was saying was that we have had our Fall. We have gone into the modern world with an inburnt knowledge of human limitations and with a sense of mystery which could not have developed in our first state of innocence— as it has not sufficiently developed in the rest of our country.[12]

What Percy knows is not merely that the Civil War, like any war, is a symbol of the Fall of Man. "Behind" southern history, Miss O'Connor declares, "deepening it at every point, has been another history." The southern writer is different from nonsouthern writers because he has "a vision of Moses' face as he pulverized our idols." The southern writer descends in the line of prophets. He has the gift and vocation of prophetic interpretation. Operating at "a peculiar crossroads where time and place and eternity somehow meet," he is a participant (not a participant-observer but a participant) in the transcen-

10 "The Grotesque in Southern Fiction," in *Mystery and Manners*, ed. Sally and Robert Fitzgerald (New York: Farrar, Straus, and Giroux, 1969), 49–50.
11 "The Regional Writer," in *Mystery and Manners*, 58.
12 *Ibid.*, 58–59.

dent mystery of the history behind history. His "problem" is to discover the "location" where he is operating.[13] Since he must fix this through his art, Miss O'Connor implies, it is necessary for him to abandon the metaphor of the novel (or the short story, Miss O'Connor's chief form) as a clock stationed in time. It is the nexus of time, place, and eternity.

We become aware that Flannery O'Connor has refocused the southern fictional imperative. Rejecting the mode of remembering—of inwardly assimilating history to memory—she has embraced the mode of revelation. Interestingly enough, she wrote two stories that illustrate her shifting focus on the necessary aesthetic of fiction in the South. One, which appears in her first book, "A Late Encounter with the Enemy," is about General Tennessee Flintrock Sash, a ninety-two-year-old Confederate veteran (who had "probably" in actuality been nothing more than a foot soldier, although he cannot remember what he was, and in fact cannot remember the war) and his sixty-two-year-old granddaughter, Sally Porker Sash, who uses her senile grandfather as a means of glorifying the ceremony attending her belated commencement from a small southern college. In "A Late Encounter with the Enemy," Miss O'Connor again evokes a comparison with James. The difference between the Jamesian figure of the South as an invalid in a wheelchair but possessed of the high historic tone and General Sash—who on every Confederate Memorial Day is wheeled into the town museum to be displayed from one to four in the afternoon—is the difference between the Jamesian respect for the culture of memory and a deliberate spoofing and degradation of it. The debasement of memory in Miss O'Connor is directed toward preparing the way to assume the vocation to prophecy. This preparation reaches toward fulfillment in a late story in the O'Connor canon entitled "Revelation." In this story, the metaphysical crossroads is precisely fixed in the vision of the operation of God's redeeming grace that Ruby Turpin beholds in the skies as she stands gripping the rail of the Turpins' pig parlor and listening to the echo of the question she has hurled at God, "Who do you think you are?"[14]

13 *Ibid.*, 59.
14 "Revelation," in *The Complete Stories of Flannery O'Connor* (New York: Farrar, Straus and Giroux, 1972), 507.

Yet this determination of the crucial crossroads has a disconcertingly abstract quality. For all of Flannery O'Connor's skill in handling setting and character, there is an incongruity between Ruby's profound question and the questioner. As a matter of fact, the whole situation in "Revelation" is unconvincing. Ruby's response to the nasty taunts of the girl from Wellesey moves into depths of a self that Ruby, as a member of her historical society, does not possess. This movement is interpreted as the working of God's grace, which surely can yield a vision beyond one's level of theological sophistication. But even in the domain of southern Protestantism visions come to those in some way prepared for them. We are not convinced that time, place, and eternity find a location in Ruby's story because it is not *her* story. It is the author's; and it is Miss O'Connor—as poet-prophet, as participant in the mystery of the history behind history—who assigns the location. Revelation originates, Miss O'Connor observes, in a descent into the writer's self that is "at the same time a descent" into the writer's region. "It will," she says, "be a descent through the darkness of the familiar into a world where, like the blind man cured in the gospels, he sees men as if they were trees, but walking." [15] In the sense of this observation, the great metaphysical juncture is located in the self (in the older term, in the soul) of the writer. Flannery O'Connor suppresses the motive of the southern literary imagination known to Faulkner, Eudora Welty, and Warren: a tension between memory and history. Ascribing to the southern writer a transcendent religiosity of consciousness, she parodies the quest to resist the historicist compulsion. An actor in the drama of existence, lacking the capacity for detached observation and suspension of judgment, she fails to realize that her concept of a simultaneous descent into the self and into the South is a way of evading the historicism of consciousness; that the problem of locating the transcendent juncture of time, place, and eternity is ironically involved with the problem of the modern self's tendency to enclose history in the self. Having no empathy with the self that internalizes history as memory so that it may survive history and its catastrophes, she oversimplifies the modern situation of the self; her stories

15 "The Grotesque in Southern Fiction," in *Mystery and Manners*, 50.

employ a series of characters who lack the sophistication to grapple inwardly with the subleties of the self as a creature of modern secular history. She lacks, perhaps refuses, an intimacy with history. Blessed by an overpowering gift of faith, she lets the Faulkner company, the survivors of history, go its way. Her vision is directed toward timeless order and the ultimate beatitude of the soul. Prophesying the irresistibility of God's grace in the life of the individual, her stories follow a compelling aesthetic of revelation. The result is that, in spite of their detailed portrayal of the manners of her region, they divest it of a tension toward historical reality.

Walker Percy may have had a harder time of it than the company of Faulkner or Flannery O'Connor. A self-conscious survivor of history and a highly self-conscious Christian, he has followed the prophetic inclination into apocalyptic eschatology. He has identified his being as a novelist with an image of the self in the loneliest possible state of being. This is the self embodied in a person who knows that the modern world either has already ended or soon will; who knows this when almost nobody else knows or even suspects it; and who knows—his most important knowledge—that he is now a survivor of a world that has ended.

Percy was trained to be a medical doctor, taking his premedical work at the University of North Carolina and his medical training at Columbia University School of Medicine, from which he was graduated with the M.D. degree. Forced to forego the practice of medicine, he took up the study of religion and philosophy, became (like Caroline Gordon, Allen Tate, and, more recently, Walter Sullivan) a convert to Roman Catholicism, and began to write essays on religious and philosophical subjects. He learned as he went along that science "is not the only way of telling the truth." Science can arrive at quantitative truth, but "it cannot utter one single sentence about what man is himself as an individual" and does not attempt to do so. When made the object of the scientific attitude, a man becomes a "great lacuna, a great vacuum."[16] Percy came to see, in the terms that I have been using, that the scientific-rationalistic focus on exis-

16 "Walker Percy: Rotation and Repetition" (an interview with Percy) in John Carr, *Kite-Flying and Other Irrational Acts* (Baton Rouge: Louisiana State University Press, 1972), 39.

tence has isolated and abstracted the self in history. Having arrived at this conception of the self in extremis, Percy turned to the novel in an attempt to imagine and describe this condition. During the twenty years he has devoted to fiction, he has published four novels. In the protagonists and antagonists of these stories, he dramatizes a relation among history, memory, and prophecy that eventually takes the form of a tension between memory and eschatology.

Aunt Emily in Percy's first novel, *The Moviegoer*, represents the southern culture of memory as characterized by a Stoic nobility of behavior joined to a gentility of manners. But her nephew, Binx Bolling, rejects her attempts to suggest that he recover the ideal of honor and self-discipline held by this culture. In his quiet but intense and struggling search for God—in the midst of the "very century of merde, the great shithouse of scientific humanism . . . where . . . the malaise has settled like fall-out"[17]—Binx, who has yet the strongest sense of time and place, knows southern ghosts when he sees them and would like to yield himself to them. But he resists them and becomes a laconic prophet of the self's redemption through the Kierkegaardian leap into faith. Yet Binx's entry into the Kierkegaardian religious state is not repeated in Percy's tales. These tend to become at once more anxious in tone, more complex in theme, and darker in substance. In *The Last Gentleman*, the internalization of southern history as memory in young Will Barrett assumes a psychopathic quality. Subject to recurrent episodes of *déjà vu* followed by prolonged spells of amnesia, Barrett is a hysteric, who even between his amnesiac periods "did not quite know what was what. Much of the time he was like a man who has just crawled out of a bombed building. Everything looked strange." Although "such a predicament . . . is not altogether a bad thing," inasmuch as Barrett, like the "sole survivor of a bombed building . . . had no secondhand opinions and . . . could see things afresh," the youthful southerner does not experience a transcendence of his condition.[18] In contrast to the prophetic role of the dour Sutter Vaught (a medical doctor who has lost his license), Barrett's role in *The Last Gentleman* does not seem to promise spiritual fulfillment of the self. One significance of Barrett's role, possibly a

17 *The Moviegoer* (New York: Knopf, 1973), 228.
18 *The Last Gentleman* (New York: New American Library, 1968), 17.

primary one, is that it assigns memory an elusive yet important place in the etiology of the modern spirit. Set in a "time near the end of the world," Percy's third novel, *Love in the Ruins*, depicts the condition of an America and a South that have followed the governing logic of the society of history and science to its culmination in an utter madness of rationality. In the final phase of the society created by the modern behavioralists, who are determined to perfect a technology of consciousness (and who are living in a citadel in an unnamed city that is obviously New Orleans), the classical-Christian concepts of the culture of memory are but a ghostly presence. And yet they are a strong, ironic memorial presence, for they supply the ostensible justification for the scientific management of the psyche. Martin Luschei points out that when Dr. Tom Moore, the hero of Percy's novel, listens to Buddy Brown run through a scientific litany it is "like Binx Bolling enduring his Aunt Emily." Brown "speaks a language of ideals drawn from the Judaeo-Christian tradition and operates on behaviorist assumptions."[19] But a greater irony in *Love in the Ruins* than the culture of memory is the ghostly presence of Utopia—of the indistinct memory of the rational paradise created by Dr. Tom Moore's ancestor, the sainted Sir Thomas More.

In his suggestion of this presence, Percy penetrates the more inaccessible nuances of the American imagination of existence. During the centuries since *Utopia* was written, the idea of the utopian community has become confused with the golden age, the Garden of Eden, heaven, paradise, and the millennium. In Sir Thomas More's mind, an unrealizable no-place, Utopia, has become a some-place to be realized on earth—a symbol of a transcendent community immanent in secular history. Representing the moment in the sixteenth century when the image of a rational society began to become a prophetic image of the future and time began to become a series of possibilities to be shaped by the mind, the utopian quest has curiously united memory and the future. The historical advancement of knowledge, the whole dynamic of linear progress, demands that man always remember that he belongs to the future. The demand became urgent upon the European taking on the aspect of the American, a

19 *The Sovereign Wayfarer: Walker Percy's Diagnosis of the Malaise* (Baton Rouge: Louisiana State University Press, 1972), 210–11.

new man in a new world. Forever on a trek toward a no-place that he has confidently believed to be *some* place, the American has moved readily in his imagination from memory to apocalypse, hardly pausing at the stage of prophecy. He might seem almost to have erased the tension between memory and history. But of course the tension has not been obliterated. The longer Utopia has been deferred, the more insistently and desperately memory has prompted us to recall that we are the people chosen solely to have a future—to realize the apocalypse of the rational state, to attain the condition of existence once proclaimed and now memorialized in the Declaration of Independence. *Lancelot*, Percy's most recent novel, is a logical development out of his fascination with utopian symbolism in *Love in the Ruins*. It explicitly dramatizes the self's internalization of American history as the memory of the future.

A leading theme in *Lancelot* is the protagonist's effort to reject memory. He deplores memory, not because it is a symptom of a diseased consciousness, but because it is banal. Confined in a psychiatric ward, Lancelot spends his time imagining a search through the ashes of Belle Isle (the ancestral home he has blown up, together with his faithless wife) for a clue to his act of destruction, one that will enable him to "endure the horrible banality" of what he has done. He suffers, he tells Percival, the priest-friend who listens to his story, not because of what he has done, but "because the past, any past . . . is so goddamn banal and feckless and useless." What clue does he seek? Not one, he says, to "the 'mystery' of Belle Isle." He continues: "No, that's not the mystery. The mystery lies in the here and now. The mystery is: What is one to do with oneself. As you get older and you begin to realize the trick time is playing, and that unless you do something about it, the passage of time is nothing but the encroachment of the horrible banality of the past on the pure future. The past devours the future like a tape recorder, converting pure possibility into banality. The present is the tape head, the mouth of time." [20]

Lancelot would recover the American remembrance of the future: the forever lost yet forever pure possibility of the future. Contemplating the chance that he may go to live with Anna (the victim of a

20 *Lancelot* (New York: Farrar, Straus and Giroux, 1977), 105.

gang rape who is a patient in the room next to him) in her father's cabin in the Blue Ridge country of Virginia, he renounces his prior vision of a new beginning at Big Sur in California. "It won't be California after all. It will be settled in Virginia, where it started."

> Don't you see? Virginia is neither North nor South but both and neither. Betwixt and between. An island between two disasters. Facing both: both the defunct and befouled and collapsing North and the corrupt thriving and Jesus-hollering South. . . .
> The Virginian? He may not realize it, but he is the last hope of the Third Revolution. The First Revolution was won at Yorktown. The Second Revolution was lost at Appomattox. The Third Revolution will begin there, in the Shenandoah Valley.[21]

Lancelot tells about a dream he has had. A young man stands in a pass over the Shenandoah Valley; a scout apparently, he must be waiting for a message. In the distance, men are singing and may be marching to a song. Their song, however, is strangely unmartial: *Oh Shenandoah we long to see you.* About leaving one paradise for another, elegiac, wistful, melancholy, this meditative lament—in which the destiny of America is forever suspended between the "green hills of the Shenandoah" and the distant "wide Missouri"— is the quintessential evocation of the strain in the American consciousness between memory and history. Brooding on the failure of the first two American revolutions, Lancelot seeks in effect to destroy this anxiety. Dreaming the American dream as a version of the gnostic nightmare of modern history, he declares that he will redeem America from the Sodom that it has become in failing to fulfill itself in its revolutionary ethos. He will do this by his own instrumentality, he says, by the sword if necessary. But, Lancelot tells Percival, he is willing to wait in order to give Percival's God, if he exists, time to act. Is Lancelot insane, removed from all reality? Or is he absolutely sane and attempting to articulate a reality he is experiencing: a struggle of the soul against its degeneration into gnostic selfhood, a conflict he can dramatize but cannot exposit? There is surely some suggestion that Lancelot is irresolute in his commitment to his self-conceived mission. There is the possibility, to be sure, that he suspects that it is a delusion of the homeless modern self. Lancelot's fury against the corruption of the American apocalypse may in fact mask a motive of far more import than that of purifying the American memory of the future. Imagining the self on the "island of Virginia," Lancelot resembles the castaway in Percy's central philosophical essay, "The Message in the Bottle," who waits for news from a newsbearer who comes from across the sea. Yet if there is a possibility that Lancelot could be redeemed by receiving a message in the wordless language of divine grace, it is negated by his ironic obligation to the historical pattern of the South, an imperative movement from memory into prophecy and apocalypse. Implicit in the element of memory present in southern fiction as far back as George Tucker's *Valley of Shenandoah* (1824), the stages of this movement may be traced broadly from Tucker to Percy, although in all the more complex southern writers the three stages are present at once, so that the movement may be described as dialectical.

But it is not until the last half of the twentieth century—when, in Percy's novels, the southern aesthetic of memory is subjected to the ethos of a profound and severe Christian existentialism—that the dialectic develops a subtle tautness between history and eternity. In "The Message in the Bottle," Percy quotes Kierkegaard on faith and knowledge: "Faith is not a form of knowledge, for all knowledge is either knowledge of the eternal, excluding the temporal and the historical as indifferent, or it is pure historical knowledge. No knowledge can have for its object the absurdity that the eternal is the historical." In his distinction between the eternal and the historical, the Danish philosopher offers a strategic opposition to the triumph of the modern society of history and science, a triumph based, as Kierkegaard sees it, on the confusion of the timeless and the temporal. For once, Percy takes exception to his mentor.[22] If it is to be meaningful, the news that the newsbearer brings to the castaway cannot be a knowledge offered as a truth *sub specie aeternitatis*, but news borne within time to a specific person, a creature of history who, yearning for the news, receives it—through faith and by the

22 See Percy's "The Message in the Bottle," *The Message in the Bottle: How Queer Man Is, How Queer Language Is, and What One Has to Do with the Other* (New York: Farrar, Straus and Giroux, 1975), 119–49.

grace of God. It is news that only the castaway, conceived as a survivor of history, can hear.

Seen in the light of Percy's gloss on Kierkegaard, the story of Lancelot ends darkly. It would seem likely that, although he may wait to give God a chance, Lancelot is not one who truly yearns for the good news and so is capable of hearing it. It may be doubtful, furthermore, if Percival, the almost silent priest who listens to Lancelot, is a valid messenger.

All of Percy's novels involve the dialectic of memory, prophecy, and apocalypse and are about survivors of history. In each one of them, the castaway, the survivor of history—specifically a survivor of the history of the American South, white, male, and of "good family"—is potentially the recipient of a salvational message. In each of his novels, Percy leaves open the question of the extent to which the message is received—whether it is received at all—but in *Lancelot*, does the novelist leave any room for hope that the saving knowledge will ever be heard? Lancelot has blocked out the possibility by listening to another message: the compelling promise that the memory of the future holds forth. This is to say, the promise of the self-actualization of the eternal as the historical, or the fulfillment of the promise that the self is God. Evidently determined to embody the absurd impulse of modernity—to incarnate the mystery of history in the finitude of the self—Lancelot is Percy's most frightening creation. Although students of southern culture have advanced the notion that the catastrophe of the Civil War made southerners wary of the danger of self-will, as it made Yankees susceptible to it, Percy recognizes in the portrayal of Lancelot that the modern will to apocalyptic selfhood is an inherent force in the southern sense of memory.

13 / The Closure of History in a Postsouthern America

> We shall never be again as we were!
>
> —Kate Croy in Henry James,
> *The Wings of the Dove* (1902)

A major motive of the twentieth-century southern literary expression is a vision of social order at once strongly sacramental and sternly moralistic. The vision, integral with its source, the classical-Christian ground of Western civilization, has been fundamental to the moral history of the nation as a whole. But the union of the sacred and the righteous in the South has borne a character derived from the southern experience of the historical displacement of the ancient community of masters and slaves, free and bond, lords and servants. For writers in the rest of the nation, this experience effectively concluded with the removal of a king from the center of order by the American Revolution. Its meaning was put in more or less conclusive perspective by Cooper, Hawthorne, and Melville. But the unresolved, problematical meaning of the experience has been the southern subject from Thomas Jefferson, John Randolph, and George Tucker to John Crowe Ransom, Donald Davidson, Allen Tate, Andrew Lytle, and William Faulkner. It echoes vividly in Robert Penn Warren, Eudora Welty, and William Styron. It sounds clearly in Walker Percy and John William Corrington, although more distantly in Flannery O'Connor.

The recognition of the southern subject has been somewhat obscured by the tendency of southern interpreters over the years to confuse the experience of displacement with the perpetuation in the South of the actual order of hierarchical, authoritative community. The confusion is evident in the assumption that a seventeenth-century Virginia plantation like Westover was an actual, not merely an attempted, transference of the English feudal estate to America. In a more complex sense, it is evident in the nineteenth-century de-

255

fense of chattel slavery. To support a historical contingency that had become an economic necessity, southerners tried to conceive their society as a restoration of the sacred community. The relation that southern men of letters bear to this effort and to the later attempt to contain the former slaves and their descendants in a sacerdotal segregation of white and black (which assumed paradoxically to affirm community) is choate with the assumption of twentieth-century southern writers that their sensibility is continuous with an old-world consciousness, in which bardic poetry integrated the divine, art, and self. But this assumption is an illusion. The South has its origins in a movement out of an old-world community already in a state of dissolution onto a vast colonial frontier transparently governed by the opportunities and accidents of history. Trying to represent the South as a unified sensibility, the southern writer has ironically implied that the very effort is a historical gesture.

This tension toward history, the essential motive in the inner drama of the southern literary mind in the present century, is nowhere displayed more succinctly and convincingly than in the critical stance that the novelist and critic Walter Sullivan takes in two remarkable meditations on southern literature, *Death by Melancholy* (1972) and *Requiem for the Renascence* (1976). The moral earnestness of his opposition to the historical destruction of the community of myth and tradition, together with his emotional grasp of the mode of life developed in the centuries when Christendom prevailed, issue with reverberant irony in his perception of the historicity of his own passionate attempt to discover a South transcending the modern condition of temporality (the condition that developed, André Malraux observes, when "clocks begin to reign over the churches"). In resisting what he perceives, Sullivan becomes both an elegist of the twentieth-century Southern Literary Renascence and a brilliant and bitter analyst of the causes and consequences of its passing. An examination in some detail of his criticism, notably with respect to its treatment of the literary vocation, suggests that in the 1960s and 1970s Sullivan has assumed the role of the sensitive and provocative theorist of southern literature that Allen Tate occupied in the 1930s and 1940s.

Among the assumptions Sullivan makes about the Southern Literary Renascence (in his interpretation, the period in southern writing from the 1920s to the mid-1940s) is that it represents a moral and spiritual entity. We are justified, I think, in placing an extraordinary emphasis on the term *state* in his subtitle to *A Requiem for the Renascence*: "The State of Fiction in the Modern South." The term conveys the notion, not merely of the state of a literary art, but of the condition of a literary dominion. It reflects the correlation of southern fiction with the South as a spiritual nation explicitly made in an essay in *Death by Melancholy* entitled "In the Time of the Breaking of Nations: The Decline of Southern Fiction":

> It is a commonplace among historians and political scientists that the whole concept of nationalism is obsolete. Although much of the world has yet to learn this, it seems to me to be undeniably true, and a Southern writer's failure to understand it will be reflected in his work. The time of the southern renascence was the time of political and social integrity of the southern nation, but now the southern nation is only a shell of its former self. Its physical characteristics have been changed by the growth of urban centers, the construction of super highways, and most of all by the innumerable products of the general postwar affluence in which the South has shared.

The concept of the Southern Renascence as coincident with, and an expression of, the "southern nation" in its political and social wholeness—a concept that so willfully disregards the reality of the South in the 1920s and 1930s—may be taken to indicate the lingering glow of the Confederacy in Sullivan's heart. But the inspiriting center of his criticism is not fundamentally any such attachment; it is a regard for "the metaphysical myth which arose from the common experience of the South" after the Civil War. Sullivan is quite willing to admit the moral fallibility of the antebellum South. He refers to the grandiose dream that Robert Barnwell Rhett and other antebellum southerners had of creating a great slave civilization extending to the Caribbean and South America. He mentions Henry Timrod, who had a vision of a beneficent cotton empire that would bring peace to the whole world. But in between the vision of a slave civilization as utopia and the full return of the gnostic impulse to the South in the affluence of the post–World War II age, Sullivan says, "something of great historical and literary significance occurred: the myth by which the South lived assumed its singular delineation and thereby allowed the renascence to take place. Divested of its gnostic character by the events of history, it was at the same time stripped of all future hope: it became entirely a myth of vanished glory. It was a paradigm, a guide, a system to live by; but no idea of restoring the old secular Eden could be entertained." Sullivan is not entirely clear as to how this mythic system operated as a guide for living. In some ways it functioned in a purely negative manner; it placed the golden age in the past, and it negated the future. It demanded that the past "be maintained at whatever cost for as long as possible." But such negativity also encouraged the survival in the South of "old moral and metaphysical values." Reverence for the past promoted the recognition of the limitations placed on human beings by nature and history. The reversal of American innocence in the South afforded the southern writer a perspective on a gnostic modernity from within a temporary but specific and coherent culture oriented toward the conviction that human existence is both moral and sacred. This was enough to bring forth the remarkable southern literary movement between the great twentieth-century wars.

The loss of the southern myth of the past and the resultant end of the modern southern literary movement as exemplified in its fiction is the burden of *A Requiem for the Renascence*. The argument is not entirely consistent. The loss is partly attributed to the decline of Protestant Christianity, which had been the "metaphysical base" of the myth. But, in Sullivan's opinion, from 1865 onward the falling off from religion was a secondary force in providing the cultural context of southern writing. The role of the family was more important. Still more significant was the role of moral authority represented by the pantheon of southern heroes, Lee, Jackson, and Forrest. Appealed to more often than God, they were not entirely infallible, "short on the sacred dimension, the mysterious in the true sense." No truly transcendent heroes like "Beowulf or Roland" appeared in the South. The heroic southerners "remained flesh and blood, worshipped though they were, and therefore, though they resisted mightily, they were ultimately to fall victim to the erosion of time." In the midst of his somewhat equivocal analysis of the deterioration of the southern myth, Sullivan suddenly comes to this thought: "Of more importance is the fact that their [the southerners'] cause, out of which the myth was born, was flawed. To worship the past meant to worship all that the past stood for, and although much of this was good, some of it was bad: the ethic was mundane, imperfect, subject inevitably to change." Calling into question not only the spiritual legitimacy of the myth but also its ethical validity, the critic virtually suggests that a myth originating in a dominantly secular society, just emerging out of its historical condition as a modern slave society, is of dubious intrinsic moral value.

Yet against his own demythologizing tendency Sullivan affirms the efficacy of the dominion of southern fiction, supported by the southern myth of the past, by contrasting it with the "new dispensation," the new state, of southern fiction that comes into being after World War II—at the point when "with the fading of the homogeneous view born of the lost war, the agrarian orientation, the mistrust of history as process, the sense of the concrete and all the other characteristics typically assigned to southern culture, the myth dies." The mark of its passing is Robert Penn Warren's *All the King's Men* (1946).

> Jack Burden's entrance into Time and History signaled the beginning of a new dispensation that boded ill for the southern artist and for the culture which had supported him. He found himself not with a tradition still vital and alive, a past still throbbing with the high drama of its heroism and losses, but with a literature about that past. The heroes were gone; the Snopses and the gnostics had arisen to take their place. Now the new Miranda, whoever and wherever she was, could merely look at novels and stories and poems about the myth that Katherine Anne Porter's Miranda had watched develop and begin to fade while she paused breathless, her emotions, her being precariously balanced between ancient loves and loyalties and the inexorable new day that had begun. For the new Miranda, the new southern writer, there is only time—only the present age and a shelf of great books about an age that she never knew.

A projection into the "new dispensation" of the character in "Old Mortality" who represents Katherine Anne Porter herself, the "new Miranda" is a symbol of the southern writer after the loss of the myth has become so complete that the writer's imagination no longer experiences its directing force. The new Mirandas are those southern writers whose careers began after Jack Burden's movement (as the novel says) "out of history into history." Flannery O'Connor and

Walker Percy are prominent among the new Mirandas. Warren, Faulkner, and Eudora Welty are notable among the old Mirandas who are transformed into new Mirandas by historical change. Doomed by a situation in which "literature dies as the culture which supports it does," the new Mirandas have vexatious careers. The great skill of Flannery O'Connor was "strained by the deterioration of myth and community, and her energies were drained by the intensity of her argument with a faithless world." Percy in *Love in the Ruins* "moves forward—not backward—into time" and so denies entirely the myth of the past. Welty in *The Optimist's Daughter* fulfills her usual high aesthetic standards but "disappoints us in the poverty" of the novel's conclusion.

But the new Miranda was capable of more sinister behavior than simply yielding to the lapsing southern situation. As he advanced in his career, no lesser figure than Faulkner began to subordinate his sense of "morality and transcendent truth" to the "amorality of art," even to the point of asserting (in the well-known *Paris Review* interview) that the "artist will and indeed should rob his grandmother in order to do his work." Because he is convinced that it masks a betrayal of morality, Sullivan will not allow Faulkner his little joke. Indeed, Sullivan's theory of southern literature finds its chief theme and conceptual center in the writer's betrayal of the moral basis of culture.

The proper contextual metaphor of the Southern Renascence, Sullivan says in *Death by Melancholy*, is that of a *Götterdämmerung*. The Renascence was the expression of the highly fruitful but final epoch of a traditional society which, for all its failings, had a definite and worthy system of values established in a comprehensive vision of existence. It was a world that understood "that the whole of things is greater than the sum of its parts." The southerner saw "history as a series of images, rather than as a sweep of theories, which is to say that his vision was not abstract, but concrete." When the southern writer realized in the 1920s and 1930s that his ordered community was dissolving, his response was to strike "his chronicle of it in the twilight of its going." By the time he had done so—with such force that the Southern Renascence had been created—the southern soci-

ety had become "largely bourgeois" and "no longer pious or respect-
ful of tradition," no longer affording the southern writer a context in
the wholeness of existence. Whereupon, conforming to the general
attitudes of modern writers who attempt to find meaning in a mean-
ingless world, he inevitably fell under the spell, already so pervasive
everywhere else, of the Joycean apotheosis of the literary artist.
Sullivan parallels Joyce's Stephen Dedalus in *A Portrait of the Artist as a Young Man* and the legend of Faust, especially as it is dramatized by Marlowe. Stephen's rejection of religion is deliberate and, in
the light of the motivation and structure of Joyce's story, intended
not merely to emphasize Stephen's commitment to art but also to indicate the deliberate surrender of his soul to pride. Not only does he
tell Cranly, echoing Lucifer, that he will not serve the Church, but
he makes it plain that if his damnation be the price of his decision
to serve art, he will risk it.

> One of the remarkable aspects of *A Portrait* is the manner in which Joyce
> is able to develop Stephen's pride to the point that it becomes a dynamic
> force in the book. Like Faustus, he considers himself spiritually and intel-
> lectually superior to the common run of humanity, and it is this phase of
> his character, not weakness of the flesh or his talents or competencies,
> that furnishes the basic motivation for the drama and makes the novel
> work. To be sure, in the strict sense, Stephen, unlike Faustus, has no di-
> rect commerce with the devil, and indeed, he thinks probably that the
> devil does not exist. But should he exist, Stephen has delivered himself
> knowingly into his hands. Finally, the most significantly, for the sake of
> increased literary power, i.e., his own kind of magic, Stephen abandons
> the sources of political and social and metaphysical order with results in
> many ways similar to those that Faustus achieved.

The logical extension of this argument, according to Sullivan, is
that Joyce himself followed the compulsion to literary power he ascribes to Stephen, rejecting Church and State and maintaining the
rejections throughout his career. Like Faust, he underwent a damnation. "From the magnificence of his previous achievement, particularly in 'The Dead' and *A Portrait* itself " he fell into "largely empty
experimentation." *Ulysses* is an intellectual masterpiece but an
"empty novel" with "no moral center." Molly Bloom's celebrated
soliloquy is "tantamount to Faustus plucking fruit in the dead of
winter." *Finnegans Wake* means nothing. Still, Sullivan asserts, the

moral vacuousness of Joyce has been universally hailed by writers. Stephen Dedalus has become the "folk hero" of the modern literati.

Finally the inquiry into the Joycean aesthetic in *Death by Melancholy* ranges beyond art into theology. Sullivan observes that Joyce, "working strictly in scholastic terms . . . furnished for the intellectuals of our age a new theology."

> Aquinas, discovering his pattern in the Christian trinity, sets forth three qualities that are required for beauty, which Joyce translates from the Latin, quite conventionally, as wholeness, harmony, and radiance. These are all familiar to us, and the first two are easily grasped. Wholeness is understood as our apprehension of the work of art as a single thing, an entity limited and separate from all the other things that are in the world. Harmony exists in the relationship of the parts of this thing which we have established as one, the pleasing arrangement of these parts as seen in terms of their various juxtapositions to each other. So far so good, and to this point, Joyce and Aquinas proceed in agreement. But there remains radiance, the *claritas* of the original: this Aquinas sees as the essence of Being, which comes from and is God. For Joyce radiance is the artistic rendition of the moment of epiphany. The artist, making use of his heightened perception, has seen and recognized in the common fabric of life some instant of ineffable significance and beauty. The recapturing of this experience in its bright coloration is the source of radiance.

The new theology, Sullivan says flatly, attributes to man the creativity of God. It bases art "not on the Being of God, but on the epiphany of the artist." The result is an alienation of the writer from the power to transcend himself. Incapable of locating the source of his imagination within a transcendent reality, he allows his vision of the South's representation of myth and community to lapse. He becomes worse off than the later Faulkner, until eventually he creates heroes like William Styron's Nat Turner, who hate the world and want out of it—heroes who desire "only to destroy and be destroyed." Overwhelmed by a melancholy beyond remedy, a figure such as Nat, or Sheriff Hank Tawes in Madison Jones's *An Exile*, are implicit images of their creators, faithless literary artists writing about faith in a faithless world.

Sullivan's comprehension of the southern situation, however, never quite moves beyond hope of remedy. Another thematic motive in his theory of twentieth-century southern literature is a rectification of the sorry moral and spiritual condition into which the writer has fallen. *Death by Melancholy* points to at least two salvational resources available to the young southern writer. One is the potential capacity of the individual writer to restore a sense of transcendence by "developing in his own soul the values he once could draw from his culture." He can "furnish for himself what every Southern novelist could claim for his birthright thirty years ago": the knowledge "that the flesh without the spirit is nothing, and the search for the life of the body, unvitalized by the soul, is in the very truest sense a search for death." Understanding this, the writer will free himself from the idea that art is God. He will find a "concept of self-environment for literary endeavor by integrating the finite and the infinite, the mundane and the spiritual," thus reclaiming the religious view. Then, through grace, he will have the lonely strength to envision the "conflicts of our age in their full significance" and to discover images of the battle between good and evil in our time, in which nothing less is at stake than the "spiritual survival of mankind." In a rather contradictory way, *Death by Melancholy* also mentions another resource possibly yet available to the young southern writer: his identity with his southern homeland and with all that this entails—love of the land, dependence on manners, a penchant for the concrete as opposed to the abstract, and an "innate sense" of the mystery of existence.

But the prospect of remedying the condition of the southern literary vocation receives comparatively minor emphasis in Sullivan's criticism. He seems hardly to believe in the chances for a renewal of transcendence either through the spiritual strength of the individual writer or through the power of place over him. The remedial suggestions rise more out of the critic's moral obligation to hope than out of his conviction of their efficacy. Significantly, they are not reasserted in *A Requiem for the Renascence*. The only writer held up in *Death by Melancholy* as an example of a post–World War II achievement of transcendence, Flannery O'Connor, is, as I have noted, cited as a new Miranda in the later book. So far as a reassertion of the moral quality integral in the writer's southern heritage is concerned, *A Requiem for the Renascence* reaches its climax in the recognition of the total inversion of this relationship in *Child of God* (1973), a novel by Cormac McCarthy, a Tennesseean whose first novel, *The Orchard Keeper*, won the William Faulkner Foundation Award in 1965. The story of a necrophile, Lester Ballard, who stocks a cave with mouldering female corpses, *Child of God* in Sullivan's interpretation is a series of "perfectly rendered depravities." An artistic achievement exceeding anything McCarthy has yet done in the genre of "grotesque local color," Sullivan says, the novel presents the southern novelist not as merely "bereft of community and myth" but as engaged in "war against these repositories of order and truth." Although his discovery of overt treason against the moral and spiritual order of literature does not altogether rub out Sullivan's hope for its renewal, the condition of such a prospect becomes extreme: the elimination of all pride and sense of distinction in the literary vocation. Only when the writer and his society as a whole accept "art as a vocation like and no better than any other" will there be any prospect for a "rejuvenation" of literature and "new and better manifestations of myth and community."

The inference to be drawn from the condition that Sullivan stipulates is drastic. Reaching out for a basic remedy for the ills of literature, he turns his theory of the Southern Renascence against itself. Conceiving of a literary rejuvenation as productive of *"new and better manifestations of myth and community"* (my italics), he raises the question of whether or not Ransom, Tate, Davidson, and other southern writers of the 1920s and 1930s were, after all, expressions of traditionalist society. He intimates that the literary vocation was not inherent in a southern *Götterdämmerung*. Yet it is interesting that, in his critical maneuvering, Sullivan, ever sensitive to the nuances of the literary spirit, establishes his theory of the Southern Renascence in a larger motivating context than he would seem consciously to seek: the quest in modern Western letters for a homeland of the literary spirit.

One fulfillment of this quest had occurred nearly a hundred years earlier, when, in the twilight of its going, writers had struck the chronicle of New England, creating a literary renascence powerful enough to make the old Puritan community appear to be (as the South was to an appreciable extent in the twentieth century) the literary center of the nation. But the literary significance of New England was not discovered by writers whose sense of vocation derived from a compacted, nationalistic New England culture. It was made by those New England writers who had come into the sense of the distinctive spiritual role of the writer in modern Western civilization. These included Emerson, Thoreau, Hawthorne, and Emily Dickinson—all those who had a vision of the profoundly self-conscious relation existing between, on the one hand, the modern poet, storyteller, and critic and, on the other, myth, tradition, history, and God (or it may be, the absence of these). Undergoing the ordeal of the depreciation of spirit in the disorders of the nineteenth century—the growing hollowness at the center of Western institutional life, the enlarging emptiness of the soul—the New England writers became estranged from the ethic of progress and the dominant values of modernity. Repudiating life in a moral and spiritual vacuum, each writer struggled with the problem of how his attitude bore on (to use a phrase from Sullivan slightly out of context) "loyalty to family, state, and the substantive forms of religion." This striving involved the writer's community with the immediate world: its landscape, people, laws, manners, and its fading but still living sense of the mystery of existence. Nonetheless, the endeavor was controlled by a commitment to a principle of self-reliance. Not necessarily Emersonian, this expressed in some way the radical Emersonian dictum, "Nothing is at last safe but the integrity of your own mind." The most original of the New England writers knew intensely the source of the geniune literary talent in modern times: a vision of the writer as an isolated yet redemptive literary consciousness.

Although Old South writers like William Gilmore Simms and Henry Timrod constantly felt rejected by their society, they were effectively cut off from the vitalizing vision of the writer's situation in modernity. Assimilated to the interests of the state by the politics of slavery, they failed to conceptualize the ironic drama of their careers or to grasp the ironic meaning of the South as a modern slave society. (Poe, who was outside the South a great deal, presents a more complex instance of the southern writer.) Following the Civil War, preoccupied not only with his psychic survival but with sheer physical survival as well, the southern writer continued to be limited in his response to the major impulses in Western literature. But things changed, and in the aftermath of World War I his education began to comprehend the modern literary self-consciousness. While he took the direction of a Hawthorne rather than an Emerson, attacking the self in favor of the traditional community, he followed a self-conscious vocation to redemptive literary mission. No southern writer, I would say, affords a better illustration of such self-consciousness than the one Sullivan admires and emulates, Allen Tate. I am thinking particularly of Tate's essay, "The Man of Letters in the Modern World."

> The man of letters sees that modern societies are machines, even if he thinks that they ought not to be: he is convinced that in its intractable Manichaeism, society cannot be redeemed. The shadowy political philosophy of modern literature, from Proust to Faulkner, is, in its moral origins, Jansenist: we are disciples of Pascal, the merits of whose Redeemer were privately available but could not affect the operation of the power-state. While the politician, in his cynical innocence, uses society, the man of letters disdainfully, or perhaps even absentmindedly, withdraws from it: a withdrawal that few persons any longer observe, since withdrawal has become the social convention of the literary man, in which society, insofar as it is aware of him, expects him to conduct himself.

This is a reflective, post-Renascent Tate giving the Phi Beta Kappa Address at the University of Minnesota in 1952. (Later he said the same things to an international literary gathering in Paris.) He is presenting to his audience "in outline the melancholy portrait of the man who stands before you." Most assuredly, this is not the portrait of a writer whose derivation lies in an integral culture. On the contrary, it depicts a distinguished man of letters whose career had its inception in the modern estrangement of the literary intelligence. Tate's figuration of the man of letters, which must be accepted as a chief symbol of the Southern Renascence, derives from the Joycean figure of the man of letters in *A Portrait of the Artist as a Young Man* and, in a larger sense, from the general context of the Joycean portrait, the alienation of the creative and critical consciousness in Western civilization.

The history of this phenomenon must be traced back into its anticipations in ancient times if we would explore it fully, but we can see its less remote origins in the tripartite separation of existence in late medieval times, which I have remarked upon elsewhere in these essays. When there were no longer two general realms of order in the West, Church and State, but three—Church, State and the polity of secular letters—the symbolism of order in the West was substantially altered, for the Republic of Letters represented the separation of consciousness from the great and intricate institutional symbolism of spiritual transcendence. This disjunction of consciousness is the most readily apparent source of the alienation of the modern writer. Ever since this began to develop, the Western literary consciousness has known a dubious relation to the spiritual dimension and so to a shaping wholeness of existence. It has been hard for a man of letters, even though he may be a Christian in personal faith, to give his primary allegiance to the Kingdom of God; as difficult as it has been for him, even though he be one of its good citizens, to give his primary allegiance to the State. The non-Christian man of letters, the one-hundred-percent agnostic humanist, say, presumably has had an easier time of it. But not necessarily. The man of letters, Christian or pagan, has lived in a world that once centered all efforts of the imagination in a compelling aspiration to represent the transcendent dominion of God. Permeated with the thought and emotion associated with this desire, Western society has transformed its religious structure into a secular structure without clearly discriminating the older religious mode of being from the newer secular mode. I think Sullivan is deeply right when he insists that for two thousand years our literature in the broad sense has been Christian. Depicting people living in societies that "to a greater or less extent held Christian beliefs and values," it has continued to refer the "moral standards against which all acts of morality and all concepts of being" are finally measured to Christian theology. But the symbol of Christendom as a world culture in which all the individual worlds of the West have been smaller worlds within the greater one has disappeared.

Facing the question of the nature of the literary vocation, the man of letters has recognized the demand that he represent the secular or humanistic polity of letters, but the demand often being ambivalent or ambiguous, the response has been equally so. A tendency to exalt the vocation to letters, to make it a transcendent calling, has been present in every literary age since Petrarch, whose public crowning with the laurel was paradoxically a certification of his estrangement. This sense of apartness has intensified as Western civilization has become not only less Christian but less literary. Under the conditions of democratic, technological materialism—of, if one may use the term with poetic latitude, "historical materialism"—the role of the literary man has become so uncertain and defensive that his need to affirm his identity is at the same time compulsive and despairing.

The displacement of the man of letters is a fundamental aspect of the career of Faulkner, of the careers of the Fugitives and Agrarians, of the careers of all the writers who belong to the southern movement in modern literature. The history of the literary mind of the South seeking to become aware of itself—of its special relation to Church and State, and of its still more special identification with the modern South—is a segment of the final stage in the drama of the dissolution of the Western moral and spiritual culture. As I have tried to indicate, Sullivan's complex consciousness is continuous with the southern effort in self-interpretation. In *Death by Melancholy*, his expectation that the vocation of the southern writer will maintain the quest for moral order amid the spiritual, political, and literary disorders of our age brings into focus the drama of his own experience as a man of letters. Compounded of hope and despair, his vision of a renewal of the Renascence in the lonely young southerner, who seizes upon what he can from the relics of the spiritual homeland that the Renascent mind has created, is one of those haunting, apocalyptic moments characteristic of the modern literary spirit. We are reminded that Sullivan has an affinity with Walker Percy, however sharply he may question Percy's existentialist premises. In *The Last Gentleman*, young Will Barrett assumes one dimension of his meaning for us as a state or quality of the southern consciousness in the middle decades of our frightful century.

> Like many young men in the South, he became overly subtle and had trouble ruling out the possible. They are not like an immigrant's son in Passaic who decides to become a dentist and that is that. Southerners have trouble ruling out the possible. What happens to a man to whom all

things seem possible and every course of action open? Nothing of course. Except war. If a man lives in the sphere of the possible and waits for something to happen, what he is waiting for is war—or the end of the world.

In the last quarter of the twentieth century, both Walter Sullivan and Walker Percy suggest, we are beginning to live in a postsouthern America, as in the final part of the last century people (including southerners) began to live in a post-New England America. The epiphany of the southern literary artist will not be repeated. The Southern Renascence will not come again. But in this postsouthern age it could be that boys from Passaic to San Francisco, from Minneapolis to New Orleans will more nearly resemble Will Barrett than the son of the Passaic immigrant. In the existentialist America (if that is what to call it) that is becoming our spiritual context, the possibility of the reopening of the metaphysical dimension of reality —of a return to a participation in the mystery of history—is presented to us through the vision of a Percy or a Sullivan.

But the possibility is strongly problematical, especially if the writer to be redeemed is a novelist. From Shakespeare on, all writers are highly sensitive to the imperative inwardness of modern society. Shakespeare in *Hamlet*, Donne in "Anatomy of the World," Arnold in "Dover Beach," Eliot in *The Waste Land*, Yeats in "The Second Coming": the poets have given the literary reaction to the heretofore unknown assertion by the human consciousness that history is immanent in the processes of consciousness. The full registration of this reaction, however, is in the novelists. Their vocation originated, in the seventeenth and eighteenth centuries, in the need for a new literary form that would express the intricacies of the falling off from the assumption of a transcendent reference for human existence. The portrayal by the novelists of the struggle for consciousness against its own imperative to internalize history—and thus to acknowledge its loss of divine authorization and its utter dependence on itself— affords an index to the novelty of modern existence. As the struggle neared its most decisive expression in the work of the twentieth-century novelists, the philosopher Benedetto Croce formulated the virtual text of the novelists—and of the social scientists—when he said: "We no longer believe . . . . like the Greeks, in happiness of life on earth; we no longer believe, like the Christians, in happiness in an other-worldly life; we no longer believe, like the optimistic philosophers of the last century, in a happy future for the human race. . . . We no longer believe in anything of that, and what *we have alone retained is the consciousness of ourselves, and the need to make that consciousness ever clearer and more evident*, a need for whose satisfaction we turn to science and art."[1]

From Cervantes through Richardson, Fielding, and Sterne, through Flaubert, Dostoevski, and Dickens, through Mann, Proust, Joyce, and Kafka, we follow the progressive drama of the closure of history in the finitude of the human consciousness. Over a shorter span of time—and with a sense of coming into it at its intensive culmination rather than at its beginning—we follow the same drama in the American novelists. There are Brown, Cooper, Poe, Hawthorne, and Melville. Most notably there is Henry James, who, by reason of his intimate grasp of the European context of America, is the first American novelist to become wholly aware of the subjective quality of the nation's historical existence. While how this is so may be abundantly illustrated by calling upon James's imagination of America in his stories, we may once again appeal for a cogent, succinct reference to that fascinating nonfiction fiction, *The American Scene*—this time to the chapter on Washington, D.C. In the monumental official seat of democratic polity, James—personified as the "restless analyst"—discovers his attention centering on the Capitol. In this massive edifice "association really reigns," the analyst says. And "in the richest, and even again in the drollest forms; it is thick and vivid and almost gross, it assaults the wondering mind." The Jamesian sense of wonder is particularly stimulated by the way in which the building symbolizes the "*democratic assimilation* of the greater dignities and majesties" connected with governmental order and power. Initially envisioning the Capitol as a place exuding a "certain large, final benignity" deriving from its service as an "estate-office" for a "huge flourishing Family," the analyst eventually has another vision —one complementary to yet quite different from the image of the Capitol as a "vast democratic lap." Strolling the "Acropolis height"

1 Quoted in H. Stuart Hughes, *Consciousness and Society: The Reorientation of European Social Thought, 1890–1930* (New York: Vintage Books, 1961), 428–29.

afforded by the "various marble fronts" of the majestic edifice on a bright early twentieth-century morning, he has the impression of being in a "playhouse gallery" that dominates—"rakes"—the whole American scene. But the gallery is also a stage, where the analyst (a relator who is as well an actor) encounters other actors.

> Though I had them [the marble fronts] in general, for contemplation, quite to myself, I met one morning a trio of Indian braves, braves dispossessed of forest and prairie, but as free of the builded labyrinth as they had ever been of these; also arrayed in neat pot-hats, shoddy suits and light overcoats, with their pockets, I am sure, full of photographs and cigarettes: circumstances all that quickened their resemblance, on the much bigger scale, to Japanese celebrities, or to specimens, on show, of what the Government can do with people with whom it is supposed able to do nothing. They seemed just then and there, for a mind fed betimes on the Leatherstocking tales, to project an image in itself immense, but foreshortened and simplified—reducing to a single smooth stride the bloody footsteps of time. One rubbed one's eyes, but there, at its highest polish, shining in the beautiful day, was the brazen face of history, and there, all about one, immaculate, the printless pavements of the State.

As Walter Sullivan, himself a novelist, is aware, novelists like Faulkner, Tate, Welty, Warren, and Percy in various ways comprehend the phenomenon that James, uncertainly but surely, describes in his symbolization of the Capitol of Washington. Taking as its model the exercise of a rational, democratic beneficence over the individual's destiny, the State—having, in the name of freeing the individual from history, abrogated its historical union with the Church—establishes its direct psychic dominance over the self. Reifying the Hegelian "secularization of the spiritual," this act, we may say, constitutes a transforming force in the structuring of history, a secular deformation, even a destruction, of the reality and authority of supratemporal history (as symbolized by the City of God). In a remarkable essay on James—a small but significant part of his immense inquiry into the symbolism of order and history—Eric Voegelin comments on the "fateful shift in Western society from existence in openness toward the cosmos to existence in the mode of closure against, and denial of, reality."

> As the process gains momentum, the symbols of open existence—God, man, the divine origin of the cosmos, and the divine logos permeating its

order—lose the vitality of their truth and are eclipsed by the imagery of a self-creative, self-realizing, self-expressing, self-ordering, and self-saving ego that is thrown into, and confronted with, an immanently closed world. This shift in the mode of existence is accompanied by various movements in literature and art which express the shift and its progress—from Mannerism, through Romanticism, to the Symbolism of James's time, and further on to Surrealism. The artists who represent these movements place themselves in the situation of deformed existence and develop symbols that will express their experience, as it were, from within the deformation. It is true, the tension between reality and its deformation can never disappear altogether or the concrete case of closure would become unrecognizable as a mode of the human condition, but the consciousness of the tension can be pushed so far back that it does not become explicitly thematic in the work itself. A Romantic or Symbolistic work of art is not an Aeschylean drama in which the full articulation of various tensions is the mode of consciousness that make the drama a tragedy.[2]

If we understand that, as Voegelin says, the "closure of existence" is the "problem" of James's work, we grasp more clearly James's insistent identification of the novel and history, of the vocation of the novelist and that of the historian. In "The Art of Fiction" (1884), James sees the historian and the novelist as committed to a "sacred office." The underlying force of this symbol of vocation derives from the feeling that the historian and novelist, as priests of the divinization of secular history, are entrusted with the moral promise of the self-conceived self of the writer unfolding its meaning as the incarnation of the closure of history. But a sense of the frightening motives of the literary vocation more or less escapes James in "The Art of Fiction," the most graphic symbol of closure in the essay being presented with little realization of its constrictive quality: "Experience is never limited, and it is never complete; it is an immense sensibility, a kind of huge spiderweb of the finest silken threads suspended in the chamber of consciousness, and catching every air-borne particle in its tissue. It is the very atmosphere of the mind; and when the mind is imaginative—much more when it happens to be that of a man of genius—it takes to itself the faintest hints of life, it converts the very pulse of the air into revelations." Much later—almost at the end of his life, and almost at the end of the society he had

2 "A Letter to Robert A. Heilman," *Southern Review*, n.s., 7 (Winter, 1971), 27.

known—James realized, and in his realization defined, the terror of his vocation. In March, 1914, he wrote a letter to Henry Adams (who had already found out that, in becoming the model of history, the mind might well have become the emblem of historical disaster).

> Of *course* we are lone survivors, of course the past that was our lives is the bottom of an abyss—if the abyss *has* any bottom; of course, too, there's no use talking unless one particularly *wants* to. But the purpose, almost, of my printed divagations [the autobiographical *Notes of a Son and Brother*] was to show you that one *can*, strange to say, still want to—or at least can behave as if one did. Behold me therefore so behaving—and apparently capable of continuing to do so. I still find my consciousness interesting—under *cultivation* of the interest. Cultivate it *with* me, dear Henry —that's what I hoped to make you do—to cultivate yours for all that it has in common with mine. *Why* mine yields an interest I don't know that I can tell you, but I don't challenge or quarrel with it—I encourage it with a ghastly grin. You see I still, in presence of life (or of what you deny to be such,) have reactions—as many as possible—and the book I sent you is proof of them. It's, I suppose, because I am that queer monster, the artist, an obstinate finality, an inexhaustible sensibility. Hence the reactions— appearances, memories, many things, go on playing upon it with consequences that I note and "enjoy" (grim word!) noting. It all takes doing— and I *do*. I believe I shall do yet again—it is still an act of life. But you perform them still yourself—and I don't know what keeps me from calling your letter a charming one! There we are, and it's a blessing that you understand—I admit indeed alone.[3]

More cogently than any other statement by James, this well-known letter evokes his fundamental apprehension of the coalescence of the novelist and the historian in the figure of the artist. In the self-conscious burden imposed on the writer by his increasing awareness of the inwardness of history, James perceives the drastic circumscription of the boundaries of reality in the modern age: history is self-consciousness and self-consciousness is history. Adams' despairing cry about the loneliness of the survivor of history provoked an empathy in (to use Voegelin's subtle description of the Jamesian mind) the "complexities of a consciousness that has distance to its want of distance."

The empathetic capacities afforded by his "distance to his want

---

3 *The Letters of Henry James*, ed. Percy Lubbock (2 vols.; New York: Scribner's, 1920), II, 360–61.

of distance" affords a fascinating perspectival pattern throughout James's career, the pattern becoming more intricate as his work advances into the twentieth century. *The Wings of the Dove* (1902) is his most subtle elaboration of one of his major themes, the Western concept of innocence as embodied in the American. In the story of the dying Milly Theale, "heiress of all the ages," this theme assumes its full symbolic import. Milly—whether we call her secular saint or angel—becomes an ineffable yet powerful fulfillment of James's long struggle to invest the art form that rose directly out of modern secularism, the novel, with transcendent meaning and authority. Yet, although the transfiguring work of Milly's redemptive act of forgiveness is completely evident in the moral awakening of Densher and Kate Croy, the two Europeans who have sought to use her so mercilessly, James's novel conveys in its overall tone a strange sense of spiritual resignation. When Densher asks Kate if their relationship can not be resumed, her reply—"We shall never again be as we were!" —at once asserts the inviolate triumph of Milly's self-sacrificing act and rings with a finality that belies their entrance upon a new, redeemed life. In a world symbolized by Henry Adams' desperate act of transforming the Virgin into a secular goddess, Milly is but a less consequential, if vastly appealing, relic of history's ravaging of the consciousness. She takes her place in the American literary imagination of history along with Adams' Virgin: a reliquary figure of spent emotion, a nostalgic emblem of the self's desire to become a living soul.

Still, James did not overtly grasp that his motive in *The Wings of the Dove*, and in all his work, is the self's assumption of the burden of history.

In an immediate sense, the Jamesian response to Adams' letter of March, 1914, was no doubt inspired by the vague unease pervading the air five months before the commencement of World War I. When it came, unexpectedly, "one huge horror of blackness," James experienced a complicated and terrifying crisis of consciousness. His delineation of this is fragmentary, but in a few letters and one or two incidental essays he indelibly suggests its intensity.[4] On August 4,

---

4 *Cf.* the arresting interpretation of the final decade of James's life in Henry Nash Smith, *Democracy and the Novel: Popular Resistance to Classic American Writers* (New York: Oxford University Press, 1978), 161–65.

1914, James wrote to Howard Sturgis: "The plunge of civilization into this abyss of blood and darkness by the wanton feat of those two infamous autocrats is a thing that so gives away the whole long age during which we have supposed the world to be, with whatever abatement, gradually bettering, that to have to take it all now for what the treacherous years were all the while really making for and *meaning* is too tragic for words." The coming of the war, he said a few days later to Rhoda Broughton, "seems to *undo* everything that was ours, in the most horrible retroactive way." In a reminiscence in 1915, James refers to the fifty years before the Great War as ones of insidious and artful beguilement. Another 1915 retrospection declares that these years should be labeled in the "very largest letters" the "Age of the Mistake." In the midst of the war, and almost at the end of his life, James expressed to Horace Walpole troubled reservations about continuing his work: "The subject-matter of one's effort has become *itself* utterly treacherous and false—its relation to reality utterly given away and smashed. Reality is a world that was to be capable of *this*—and how represent that horrific capability, *historically* latent, historically ahead of it? How not on the other hand *not* represent it either—without putting into play mere fiddlesticks?"

Asserting how little his imagination comprehended the nature of the historical society that he belonged to, James, by overstatement, indicates his deep sensitivity to its character. Blindly dedicated to the creation of heaven on earth, it was the society that in the later nineteenth century completed the transfer of man, world, and God into mind. Inescapably a part of it, James shared its belief that modernity—modeled on a growing acuity of intellect and a progressive refinement of consciousness—was moving toward a higher degree of civilization than had yet been known. Forced to recognize that this movement was an illusion, James was up against the fact that his source of being—his mind, his consciousness—was treasonable to itself. Yet the outbreak of the war was strangely and powerfully a confirmation and justification of James's vocation. With singular perceptiveness James saw himself as the embodiment, we may say, of the secularization of the spiritual: as the modern artist, that queer monster whose meaning quite explicitly and self-consciously is his closure of history in the self—in, that is to say, his self-willed, yet deeply unwilling, deformation of the reality of God. Ten years before World War I, when he had seen the shameless, detached, and no doubt Satanic, visage of history looming above the American Capitol, James had looked, we may suppose, on a face palpably his own. There is a kind of terror in thinking that he was a survivor looking upon what he had survived, and still must survive.

PS 88 .S45

Simpson, Lewis P.

The brazen face of his

DEMCO